Piece Together Praise

Piece Together Praise

A Theological Journey

Poems and Collected Hymns Thematically Arranged

Brian Wren

Stainer & Bell, London, England,
and Hope Publishing Company,
Carol Stream, Illinois, USA

First published in 1996 by
Hope Publishing Company, Carol Stream, IL 60188, USA, and
Stainer & Bell Limited, P.O. Box 110, Victoria House, 23 Gruneisen Road,
London N3 1DZ, England.

All rights reserved. This book is copyright under the Berne Convention. It is fully protected by the British Copyright, Designs and Patent Act 1988. No part of the work may be reproduced, stored in a retrieval system, or transmitted in any form by any means, electronic, mechanical, photocopying or otherwise without the prior permission of the publishers:

Hope Publishing Company for the USA, Canada, Australia and New Zealand, and Stainer & Bell Limited for the rest of the world.

For permission to reproduce anything in this work, except where copyright is credited as owned or controlled by third parties:
* Everywhere except the USA, Canada, Australia and New Zealand, contact Stainer & Bell, address above, phone 0181-343-3303, fax 0181-343-3024.
* In the USA, Canada, Australia and New Zealand, contact Hope Publishing Company, address above, phone 630-665-3200, fax 630-665-2552.

British Library Cataloguing-in-Publication Data
A catalogue record of this book is available from the British Library

ISBN: 0 85249 835 7 (World excluding USA, Canada, Australia and New Zealand)
ISBN: 0 916642 62 3 (USA, Canada, Australia and New Zealand)

Library of Congress Catalog Card No. 96-075969

Cover Photograph by Fannie Hirst
Typesetting and Cover Design by Brian Wren
Printed in Great Britain by Galliard (Printers) Ltd, Great Yarmouth, England

Contents

	Page
Welcome and Introduction	vii
How to Use this Book	ix
Worship-Planner's Guide	xi

Poems and Hymns

Seeking and Being Found 1
Questions about Life, Faith, and God

Hearing the Spoken Word 9
God's Covenant in History and Revelation in Jesus Christ

Becoming Whose We Are 57
A Covenant People, Worshipping and Working

Living in the World God Loves 105
Creation, Suffering, Peace and Justice

Seasons of Life 127
Birth, Childhood, Love, Trials, Mortality, Hope

In the End, God 149
Eternal Life and New Creation

Our Lives Be Praise 155
Praising God: Creator, Mystery, Trinity

Appendix and Indexes

Lift Heart and Voice: The Great Thanksgiving in Song 174
Hymns Not Included 177
Poems and Lyrics 180
Index of Metres 186
Index of Box Notes on Theological Themes 189
Index of Scripture References 190
Index of First Lines with Tunes 193

Painting many pictures
in the hall of faith,
seeking God we gather,
happily, or grieving,
doubting or believing,
and piece together praise.

Sewing many stories
in a quilt of love,
friends of God, we gather,
variably able,
at a common table,
and piece together praise.

Brian Wren - See No. 75
© 1995 Hope Publishing Company for the USA,
Canada, Australia and New Zealand
and Stainer & Bell Limited for all other territories.
All rights reserved.

The quilt in the cover photograph was made
by Marion Dahl, of Crosby, North Dakota,
from materials in the sewing box
of Norma Heafield, Lindsay, Montana.
Each piece of fabric has stories or memories
of members of the Heafield family,
pieced together to make a patterned whole.

Welcome and Introduction

Welcome to this book. I hope it will be useful: as a spiritual journey, a resource for planning worship, a work of theology, or for religious education.

Ten months ago, my publishers asked me to anthologise all the hymn-texts I have written. Rather than arrange them tediously from A to Z, I took the opportunity of setting them out thematically, as a statement of belief in the form of a journey.

These hymns and poems have come about in a variety of ways. Some arise from my life story and faith journey (e.g. 1, 4, 20, and 39), others from chance events, like seeing people at prayer on a transatlantic flight (6), hearing a tune and wanting to write for it (19), or being annoyed by a sermon (13). Sometimes a work of theology excites me to respond by shaping its impact into a faith statement or song (e.g. 23, 29). Many hymns have been requested or commissioned, often giving a topic I would not otherwise have explored and the challenge and delight of discovery (e.g. 17, 47, 60, 68, and 116).

The sum total of items, and their arrangement, come from the interplay of serendipity and intent, including interaction with others, changing opportunities of a working life, sufficient time overall, and a sense of vocation to express the fullness of Christian faith, as best I can. As I thus "piece together praise," the result is, among other things, a work of theology. In a systematic theology, some things would come out differently, but I would still begin with Jesus, the most reliable source for knowing God, and end with praise (see further on p. 104).

I am deeply grateful to literally hundreds of people and communities, who enable, encourage and resource my life and writing. My particular thanks go to Stainer & Bell, for requesting and publishing this work, Hope Publishing Company, for many years of covenantal relationship, the College and Church to whom the work is dedicated, and my partner in marriage, Susan Heafield, for love, truth, friendship, wisdom, skill and critique: in a word, for true partnership.

Brian Wren, Goodwin's Mills, Maine, USA
April 1996

This work is dedicated to
the United Reformed Church
of Great Britain
and to
Mansfield College, Oxford,
in gratitude to God
for their tradition,
polity, and life,
which nourish
and sustain me.

How To Use This Book

Worship and Preaching

For readings, prayers, sermon ideas, quotations:
- Worship Planner's Guide
- Index of Scripture References.

For musical uses:
- Index of First Lines with Tunes

A Work of Theology

Consider and critique
- the order of the work;
- its shape and format;
- its individual items;

See also:
- Box Note, p. 104
- Worship Planners Guide
- Indexes.

Education
(Adult and youth)

- Use the book, or sections of it, for study and worship
- Find particular themes in the Worship Planner's Guide

A Spiritual Journey

- Browse, using any page for thought and meditation
- Choose and read a section
- Compare your journey with my own

Worship Planner's Guide

Topics and Themes for Easy Reference

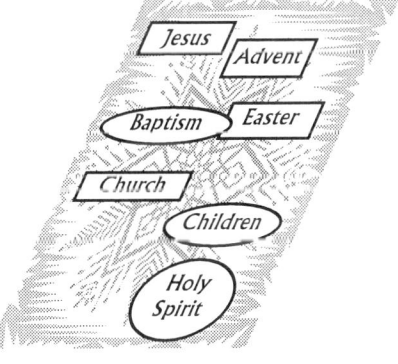

Times

The Christian Year

References are to hymn numbers, unless page numbers are specified. Box Notes on theological themes are in bold type. Items from the Appendix are in italics.

Advent - Preparing for Jesus
Jesus comes today 13
Sing and tell our Saviour's story 9
This is a story full of love 10
Welcome the wild one 24
When God is a child 16
Who comes? 12
Will you come and see the light? 14

Advent - Our Final Destiny
Arise, shine out 164
Christ will come again 163
When all is ended 161
Will God be Judge? 160
With humble justice 162

Christmas
As in a clear dawn 47
Good is the flesh 23
Hail, undiminished love 15
Her baby, newly breathing 19
If I could visit Bethlehem 21
Oh, how joyfully! 17
Sing my song backwards 53
When a baby in your arms 18
You were a babe of mine 20

Massacre of the Children
Child, when Herod wakes 22

Epiphany
A man of ancient time and place 30
Hail, undiminished love 15
Will you come and see the light? 14

Jesus:
Box Notes:
Choice and Chance .... page 40
For Women and Men? .... page 35
Human Stranger .... page 17
Jesus - Christ .... page 23

- Baptism
Welcome the wild one 24
What was your vow and vision? 25

- Temptation
How perilous the messianic call 26

- Life Work
A dancer's body leaps and falls 48
A man of ancient time and place 30
Can a man be kind and caring? 31
Daughter Mary 28
This is a story full of love 10
Woman in the night 29

- Healing
A woman in the crowd 27

- Teaching
Here and now, if you love 32

- Transfiguration
Jesus on the mountain peak 34

- Facing Death
Doom and danger Jesus knows 36
I am going to Calvary 35

Ash Wednesday
Dust and ashes 83

Lent
A dancer's body leaps and falls 48
Come, Holy Breath 82
Look at this man 33
Made one in Christ, we gather 78

Palm/Passion Sunday
Doom and danger Jesus knows 36

Holy Week
God, thank you for the Jews 90
Made one in Christ, we gather 78
The gifts of God 142

And Seasons

Maundy Thursday
As Jeremiah took a jar 38
Great God, your love 84
Made one in Christ, we gather 78
On the night before he died 37
Praise the God who changes places ... 177

Good Friday
A body broken on a cross 58
Dying love has been my birth 43
God is One, unique and holy 179
God remembers 42
God, thank you for the Jews 90
Here hangs a man discarded 39
Holy Spirit, storm of love 40
When pain and terror 41

Easter Vigil
A dancer's body leaps and falls 48
Joyful is the dark 45
Made one in Christ, we gather 78
The waiting night 46

Easter Sunrise
As in a clear dawn 47

Easter
Christ crucified now is alive 51
Christ is alive! 52
Christ is risen! Shout hosanna! 49
Easter Light 193

Easter Season
Box Note:
Easter Joy-Action for Justice ... page 48
A woman in a world of men 55
Dear Christ, uplifted from the earth 44
Faith moving onward 54
Jesus is good news to all the poor 50
Sing my song backwards 53

Ascension
Christ is alive! 52
Jesus is with God 56
Peace is my parting-gift to you 109

Pentecost
(See also Holy Spirit)
As in a clear dawn 47
Great soaring Spirit 130
There's a spirit in the air 101

After Pentecost
By purpose and by chance 81

Trinity Sunday
(See God- Glorious Trinity)

All saints
A cloud of witnesses around us 74
All saints? 70
We are not our own 62

Other Events

Columbus Day (USA)
The gospel came with foreign tongue .. 92

Fathers' Day
Bring many names 173
Dear Mother God (see Stanza 4) 176
How can we name a love? 136

Graduation - see Transitions

Harvest Thanksgiving
Come, cradle all 112
Praise God for the harvest 114
Thank you, God, for water etc. 111
We plough and sow 115

July 4th (USA) - see Patriotism

Worship

Memorial Day (USA)
A child, a woman and a man 126
I love this land 124
Weep for the dead 120

Mothers' Day
As a mother comforts her child 170
Bring many names 173
Dear Mother God 176
How can we name a love? 136

New Year (See also Transitions)
Ever-journeying Friend 107
Look back and see 72
Sing praises old and new 85
This is a day of new beginnings 159

Presidential Election (USA)
Jesus comes today 13

Reformation Sunday
Outgoing God 87
Sing and tell our Saviour's story 9

Remembrance Sunday (UK)
A child, a woman and a man 126
I love this land 124
Weep for the dead 120

Thanksgiving (USA)
Come, cradle all 112
Praise God for the harvest 114
Thank you God, for times 135
Thank you, God, for water etc. 111
The gospel came 92
We plough and sow 115

World Communion Sunday (USA)
Far and wide the gospel travels 103
(See also: Communion)

Worship and Sacraments

After Communion
There's a spirit in the air 101

Baptism - Infants
Born into love 138
The light of God is shining bright 139
Wonder of wonders 137

Baptism / Reaffirmation of Baptism
In water we grow 61
Water, splashing hands and face 60
What was your vow and vision? 25
When anyone is in Christ 95

Beginning of Worship
Acclaim with jubilation 168
By purpose and by chance 81
Come let us praise 11
Eternal Wisdom, timely Friend 166
God of many names 7
Great God, your love 84
How great the mystery of faith 79
How shall I sing to God? 150
In Christ, our humble head 71
Let all creation dance 167
Made one in Christ, we gather 78
Praise the God who changes places ... 177
Praise to the Maker 169

Blessing and Benediction
Go now in peace 148
May the Sending One sing in you 110
Peace is my parting gift 109

And Sacraments

Communion
As Jeremiah took a jar 38
At the table of the world 98
Break the bread of belonging 125
Far and wide the gospel travels 103
God is One, unique and holy 179
Great God, your love 84
Great Thanksgiving in Song, The ...... page 174
I come with joy 97
On the night before he died 37
This is a day of new beginnings 159
This we can do 129
Water, splashing hands and face 60
We are not our own 62
We bring, you take 99
We meet as friends at table 96
When minds and bodies 181
You are my body 100

Confession and New Life
Box Note: "Sin" .... page 74
All-perceiving Lover 149
Come, Holy Breath 82
Great God, your love 84

Confirmation and Commitment
To Christ our hearts now given 102
We are not our own 62
We are your people 63
What was your vow and vision? 25
When anyone is in Christ 95
(See also: Following Christ)

End of worship
Ever-journeying Friend 107
This is a day of new beginnings 159
We want to love 133

Funeral and Memorial (Children)
We are the music angels sing 157

Funeral and Memorial (General)
God, let me welcome 156
Grief of ending 153
Let hope and sorrow now unite 158
When grief is raw 154
When joy is drowned 155

Holy Union   See Love Commitments

Love Commitments
As man and woman 185
God, the All-Holy 145
I'll try, my love, to love you 140
Life is great 144
Love makes a bridge 147
This is a day of new beginnings 159
Wedding Wishes 202
When love is found 146

Marriage   See Love Commitments

Naming / Blessing / Infant Dedication
Born into love 138
The light of God is shining bright 139
Wonder of wonders 137

Ordination and Installation
By contact with the Crucified 66
Come, celebrate the call of God 67
Love alone unites us 64
We are your people 63
Where shall Wisdom be found? 65

Sunday
Made one in Christ, we gather 78

Worship
Box Note: Worship Order .... page 71
Against the clock 77
How good to thank our God 80

Topics

Topics and Themes in Alphabetical Order

Bible
Deep in the shadows of the past 86
Outgoing God 87

Cherishing the Earth
Come, cradle all 112
Great Lover, calling us to share 134
Let all creation dance 167
Only One Earth 196
Praise God for the harvest 114
Thank you, God, for water etc. 111
Water in the snow 113
We plough and sow 115

Children
How deep our Maker's grief 117
I am going to Calvary 35
I met three children in the street 178
I'll try, my love, to love you 140
The gifts of God 142
The light of God is shining bright 139
True friends 143
When children pray 141
When God is a child 16
Who is God? 5

Children - boys
Can a man be kind and caring? 31

Christ - See Following Christ

Christians and Jews
Box Notes:
    Covenant .... page 10
    Living Faith .... page 12
    Was Paul Converted? ...... page 139
Acclaim God's saving news 8
God, thank you for the Jews 90
Who comes? 12
Will God be Judge? 160

Christians and Other Faiths
    Box Note .... page 7
Each seeking faith 6
Will God be Judge? 160

Church:

- Anniversaries
See Covenant and Commitment

- Christ's people
Christ loves the Church 94
How perilous the messianic call 26

- Covenant and Commitment
A cloud of witnesses around us 74
A Stranger, knocking on a door 88
Acclaim God's saving news 8
All saints? 70
By purpose and by chance 81
Ever-journeying Friend 107
In Christ, our humble head 71
Joy has blossomed out of sadness 89
Look back and see the apostles' road ... 72
Love alone unites us 64
Outgoing God 87
Sing praises old and new 85
Source of All, Sustaining Spirit 73
This is a day of new beginnings 159
To Christ our hearts now given 102
Water, splashing hands and face 60
We are your people 63
We meet as friends at table 96
What shall we love and honour ? 3

- Evangelism
To Christ our hearts now given 102
We offer Christ 105

And Themes

Church:
- Global Community
Far and wide the gospel travels 103
In great Calcutta Christ is known 104
Once, from a European shore 91
We offer Christ 105

- Lament and Repentance
Once, from a European shore 91
The gospel came with foreign tongue .. 92

- Leadership
A prophet-woman broke a jar 68
By contact with the Crucified 66
Where shall Wisdom be found? 65

- Mission and Purpose
Box Note: Who has the Gospel ..... page 96
A body broken on a cross 58
A cloud of witnesses around us 74
Come, build the Church 93
Go forth in faith 106
Holy Spirit, storm of love 40
Holy Weaver, deftly intertwining 76
Not only acts of evil will 121
Outgoing God 87
Sing together on our journey 108
We are your people 63

- Stewardship
Joy has blossomed out of sadness 89
(See also Covenant and Commitment)

- Unity (Local to Global)
Dear Christ, uplifted from the earth 44
Far and wide the gospel travels 103
Love alone unites us 64
Painting many pictures 75
Sing together on our journey 108
The walls of separation 200
We are your people 63
When minds and bodies meet 181

City
Arise, shine out 164

Darkness and Light
Box Note .... page 46

Evil
God, give us freedom to lament 119
How deep our Maker's grief 117
Speechless in a world that suffers 116
The horrors of our history 118
When all is ended 161
Will God be Judge? 160

Exile and Migration
Break the bread of belonging 125

Final Destiny (Eschatology)
Box Note .... page 129
See also: Advent

Following Christ:
- The Gospel Call
A body broken on a cross 58
A Stranger, knocking on a door 88
Look at this man 33
Woman in the night 29

- Coming Out of Hiding
All-perceiving Lover 149

- Conversion and New Birth
Dying love has been my birth 43
I have no bucket 1

- The Way of Service
Spirit of Jesus 131

- A Peacable Way
A child, a woman and a man 126
God of Jeremiah 127
Love is the only hope 123
True friends 143
We want to love 133

- Through Trial and Trouble
When on life a darkness falls 151

- The Way of Praise
A Stranger, knocking on a door 88
Christ is alive! 52
Jesus, as we tell your story 59
Sing my song backwards 53
When anyone is in Christ 95

xvii

Topics

God:
Box Notes:
- God - and Evil .... page 42
- Can God grow? .... page 133
- Covenanted Praise .... page 157
- Divine Pronouns .... page 5
- God's Holy Name .... page 6
- The Weaver .... page 3

- Covenant and Presence
Acclaim God's saving news 8
As a mother comforts her child 170
Come let us praise 11
God, give us freedom to lament 119
Great Lover, calling us to share 134
This is a story full of love 10
Water, splashing hands and face 60

- Loving Creator
Acclaim with jubilation 168
As a mother comforts her child 170
Eternal Wisdom, timely Friend 166
Let all creation dance 167
Life is great 144
Thank you, God, for water etc. 111

- Grace and Healing
I have no bucket 1

- Mysterious and Wonderful
Are you the friendly God? 2
God remembers 42
I met three children in the street 178
What shall we love? 3

- Praise and Thanksgiving
A cloud of witnesses around us 74
Acclaim with jubilation 168
Bring many names 173
Come let us praise 11
Dear Mother God 176
Eternal Wisdom, timely Friend 166
God is One, unique and holy 179
God of many Names 7
Great Lover, calling us to share 134
Holy Weaver, deftly intertwining 76
How can we name a love? 136
How shall I sing to God? 150

How wonderful the Three-in-One 182
Joyful is the dark 45
Let all creation dance 167
Name Unnamed 174
Praise God from whom 172
Praise God, the Giver and the Gift 165
Praise lifts our spirit high 171
Praise the God who changes places ... 177
Praise the Lover of Creation 180
Praise to the Maker 169
Sing praises old and new 85
Tree of Fire 175
When minds and bodies 181
Who is God? 5
Who is She? 4

- Revealed as Trinity
Ever-journeying Friend 107
God is One, unique and holy 179
God, the All-Holy 145
How wonderful the Three-in-One 182
I met three children in the street 178
Jesus is with God 56
Joy has blossomed out of sadness 89
May the Sending One sing in you 110
Praise God from whom all 172
Praise God, the Giver and the Gift 165
Praise the God who changes places ... 177
Praise the Lover of Creation 180
Praise to the Maker 169
Source of All, Sustaining Spirit 73
When minds and bodies 181
Who is She? 4

Grief / Bereavement
See Funerals and Memorials

Guilt or Lament? Box Note: .. page 84

Health and Healing
A woman in the crowd 27
Christ will come again 163

HIV/AIDS
When illness meets denial 152

And Themes

Holy Spirit
Come, Holy Breath 82
Great soaring Spirit 130
Source of All, Sustaining Spirit 73
Spirit of Jesus 131
There's a spirit in the air 101
We want to love 133

Hope
Faith moving onward 54

John the Baptist
Welcome the wild one 24

Joseph, father of Jesus
You were a babe of mine 20

Journey
Ever-journeying Friend 107
Sing together on our journey 108

Justice between generations
Box Note: Justice, Peace & Love ... page 92
God, let me welcome timely death 156

Justice, Social
See Peace with Justice

Language
Box Notes:
    Divine Pronouns .... page 5
    God's Holy Name .... page 6
    God - The Weaver .... page 3
We cannot be beguiled 201

Love
Love is the only hope 123

Mary, mother of Jesus
Daughter Mary 28
Her baby, newly breathing 19

Mortality and Hope
God, let me welcome timely death 156
We are the music angels sing 157

Music
Acclaim with jubilation 168
Give thanks for music-making art 69
How shall I sing to God? 150
Painting many pictures 75
Praise lifts our spirit high 171
We are the music angels sing 157

Pain and Suffering
God, give us freedom to lament 119
How deep our Maker's grief 117
Speechless in a world that suffers 116
The horrors of our history 118
When all is ended 161
When illness meets denial 152
When pain and terror 41
Will God be Judge? 160

Patriotism / Nation / War
A child, a woman and a man 126
I love this land 124
The walls of separation 200
Weep for the dead 120

Peace
A child, a woman and a man 126

Peace with Justice
Box Notes:
    Easter Joy-Action for Justice . page 48
    Justice, Peace and Love ...... page 92
Break the bread of belonging 125
Christ will come again 163
Come, build the Church 93
Come, cradle all 112
Dust and ashes 83
Faith moving onward 54
Go forth in faith 106
Here am I 57
Here and now, if you love 32

Topics and Themes

Peace with Justice (cont.)
Holy Spirit, storm of love 40
How good to thank our God 80
Jesus is good news to all the poor 50
Jesus is with God 56
Lead us in paths of truth 132
Listening 195
Love is the only hope 123
Not only acts of evil will 121
Praise God for the harvest 114
Prophets give us hope 128
Say "No" to peace 122
Spirit of Jesus 131
The walls of separation 200
This we can do 129
We want to love 133
When all is ended 161
With humble justice 162

Prayer
When children pray 141

Prophets
God of Jeremiah 127
Prophets give us hope 128

"Sin": Box Note: .... page 74

Theology: Box Note .... page 104

Transitions
Ever-journeying Friend 107
Go forth in faith 106
Go now in peace 148
Great soaring Spirit 130
I Promise (Farewell Song) 194
Love makes a bridge 147
Thank you, God, for times 135
This is a day of new beginnings 159
When joy is drowned 155
When on life a darkness falls 151

Wisdom
Where shall Wisdom be found? 65

Women and Men
Box Note:
   Jesus - For Women and Men? ... page 35
A man of ancient time and place 30
A prophet-woman broke a jar 68
A woman in a world of men 55
All-perceiving Lover 149
Can a man be kind and caring? 31
The light of God is shining bright 139
When anyone is in Christ 95
Woman in the night 29

Worship Arts (see also Music)
Holy Weaver, deftly intertwining 76
How great the mystery of faith 79
Painting many pictures 75

Seeking and Being Found

Questions about Life, Faith, and God

I sought thee long, and afterward I knew
thou moved'st my soul to seek thee, seeking me.
It was not I that found, O Lover true.
No - I was found by thee.

Anonymous, 1890, adapted

Seeking

1

I have no bucket, and the well is deep.
   My thirst is endless, and my throat is dry.
     I ask you, stranger, silent at my side,
   can words refresh my longings if you speak?
I have no bucket, and the well is deep.

Can love unbar the strongrooms of the mind
   and scour the tombs and warrens underground
     for toys and treasures lost, or never found,
   for all I cannot name, yet ache to find?
I have no bucket, and the well is deep.

Who are you, strange yet friendly at my side,
   and can you see and judge, yet understand
     my hidden self, and heal with wounded hands?
   Are you the path, the gateway and the guide,
the keys, the living water, and the light?

Come break the rock, and bid the rivers flow
   from deep unending wells of joy and worth,
     for tears, for drinking, drowning and new birth,
   and I shall find and give myself, and know
the keys, the living water, and the light.

© 1986 Hope Publishing Company for the USA, Canada, Australia and New Zealand and Stainer & Bell Limited for all other territories. All rights reserved.

September 1984. A personal reflection, dealing with recovered childhood memory, drawing on John chapter 4. The second stanza is indebted to *The Tombs of Atuan*, by Ursula LeGuin.
Metre: 10.10.10.10.10.
Numbers 20:9-11; John 4:11-15; 7:37-38.

And Being Found

2

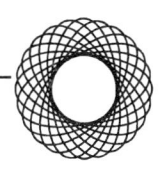

Are you the friendly God, shimmering, swirling, formless,
   nameless and ominous, Spirit of brooding might,
   presence beyond our senses, all-embracing night,
the hovering wings of warm and loving darkness?
   If hope will listen, love will show and tell,
     and all shall be well, all manner of things be well.

Are you the gambler-God, spinning the wheel of creation,
   giving it randomness, willing to be surprised,
   taking a million chances, hopeful, agonized,
greeting our stumbling faith with celebration?
   If hope will listen, love will show and tell,
     and all shall be well, all manner of things be well.

Are you the faithful God, watching and patiently weaving,
   quilting our histories, patching our sins with grace,
   dancing ahead of evil, kissing Satan's face,
till all of our ends are wrapped in love's beginning?
   If hope will listen, love will show and tell,
     and all shall be well, all manner of things be well.

© 1989 Hope Publishing Company for the USA, Canada, Australia and New Zealand and Stainer & Bell Limited for all other territories. All rights reserved.

A workshop group in July 1985 "brainstormed" names and titles of God. Some of the more adventurous metaphors caught my imagination, and I brought them together in this text. The last line of the refrain is taken from *Revelations of Divine Love*, by the 13th Century English mystic, Julian of Norwich.   Metre: Irregular   Matthew 26:48-50

> **God, the Weaver.** To speak of the Holy Weaver (76) who "quilts our histories" (above), suggests that, while each individual is unique and precious, God also values the social fabric of human life, and moves through human history, seeking not a "simple fishing-ground for souls" but "a world more joyful and humane" (134). So I praise the divine Spirit, who mends with a song, "quilting and liltingly weaving peoples and histories, beauty and pain, wickedness, glory and grieving" (169). The metaphor also describes life together in the church ("come, Spirit, weave us into one" - 100) and our individual lives, as we pray that "weaving and mending," the Spirit will "make every ending God's new beginning, glowing with grace" (145). Though I neither quilt nor weave, the metaphor spoke to me early, long before I met it in feminist theology: a 1961 hymn on church unity promises Christ that "we will not question or refuse...the pattern you weave" (186).

Seeking

3

What shall we love and honour most of all?
  No place, no thing, ambition or idea,
  no person, land, or tribe, however dear.
You are the Holy One. You stake your claim;
you give us life and breath; you call our name.

What name is yours? Whom shall we say has called?
  "The One, the Breath, the Wellspring, Adonai,
  the Light, the Lover, Abba, El Shaddai,
I WILL BE WHO I AM, come trust in me.
I have no name. I AM WHO I WILL BE."

What needs must we refuse to idolize? —
  "Controlling, feeling high, and having more,
  submissive hiding, winning, keeping score,
the tribe, the trend, and privacy in walls.
Bow down to none of these. Your Maker calls."

What shall we be? — "A people of the Book,
  who meet to make a freeing, healing space
  where all can enter, stay, and grow in grace,
Christ's story lived, good news, a hopeful song,
an open house, where many can belong."

Then let us live for you, our God, our Guide,
  born of the Spirit, learning how to pray,
  alive in Christ, our hope, our living Way.
Come, breathe through all we say and think and do,
that we may have no other gods but you.

© 1993 Hope Publishing Company for the USA, Canada, Australia and New Zealand and Stainer & Bell Limited for all other territories. All rights reserved.

June 1993, commissioned by Canterbury United Methodist Church, Birmingham, Alabama, and based on Joshua 24, especially the call to "choose this day whom you will serve" in vv. 14-15, the congregation's mission and service theme for the year. The original had a refrain, "And as for me and my house, we will walk with God," quoting v. 15.
Metre: 10.10.10.10.10.
Exodus 3:13-15; Deuteronomy 5:6-7; 6:4-5; Joshua 24:14-15.

And Being Found

4

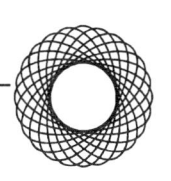

Who is She,
    neither male nor female,
      maker of all things,
      only glimpsed or hinted,
    source of life and gender?
She is God,
    mother, sister, lover;
      in her love we wake,
    move and grow, are daunted,
triumph and surrender.

Who is She,
    mothering her people,
      teaching them to walk,
      lifting weary toddlers,
    bending down to feed them?
She is Love,
    crying in a stable,
      teaching from a boat,
      friendly with the lepers,
bound for crucifixion.

Who is She,
    sparkle in the rapids,
      coolness of the well,
      living power of Jesus
    flowing from the scriptures?
She is Life,
    water, wind and laughter,
      calm, yet never still,
    swiftly moving Spirit,
singing in the changes.

Why is She,
    mother of all nature,
      longing to give birth,
      gasping yet exulting
    to a new creation?
She is Hope,
    never tired of loving,
      filling all with worth,
      glad of our achieving,
lifting all to freedom.

© 1986 Hope Publishing Company for the USA, Canada, Australia and New Zealand and Stainer & Bell Limited for all other territories. All rights reserved.

July 1983. God, beyond male and female, creates femaleness and maleness jointly in the divine image (Genesis 1:26-28), so can be glimpsed in language and metaphors drawn from both female and male experience, provided we recognise (§1) that God is "neither male nor female, only glimpsed or hinted, source of life and gender."
Metre: 3.6.5.6.6.D.
Genesis 1:26-28; Hosea 11:1-4; Mark 4:1; Revelation 21:1-5.

Divine Pronouns My German grammar says, "Die Kohle ist hart, sie ist nicht weich." The noun *Kohle* is feminine, so takes the feminine pronoun, *sie*. But it would be incorrect to translate, "the coal is hard; *she* is not soft." Like biblical Greek and Hebrew, German has *grammatical* gender, related only partially to sexual gender: God-as-he in Hebrew and Greek, though "masculine," is probably less strongly male than God-as-he in English, where "he" and "she" denote sexual gender. If we want to make it clear that "God is not a he, God is not a she, God is not an it or a maybe" (178), the options are: invent a new pronoun (many have failed), go without pronouns (easy in prayer if your heart is where your mouth is, trickier when reading scripture); use both "he" and "she" (but not in the same breath); or use "she" for a while, on the grounds that "he" is overdone. See Elizabeth Johnson, *She Who Is* (New York: Crossroad, 1992, pp. 241-245), who also quotes the above hymn (p. 191).

Seeking

Who is God -	God is young,
young or old?	God is old,
near or far?	God is she,
she or he?	God is he,
All of these	mother's kiss
and none at all,	and father's hug,
loving all,	loving all,
loving me.	loving me.

© 1993 Hope Publishing Company for the USA, Canada, Australia and New Zealand and Stainer & Bell Limited for all other territories. All rights reserved.

June 1988. Research apparently shows that children routinely think of God as a male being. This song, written for children and adults together, nudges aside that false impression.
Metre: 3.3.3.3:3.4.3.3.

> **God's Holy Name.** "Holy is the Name Un-named" (175). In English translations of the Hebrew Bible ("Old Testament"), "The LORD" renders the word, *yhwh*, God's mysterious name. Ancient Hebrew did not write its vowels, but speakers knew what to say, as we would if faced with, "W gthr t wrshp Gd, nd prse Gd's hly nm."
>
> Though Jewish faith didn't speculate much about the meaning of *yhwh*, it probably meant, "the One who Is" or "the One who makes things happen." At first spoken freely, it was later left unsaid - perhaps because speaking someone's name meant having power to summon them, which no-one could dare do with God.
>
> So when Hebrew-speakers came to *yhwh* as they sang a Psalm or read a prophecy, they substituted either *Elohim* (God) or *Adonai* (chieftain, governor). English translations adopted these substitutions (which are not in the biblical text), rendering Adonai as "lord," capitalized as "the LORD."
>
> One effect of this "trans-substitution" was to give the divine Name an overload of male overlordship at variance with the meaning of *yhwh* (though admittedly present elsewhere). Because the Psalms are peppered with the name of God, endless repetition of THE LORD, THE LORD, forms a false image of God as male and overbearing.
>
> To translate *yhwh* as "Yahweh" is offensive to Jews, because it profanes the divine name. Because *adonai* and *elohim* are *substitutions*, not in the text, one option is to transliterate, saying "Adonai" (acceptable to Jews, and suitably mysterious for most English speakers), "Elohim," or "El-Shaddai" (another Hebrew title). Or we can seek reverent substitutions of our own, such as "Holy One" or "Living One" (See *God Beyond Gender*, Gail Ramshaw [Minneapolis: Augsburg Fortress, 1995], chapter 5).
>
> The hymn-poems in this collection explore diverse ways of meeting God: as She (4), as the "Name Un-named, hidden and shown" (174, 175), and as the "God of many Names, gathered into One" (7), working always in a trinitarian framework (e.g. 4, 145, 169). Because *yhwh* became, literally, the "Name Un-named," this title is used as the repeated refrain of 174 and 175, interspersed with varied glimpses of the divine.

And Being Found

6

Each seeking faith is seeking light,
and light dawns on our seeking
    when clashing tongues combine
    to pray that light will shine
and guide and gather all on earth
    in peaceful greeting.

Each seeking faith is seeking truth,
for truth is lived by seeking,
    and though our faiths conflict,
    no dogma can restrict
the power of truth set free on earth
    in honest meeting.

Each loving faith is seeking peace,
and peace is made by seeking
    to spin the strands of trust
    in patterns free and just,
till every family on earth
    is in safe keeping.

Each living faith is seeking life,
and life flows through our seeking
    to treasure, feel and show
    the heart of what we know.
In every faith the Light, the Life,
    is shining, speaking.

© 1989 Hope Publishing Company for the USA, Canada, Australia and New Zealand and Stainer & Bell Limited for all other territories. All rights reserved.

Flying to the USA in January 1987, I saw orthodox Jews reading Hebrew journals while a Muslim behind them bowed forward in prayer. Including myself, and no doubt many others, here were three world faiths in one enclosed space, a parable of life on planet earth. The first stanza was written on the plane, the remainder during the next two weeks. The adverbs are carefully chosen: not all expressions of religious faith are seeking, loving, peaceful or living.
Metre: 8.7.6.6.8.5.

> **Christians and Other Faiths.** "Will clashing faiths be honoured and fulfilled, as pilgrims dance in galaxies of truth? Faith says, Amen, we know not how or when, but being found, are seeking yet to find." (160). If I lived in a Christian minority among Hindus, Buddhists, and Muslims, I would probably write more about "the Spirit's new, surprising word, in ours or other faiths, or none" (58). But "Each seeking faith" has guidelines: (a) "our faiths conflict" (all religions are not the same); (b) though different faith world-views seem like different "galaxies," we have to choose which values can be held in common and which cannot, and I choose honesty, justice, openness ("seeking") and peace ("the power of truth...in honest meeting, " "patterns free and just"), against coercion, fanaticism and uncommitted relativism; (c) our task is not to abandon our faith, but to *"treasure, feel, and show* the heart of what we know" and share it, while being challenged and changed for good by the other's truth. On a planet with many faiths, and in a universe with many likely life-forms, I sense a purpose which, "weaving dark and light, as deep and restless as the sea, is overcast with mystery, and ranges far beyond our sight" (166), yet affirm that Jesus Christ is "the truth about God." From knowing Christ, I believe that, while "G-o-d" is far more complex and mysterious than any story, code, faith, or symbol system can know and express, She-He-They-It is not untruthfully or deceitfully "more," but faithfully, wonderfully and lovingly "more."

"Come And Meet Us"

7

God of many Names
gathered into One,
in your glory come and meet us,
Moving, endlessly Becoming;
God of Hovering Wings,
Womb and Birth of time,
joyfully we sing your praises,
Breath of life in every people—
Hush, hush, hallelujah, hallelujah!
Shout, shout, hallelujah, hallelujah!
Sing, sing, hallelujah, hallelujah!
Sing, God is love, God is love!

God of Jewish faith,
Exodus and Law,
in your glory come and meet us,
joy of Miriam and Moses;
God of Jesus Christ,
Rabbi of the poor,
joyfully we sing your praises,
crucified, alive for ever—
Hush, hush, hallelujah, hallelujah!
Shout, shout, hallelujah, hallelujah!
Sing, sing, hallelujah, hallelujah!
Sing, God is love, God is love!

God of Wounded Hands,
Web and Loom of love,
in your glory come and meet us,
Carpenter of new creation;
God of many Names
gathered into One,
joyfully we sing your praises,
Moving, endlessly Becoming—
Hush, hush, hallelujah, hallelujah!
Shout, shout, hallelujah, hallelujah!
Sing, sing, hallelujah, hallelujah!
Sing, God is love, God is love!

© 1986 Hope Publishing Company for the USA, Canada, Australia and New Zealand and Stainer & Bell Limited for all other territories. All rights reserved.

February 1985. A prayer that we may meet (or rather, be met by) divine holiness. Exodus 3:14 inspires the conviction of God, "moving, endlessly becoming," because the Hebrew shows an incomplete action: possible translations include "I am who I am," "I am who I will be," "I will be who I will be," and "I will be who I am."   Metre: 5.5.8.8.D. Refr.
Exodus 3:14; Psalm 104:29-30 ("Breath of life in every people"), John 1:38; 3:2; 3:26-28.

Hearing the Spoken Word

God's Covenant in History and Revelation in Jesus Christ

Hark the glad sound! The Saviour comes,
the Saviour promised long.
Let every heart prepare a throne,
and every voice a song.

Philip Doddridge (1702-1751)

God With Us

8

Acclaim God's saving news,
first given to the Jews,
    and give them honoured place;
through years of good and ill,
they praise and cherish still
    the covenant of grace.

Let us, like them, agree:
"Your people we will be,
    and by our journey trace
your love most good and just,
as we obey and trust
    the covenant of grace.

Your holiness sublime,
surpasses space and time,
    yet has a human face;
in Jesus seen and shown,
we treasure and make known
    the covenant of grace.

In Christ we safely name
our failure, fear and shame,
    and need no hiding place,
accepting like a child,
reborn and reconciled,
    the covenant of grace.

Forgiving and fulfilled,
we hope to be, and build,
    a friendly, freeing space
for healing, growth and prayer,
where many seek and share
    the covenant of grace.

We pray, in all we do,
that knowledge old and new
    may nimbly interlace
with caring deep and just,
that others too may trust
    the covenant of grace."

© 1995 Hope Publishing Company for the USA, Canada, Australia and New Zealand and Stainer & Bell Limited for all other territories. All rights reserved.

March 1995. Commissioned for the tenth anniversary of Grace Covenant Presbyterian Church, Overland Park, Kansas, whose name suggested the theme and repeated phrase, "the covenant of grace." The writing process included listing feasible rhyming words with "grace" (working backwards from the last line of each stanza), seeking to honour the living reality of Jewish faith, and giving thanks for our incorporation into God's covenant.   Metre: 6.6.6.D.

> **Christians and Jews: Covenant.** Christian theology has begun to lament and repent of the anti-Judaism which, allied with anti-Semitism, "paved the devil's way to Auschwitz and the Holocaust" (90). Liturgy has not caught up with theology. If your hymnal praises God as Creator, adds a generic reference to providence, then jumps through "O Come, O Come Immanuel" into the promised coming and life, death and resurrection of Jesus, it continues theological anti-Judaism by ignoring God's actions in history, and God's historic covenant with the people of Israel. The Christian year needs a space to celebrate God's love in all human history, and to re-tell the story of Israel, recognizing that "in this story we belong" (60). To do so means trying to clarify our understanding of "Jewishness" as cultural identity, our attitude to the State of Israel and the Israel-Palestine conflict, and our appreciation of Judaism as a living faith, with which we hope to "walk at last in love." (160). Several hymns in this collection take up these themes. Christian faith should gladly "acclaim God's saving news, first given to the Jews, and give them honoured place" (8, above).

In History

9

Sing and tell our Saviour's story,
    starting from creation's birth,
God's design for human glory,
    love embracing all the earth.
Joyful news we have to tell,
whispered long in Israel,
    then in Jesus clearly spoken,
    bread of life from body broken.

Celebrate our founding vision,
    simple truth to set us free,
sung, or argued with precision,
    carried far by land and sea:
"God in Christ is fully known.
Trust in God's great love alone.
    All can meet our Friend and Saviour
    in the heart, and in the scripture."

Marvel at the Word, unbounded,
    grandly spreading time and space,
gladly then in Jesus grounded,
    smiling in a Jewish face,
life surrendered and begun,
freed to live in everyone:
    meet the Christ in men and women,
    in our elders and our children.

Gather now to pray and listen.
    Heed the Word we need to hear,
teaching, touching every person,
    easing grief and ending fear.
Singing, bringing heart and mind,
all who seek will fully find
    at the pulpit and the table
    love to challenge and enable.

Give our thirsty sons and daughters,
    not our culture's ebb and flow,
but the Spirit's living waters,
    welling from the Rock below.
See and seek the distant gleam,
justice, flowing like a stream.
    Move with eager exploration,
    ready still for reformation.

© 1993 Hope Publishing Company for the USA, Canada, Australia and New Zealand and Stainer & Bell Limited for all other territories. All rights reserved.

March 1993. Commissioned for the 125th anniversary of Third Reformed Church, Holland, Michigan. If I tell you a story about someone, you will know them better than if I try to describe what they are like. Similarly, we get to know God, not by listing God's character-traits, but by telling the story of God's grace in history and self-disclosure in Jesus Christ. For Third Reformed, a church in the tradition of John Calvin, it was appropriate to use a Genevan Psalm tune (GENEVAN 12), which I encouraged them to sing with energy, as the joyful dance it is.
Metre: 8.7.8.7.7.7.8.8.
Numbers 20:10-11; Amos 5:24; John 1:1-3; 1 Corinthians 10:4.

God With Us

10

This is a story full of love,
   a song to set us free,
of God, the Wisdom and the Word,
   the keystone and the key.

For Wisdom guides the flow of life
   and governs, hour by hour,
the forces of the universe,
   the fragrance of a flower.

And faith, awakened, hears the Word
   that Abraham must move
and slaves of Pharaoh take the road
   to freedom, law and love.

The Wisdom and the Word are one
   when flesh and bone and breath
reveal the human face of God,
   the child of Nazareth.

Disfigured on a Roman cross,
   extinguished and absurd,
by faith we praise the power of God,
   the Wisdom and the Word.

Arising over earthly powers
   our Saviour has begun
to catch them in a web of love
   and weave them into one.

    Praise God, the Wisdom and the Word,
      till all the world can see
      that Jesus is the first and last,
      the keystone and the key.

© 1986 Hope Publishing Company for the USA, Canada, Australia and New Zealand and Stainer & Bell Limited for all other territories. All rights reserved.

April 1985. Written for William Rowan's fine tune, TIMOTHY, which suggested the first line as I sang it. The hymn joins two key titles of Christ, as Wisdom of God and Word of God.
Common Metre (8.6.8.6.)
Genesis 12:1-9; Exodus 3:7-12; Proverbs 3:19-20 and 8:22-31; John 1:1-16; 1 Corinthians 1:18-31 and 2:6-8; Colossians 1:13-20 and 2:9-15; Revelation 22:13.

> **Christians and Jews - Living Faith.** Christian anti-Judaism is the shadow side of our praise for Jesus as Christ, because "believing Christ had come, we (the Church) cursed them as forever wrong" (90). Here, as elsewhere, we need to deal with historic, collective, and systemic sins which shape us without necessarily being expressed in every individual's actions. Though I have written of the Wisdom of God "shining in Israel's *past*" (85), I now watch my language more carefully, and try to speak clearly of Judaism as faith in God with a life of its own, as "through years of good and ill, they praise and cherish still, the covenant of grace" (8). Jewish faith has much to give us, not least its love of God's justice and wrestling with God's absence. When Christians seek reconciliation with believing Jews, we should come barefoot, not condescending, and ask that God may "help us, who long to mend our ancient parting of the ways, to recognize their faith, and utter Jesus' name, not in polemic but in praise, till all our hopes are made complete" (90).

In History

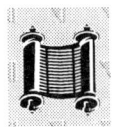

11

Come let us praise what God has done,
and all that God will do,
whose love is older than the sun,
and yet forever new.

When slaves in Egypt, long ago,
were pleading to be free,
God said, through Moses, "Let them go!",
and led them through the sea.

Remembering that old surprise,
in exile and despair,
the prophets cried, "Awake! Arise!
The way of God prepare!"

God's freeing love again was shown:
By pagan king's decree
the people came rejoicing home,
for all the world to see.

And what of Christ, who rose from death
when life and hope were lost,
and gave us, by the Spirit's breath,
the power of Pentecost?

Through many years, and still today,
Christ, endlessly alive,
has travelled with us on our way,
and waits where we arrive.

Let everything that God has done
our faith and hope renew
to love and honour everyone
and show what God can do.

© 1996 Hope Publishing Company for the USA, Canada, Australia and New Zealand and Stainer & Bell Limited for all other territories. All rights reserved.

February 1996, commissioned for the 275th Anniversary of White Clay Creek Presbyterian Church, Newark, Delaware. In the ballad style of the Scottish Metrical Psalms, this hymn tells the story of God's deliverance, believing that the oldest thing we know about God is that God does new things.
Common Metre
Exodus 8:20 and 14-15; Isaiah 40:1-3; 43:16-21 and 45:1-7, 13-14; Lamentations 3:22-23.

Jesus of Nazareth

12

Who comes? A child,
delivered on a stable floor.
His mewing, newborn cry
    is all that God can say
    of costly, unprotected love
    in Christ, alive today.
Come, singing fire
    of truth, compassion, right,
        and melt our hardened apathy,
        till love is new and bright.

Who comes? A Jew,
declaiming from a prophet's scroll.
His liberating cry
    is all that God can say
    of seeking, giving, freeing love
    in Christ, alive today.
Come, singing breeze,
    from worlds already new.
        Blow in and out of weary minds
        till faith is singing too.

Who comes? A man,
in dying moments on a cross.
His godforsaken cry
    is all that God can say
    of faithful, never-ending love
    in Christ, alive today.
Come, singing light
    from new creation's dawn,
        where trees of healing deck the streets,
        and joy is newly born.

© 1986, 1996 Hope Publishing Company for the USA, Canada, Australia and New Zealand and Stainer & Bell Limited for all other territories. All rights reserved.

July 1983. A poem in which we hear the story of Jesus (a child, a Jew, a crucified man) as the full disclosure of God's love ("all that God can say") and greet the Spirit of God breaking into the present from the new world yet to be.
Metre: 4.8.6.6.8.6.4.6.8.6.
Mark 15:34; Luke 2:7 and Luke 4:16-21; Acts 2:3; Revelation 22:1-2.

Promised Coming

13

Jesus comes today!
Prepare to meet your God!
  No Presidential cavalcade
  encircles him with might;
    the shepherds kiss a worker's child
    who loves till all are reconciled:
      Prepare to meet your God!

      Jesus comes today!
      Prepare to meet your God!
        No massed Convention roars its praise
        to hail the new messiah;
          love has no powers to lay aside,
          so crowds will have him crucified:
            Prepare to meet your God!

            Jesus comes today!
            Prepare to meet your God!
              No Primaries can pave his way
              to be the people's choice;
                he chooses us, and calls our name,
                and life can never be the same:
                  Prepare to meet your God!

© 1986 Hope Publishing Company for the USA, Canada, Australia and New Zealand and Stainer & Bell Limited for all other territories. All rights reserved.

March 1984. Written in response to a request for hymns for advent, this hymn contrasts the coming of Jesus with an American Presidential campaign, from the primaries (§3) where party members vote for the person of their choice, to the party convention (§2) where the candidate is chosen, to the inauguration cavalcade (§1). The logic of the advent story led me to reverse the campaign's chronological order, with the unforeseen result that the hymn does what Jesus does - reverse our priorities and expectations.
Metre: 5.6.8.6.8.8.6.
Amos 4:12; Mark 2:13-14; Luke 2:16-20.

Jesus of Nazareth

14

Will you come and see the light from the stable door?
   It is shining newly bright, though it shone before.
     It will be your guiding star, it will show you who you are.
Will you hide, or decide to meet the light?

Will you step into the light that can free the slave?
   It will stand for what is right, it will heal and save.
     By the pyramids of greed there's a longing to be freed.
Will you hide, or decide to meet the light?

Will you tell about the light in the prison cell?
   Though it's shackled out of sight, it is shining well.
     When the truth is cut and bruised, and the innocent abused,
will you hide, or decide to meet the light?

Will you join the hope, alight in a young girl's eyes,
   of the mighty put to flight by a baby's cries?
     When the lowest and the least are the foremost at the feast,
will you hide, or decide to meet the light?

Will you travel by the light of the babe new born?
   In the candle lit at night there's a gleam of dawn,
     and the darkness all about is too dim to put it out:
will you hide, or decide to meet the light?

© 1993 Hope Publishing Company for the USA, Canada, Australia and New Zealand and Stainer & Bell Limited for all other territories. All rights reserved.

April 1989. May be sung complete, or by adding a stanza per Sunday, thus:
1 - Advent Hope;   3 - John the Baptist;
2 - Law and Prophets;   4 - Mary's Magnificat;   5 - Christmas Day.
Commissioned by Christian Aid, London (Aid and Development Agency for the British Churches) with whom I have long and glad association. I chose KELVINGROVE as a suitable folk tune.
Metre: 12.12.14.10.
Matthew 2:1-2(§1) and 11: 2-15(§3); Mark 10:31(§4); Luke 1:46-55(§4); John 1:5(§5 line 3) and John 8:12(§5).

Birth

15

Hail, undiminished love,
   destroyed, yet resurrected,
   foreshadowed and foreseen,
yet always unexpected.

Through old, familiar forms,
   in weekly repetition,
   God startles us with grace,
yet makes no imposition:

Exotic angel hosts
   can show us nothing stranger
   than pregnancy and birth,
and parents at a manger.

No scripture, star or sign
   can guarantee the Saviour:
   a child, a man, a life
are all there is on offer.

He calls us to decide—
   for love, or domination,
   for tenderness, or pride,
for justice, or oppression.

Hail, unexpected love
   in old, familiar story:
   this ordinary birth
is Christ, the hope of glory!

© 1986, 1996 Hope Publishing Company for the USA, Canada, Australia and New Zealand and Stainer & Bell Limited for all other territories. All rights reserved.

February 1984, inspired by an advent sermon by a friend, Charles Allen, to whom it is dedicated.
Metre: 6.7.6.7.

Jesus: Human Stranger. Against the Scandinavian Jesus of Sunday school pictures, and the Divinely Sweet Jesus of 1890s middle-class piety, my generation celebrates the humanness of Jesus of Nazareth. If Jesus was not fully *human*, then God was not with us in the flesh. If Jesus was *fully* human, he was, as all humans are, unique in personality, gender, culture, language, and life span. Being human, Jesus becomes closer, yet remains the intimate stranger, "a man of ancient time and place, with foreign speech and foreign face" (30). As a newborn infant, his eyes had "yet to name or trace the world of shape and colour, or recognise a face" (19). He was Mary's child (18, 19), Joseph's son (20), a Jewish man of the first century (12, 25, 26). Celebrating the humanness of Jesus shows me who God is. "Humanity" and "divinity" are not opposites yoked in a hybrid humanoid: it is through Jesus, as human, that I have knowledge of God, as "holiness eternal is perfectly expressed" in the infant's "hands that clutch unthinking, and lips that tug the breast" (19), or as this man of ancient time and place "reveals the glory, power and grace of costly, unexpected love" (30). Because the divine Word became flesh in Jesus, we should value and enjoy the human body, and celebrate our embodied life: "good is the flesh that the Word has become," "good is the body for knowing the world," and "good is the body from cradle to grave" (23).

Jesus of Nazareth

16

When God is a child
there's joy in our song.
The last shall be first
and the weak shall be strong,
and none shall be afraid.

Hope is a star that shines in the night,
leading us on till the morning is bright.

Peace is a ribbon that circles the earth,
giving a promise of safety and worth.

Joy is a song that welcomes the dawn,
telling the world that the Saviour is born.

Love is a flame that burns in our heart.
Jesus has come and will never depart.

When God is a child
there's joy in our song.
The last shall be first
and the weak shall be strong,
and none shall be afraid.

17

Oh, how joyfully,
Oh, how hopefully,
waits the world on Christmas Eve!
    Love comes healing,
    God revealing
Friends, be joyful and believe!

Oh, how joyfully,
Oh, how peacefully,
sleeps the world on Christmas Night!
    Sins are covered,
    grace discovered.
In our darkness shines the light!

Oh, how joyfully,
Oh, how thankfully,
wakes the world on Christmas Morn!
    God has spoken,
    death is broken,
Alleluia! Christ is born!

© 1989 (No. 16) and 1993 (No. 17) Hope Publishing Company for the USA, Canada, Australia and New Zealand and Stainer & Bell Limited for all other territories. All rights reserved.

Birth

18

When a baby in your arms
grips your little finger tight,
but cannot tell you why,
or say your name,
remember Christmas,
a shining star above,
and tiny fingers,
clutching from the cradle,
holding you with love, eternal love.

When a baby in your arms
gives a yelling, bawling cry,
then wails a nameless need
you can't ignore,
remember Christmas,
a shining star above,
and hear the crying,
crying from the cradle,
calling you with love, eternal love.

When a baby in your arms
gazes deep into your eyes,
and you're the only face
that baby knows,
remember Christmas,
a shining star above,
and eyes a-gazing,
gazing from the cradle,
meeting you with love, eternal love.

© 1993 Hope Publishing Company for the USA, Canada, Australia and New Zealand and Stainer & Bell Limited for all other territories. All rights reserved.

December 1991. If Jesus was fully human, it follows that he was truly a newborn infant, without speech or developed intellect. If Jesus was the Word of God in human flesh, God can meet us through what infants unthinkingly do, if we are willing to hear, see, and be grasped by them.
Metre: 7.7.6.4.5.6.5.6.5.4.

Notes on Nos. 16 and 17 (opposite page)

"When God is a Child" - Advent 1985, revised 1987, based on four Advent themes: hope, peace, joy and love. Each Sunday adds a new stanza, all four being sung in the final week. Add symbols, for visual effect, thus - week 1: a star, made with foil or other material; week 2: a multicoloured ribbon, held aloft; week 3: a mobile of musical symbols, or a windchime; week 4: a lighted candle.
Metre: Irregular
Isaiah 12:2 and 35:3-4; Mark 10:31; 2 Corinthians 12:10.

"Oh, How Joyfully" - July 1990, for the Brethren-Mennonite Hymnal Council, as a re-envisioning in English of the German "O du fröliche" (Johann D. Falk and Heinrich Holzschuher, trans. Harris Loewen). As often with German and French, the original takes more syllables per unit of meaning than does English. To avoid sounding "thin," a verse translation must add, rather than subtract meaning.
Metre: 5.5.7.4.4.7.

Jesus of Nazareth

Her baby, newly breathing,
  with wailing needful cry,
    by Mary kissed and cradled,
      is lulled in lullaby.
        Long months of hope and waiting,
      the thrill and fear of birth,
    are crowned with exultation,
and God is on the earth.

The eyes that gaze at Mary
  have yet to name or trace
    the world of shape and colour,
      or recognize a face;
        yet Holiness Eternal
      is perfectly expressed
    in hands that clutch unthinking,
and lips that tug the breast.

The milk of life is flowing
  as Mary guides and feeds
    her wordless Word, embodied
      in infant joys and needs.
        Enormous, formless strivings,
      and yearnings deep and wide,
    becradled in communion,
are fed and satisfied.

How mother-like the Wisdom
  that carried and gave birth
    to all things, seen and unseen,
      and nurtured infant earth:
        unstinting, unprotected,
      prepared for nail and thorn,
    constricted into maleness,
and of a woman born.

© 1989 Hope Publishing Company for the USA, Canada, Australia and New Zealand and Stainer & Bell Limited for all other territories. All rights reserved.

In November 1987, I heard Hal Hopson's MERLE'S TUNE, and wanted to write for it. The poem grew by listening to women's experience of pregnancy, birthing and nursing. The women with whom I conversed often said, "No, its not like that," or "That's a male viewpoint. It was like this...," and I had to try again. I reworked the final stanza several times, till the opening lines came suddenly, like a surprise gift which exactly meets a need. The Nicene creed is echoed in §4, line 3.
Metre: 7.6.7.6.D. Iambic   John 1:14

Birth

20

You were a babe of mine.
I watched you born, and wept
with joy to see your sticky head.
I held you in my arms.
I watched you, awe-struck, as you slept.
   I love you, Christ of God:
   you were a babe of mine.

You were a boy of mine.
You wallowed in the sand.
You copied me at work, and played
with hammer, wood and nails.
You talked to me, and held my hand.
   I love you, Christ of God:
   you were a boy of mine.

You were a youth of mine.
Quite suddenly you grew,
and questioned all my words and ways.
I felt you breaking free.
I raged, admired, and feared for you.
   I love you, Christ of God:
   you were a youth of mine.

You were a son of mine,
full grown, my hope and pride.
You went your puzzling way, a man
so ready, fine and young:
life broke in me the day you died.
   I love you, Christ of God:
   you were a son of mine.

      You are the life of all,
      the Christ, the Chosen One.
      You loved and gave yourself for me;
      As I belong to you,
      new worlds are born, new life begun.
         I love you, Christ of God:
         you are the life of all.

© 1980, 1996 Hope Publishing Company for the USA, Canada, Australia and New Zealand and Stainer & Bell Limited for all other territories. All rights reserved.

December 1972, for a Christmas card, revised 1994. "Joseph's Carol" explores what it might have meant to know Jesus in person, as infant, child, youth and adult, from birth to death. Though both painful and wonderful, such knowledge would give no special advantage. To believe that this all-too-familiar person was God's Messiah would have meant a venture of faith, as it does now. The poem draws on my experience as teenager and parent.
Metre: 6.6.8.6.8.6.6.
Galatians 2:20; 2 Corinthians 5:16-18.

Jesus of Nazareth

If I could visit Bethlehem,
    what presents would I bring?
If I could see what happened then,
    what would I say or sing?

    I wouldn't take a modern toy,
        but gold to pay for bread,
    some wine to give his parents joy,
        and wool to warm his bed.

    I'd learn some simple words to speak
        in Aramaic tongue.
    I'd cradle him, and kiss his cheek,
        and say, "I'm glad you've come."

If Mary asked me who I was
    and what her child would do;
I wouldn't talk about the cross,
    or tell her all I knew.

    I'd say, "He'll never hurt or kill,
        and joy will follow tears.
    We'll know his name and love him still,
        in twenty hundred years."

I cannot visit Bethlehem,
    but what I can, I'll do:
I'll love you, Jesus as my friend,
    and give my life to you.

© 1990 Hope Publishing Company for the USA, Canada, Australia and New Zealand and Stainer & Bell Limited for all other territories. All rights reserved.

November 1988. Dedicated to Summertown United Reformed Church, Oxford, and first sung there in December 1988. The hymn imagines us as time travellers, and asks what we would do, say, and give, if we could go back to Bethlehem. When I ask children what they would take, they are as theologically practical as this hymn.
Common Metre

Birth

22

Child, when Herod wakes,
and hate or exploitation
swing their dripping swords,
from your cross and cradle
    sing a new song.

Child, when Caesar's laws
choke love or strangle freedom,
calling darkness light,
from your cross and cradle
    sing a new song.

Child, when Caiaphas
sends truth to crucifixion
to protect his prayers,
from your cross and cradle
    sing a new song.

Child, your helpless love
brings death and resurrection:
joyfully we come
to your cross and cradle
    with a new song—
    Alleluia!

© 1993 Hope Publishing Company for the USA, Canada, Australia and New Zealand and Stainer & Bell Limited for all other territories. All rights reserved.

December 1973. Herod, Caesar and Caiaphas are historical figures, yet also archetypes, who stand for typical and recurring abuses of political, religious, and economic power.
Metre: 5.7.5.6.4.
Psalm 98:1-2; Isaiah 5:20; Matthew 2:7-18; John 11:47-53; Revelation 5:9a.

> **Jesus - Christ.** When I first came to church, a "teenage seeker" before either word was invented, I met Jesus as the joy-giving meaning of life, and as the truth about God. The "how" of this, as I heard it preached, was less persuasive: a moral example I couldn't follow, or the one who saved me from personal sin by getting in the way of God's wrath. I now see Jesus as bringing God's radical message for all human relationships, calling us to decide "for love or domination, for tenderness or pride, for justice or oppression" (15). In his own life story, he does this by bringing outcasts to rebirth, lifting the humble, shifting the proud, and ending domination (26, 28). Whatever our theories of "atonement," Jesus becomes "Christ" to us as we "sing and tell our Saviour's story" (9). For if we tell how Jesus lived and led, and treasure all he did and said ("teacher, healer, Spirit-filled, peasant-prophet, captured, killed"), we find that "from his life the Spirit soars, all of history explores, reaching us and seeking all"(60). Because Jesus lived completely with God and for God, faithful to the point of death, his "life surrendered and begun" has been "freed to live in everyone." Instead of a GodHuman freak no-one can imitate, the One who meets us in Jesus is "*longing in all*, as in Jesus, to dwell" (23), as we "meet the Christ in men and women, in our elders and our children" (9). So I "marvel at the Word unbounded, grandly spreading time and space, gladly then in Jesus grounded, smiling in a Jewish face" (9), believing that "Christ is our sign, our window into God," whose freeing life, "unfinished by a cross, awakens hope, and points a way ahead" (160).

Jesus - Word in Flesh

Good is the flesh that the Word has become,
    good is the birthing, the milk in the breast,
    good is the feeding, caressing and rest,
    good is the body for knowing the world,
Good is the flesh that the Word has become.

Good is the body for knowing the world,
    sensing the sunlight, the tug of the ground,
    feeling, perceiving, within and around,
    good is the body, from cradle to grave,
Good is the flesh that the Word has become.

Good is the body, from cradle to grave,
    growing and ageing, arousing, impaired,
    happy in clothing, or lovingly bared,
    good is the pleasure of God in our flesh,
Good is the flesh that the Word has become.

Good is the pleasure of God in our flesh,
    longing in all, as in Jesus, to dwell,
    glad of embracing, and tasting, and smell,
    good is the body, for good and for God,
Good is the flesh that the Word has become.

© 1989 Hope Publishing Company for the USA, Canada, Australia and New Zealand and Stainer & Bell Limited for all other territories. All rights reserved.

August 1986, revised 1987, inspired by James Nelson's book, *Between Two Gardens* (New York: The Pilgrim Press, 1983). An ancient mis-diagnosis of the human condition (Manichaeism) sees sexuality and the body as unclean and disgusting. Manichaeism is still with us, in the anger and disgust expressed in church conflicts about sexuality, and the awkwardness still felt by many when talking about sex and bodily life in church settings, such as public worship. The hymn celebrates the logical consequences of believing that the Word became FLESH, and that God loves matter and affirms it as good. God's embodied human life in Jesus (incarnation) is seen, not as distancing God-in-Christ from everyone else, but as the beginning of divine indwelling in us all.
Metre: 10.10.10.10.10. Dactylic
Genesis 1:31; John 1:14.

Jesus - Baptism

24

Welcome the wild one, the desert declaimer,
urgently, awesomely, crying his news:
   "Now, listen now! There is One who comes after!
   I am unfitted to fasten his shoes."

Camel-hair coated, unkempt and unbending,
living off grasshoppers, honey and briars,
   knee-deep in water, he hails the impending
   flame-giving Spirit's enveloping fires.

Hear from the herald the king who's expected:
world-ending wrath is the power he describes,
   God's own anointed, outspoken, uncensored,
   judging the palace, the priests and the scribes.

See now the young one who lingers and listens,
standing intent in the buzz of the throng,
   waiting in line, on the brink of decisions,
   seeking the Spirit that beckons through John.

Gaspingly drenched by the people's baptiser,
drowned in the grief of our groanings and cries,
   bowing beneath God's unfettered outsider,
   rising envisioned, he opens his eyes.

Welcome God's Love-Child, anointed, invested,
   desert-impelled by the Spirit within.
World-making love, shining, tempered and tested,
   now is at hand - let salvation begin!

© 1989 Hope Publishing Company for the USA, Canada, Australia and New Zealand and Stainer & Bell Limited for all other territories. All rights reserved.

April 1986, for the Hymn Society of America's search for new Advent hymns, one of two hymns published in the October 1986 issue of *The Hymn*. Hymn-poet Tom Troeger's skill with imagery and onomatopoeia prompted me to try being similarly adventurous, though he's not to blame if it doesn't succeed.
Metre: 11.10.11.10. Dactylic
Matthew 3:1-17; Mark 1:1-14; Luke 3:1-22.

Jesus - Baptism

25

What was your vow and vision,
    revealed and recognised,
Christ, when you came to Jordan
    and asked to be baptised?
Was there a sudden splendour
of prophets, priests and kings,
    a wind that stirred the waters,
    a blur of mighty wings?

Was this God's call, the crowning
    of all you had become:
"Go, show and tell my coming,
    my own, my chosen one"?
Did scripture join with scripture,
revealing in surprise
    the triumph of a servant
    rejected and despised?

We meet you at the water
    and ponder why and how,
in hope that we may follow
    where God is going now,
anointed by your Spirit,
reborn, and energised,
    through deed and word proclaiming:
    "In Christ we are baptised!"

© 1975, 1994 Hope Publishing Company for the USA, Canada, Australia and New Zealand and Stainer & Bell Limited for all other territories. All rights reserved.

We don't know the inner life of Jesus, but the stories of his baptism direct us to seek the meaning of our own. This hymn meets Jesus as the Christ of God, so remembers Israel's story with God in the historical meanings of "anointing" and the phrase, "sudden splendour (=visionary experience) of prophets, priests and kings."
Metre: 7.6.7.6.D.
Isaiah 9:1-6 and 53:1-3; Matthew 3:13-17; Mark 1:9-11; Luke 3:21-22.

And Temptation

26

How perilous the messianic call! —
to hear a voice, discover hidden pow'rs,
and feel the tempting urge to work for God
by winning wars, or fame, or dazzled hearts!
How sweet the call our true Messiah brings:
"Come, let us be a messianic people,
loving justice, trusting love,
finding strength and giving power,
living faithfully with God."

How marvellous the messianic claim! —
a man who kneels, with simple dignity,
God's chosen leader, washing dirty feet;
to women, hope; to all, enabling love;
to men, a model; friend of every child.
"Come, let us be a messianic people...

How scandalous the messianic way —
befriending outcasts, going far from home,
to be rejected, captured, crucified,
and then arise, amazingly alive
in youth and elder, foreigner and slave!
"Come, let us be a messianic people...

How beautiful the messianic hope! —
our lives reborn, set free from dreary need
to domineer, or hide, or be enslaved,
made strong in Christ to clash, forgive, and grow,
as leaders kneel, and call us with a song:
"Come, let us be a messianic people,
loving justice, trusting love,
finding strength and giving power,
living faithfully with God."

© 1994 Hope Publishing Company for the USA, Canada, Australia and New Zealand and Stainer & Bell Limited for all other territories. All rights reserved.

June 1994, commissioned for the 30th anniversary of Messiah United Methodist Church, Springfield, Virginia, whose name suggested the theme. Recent cults remind us of the danger of believing that God has called you to be a spiritual leader, with paranoia and megalomania as frequent results. The record shows Jesus as confident yet non-domineering, seeking to empower his followers to become a community living the way of love, not domination.
Metre: 10.10.10.10.10. Refr.
Matthew 4:1-11, also 20:20-28; Mark 1:12-13; Luke 4:1-30; John 13:1-20.

Jesus

27

A woman in the crowd
quietly hides her defiling blood.
  "Who can tell
  twelve years of tiredness,
  longing to be well?"
Yet trusting her spirit,
  refusing to be cowed,
    she touches a coat-sleeve,
    and feels God is good.
      Health is gospel! All is well!
      Hosanna! Hosanna!
      God is always good.

A beggar, always blind,
washes his face and is dazzled by light.
  "How can he,
  punished by blindness,
  claim that he can see?"
Yet trusting his spirit,
  while many close their mind,
  he greets God in Jesus
  and sharpens his sight.
      Health is gospel! All is well!
      Hosanna! Hosanna!
      God is always good.

An immigrant from Tyre
argues for scraps from the table of grace.
  "Should her child
  get special treatment,
  foreign and defiled?"
Yet led by the Spirit,
  she senses the Messiah,
  and knows that he comes
  for the whole human race.
      Health is gospel! All is well!
      Hosanna! Hosanna!
      God is always good.

© 1986 Hope Publishing Company for the USA, Canada, Australia and New Zealand and Stainer & Bell Limited for all other territories. All rights reserved.

July 1983, for a study pack, *Health is Gospel* (Methodist Church Overseas Division, London).
Jesus' healings enacted the good news he preached.
Metre: Irregular
Matthew 15:21-28; Mark 5:25-34; John 9:1-41.

Life Work

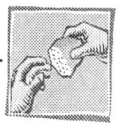

28

Daughter Mary, saying yes
    to the angel's visitation,
        no disgrace shall cloud your face.
           Thrill us with your expectation:
           As in heaven, so on earth,
           God will work salvation,
        as the child you bring to birth,
    checks the wealthy, feeds the poor,
ending domination.

Mother Mary, crying no
    at your son's disruptive vision,
        he must roam away from home,
           breaking family cohesion:
           Planting heaven here on earth,
           God's new invitation
        brings the outcasts to rebirth,
    lifts the humble, shifts the proud,
ending domination.

Sister Mary, pierced and torn,
    as the child your arms protected,
        chokes and dies before your eyes,
           trust again the unexpected:
           Love has broken free on earth!
           Death and domination
        tumble as the Spirit's mirth,
    weaving friendship, sparking hope,
sings of new creation.

© 1989 Hope Publishing Company for the USA, Canada, Australia and New Zealand and Stainer & Bell Limited for all other territories. All rights reserved.

November 1986, for a Christmas card, meeting Mary as the daughter of her parents, the mother of Jesus, and our sister in Christ.
Metre: 7.8.7.8.7.6.7.7.6.
Mark 3:20-21, 31-35; Luke 1:26-38, 46-55; John 19:25-27.

Jesus

29

Woman in the night,
   spent from giving birth,
   guard our precious light;
peace is on the earth.
   Come and join the song,
   women, children, men.
   Jesus makes us free to live again!

Woman in the crowd,
   creeping up behind,
   touching is allowed:
seek and you will find!
   Come and join the song,
   women, children, men.
   Jesus makes us free to live again!

Woman at the well,
   question the Messiah;
   find your friends and tell:
drink your heart's desire!
   Come and join the song,
   women, children, men.
   Jesus makes us free to live again!

Woman at the feast,
   let the righteous stare;
   come and go in peace;
love him with your hair!
   Come and join the song,
   women, children, men.
   Jesus makes us free to live again!

Woman in the house,
   nurtured to be meek,
   leave your second place,
listen, think and speak!
   Come and join the song,
   women, children, men.
   Jesus makes us free to live again!

Women on the road,
   from your sickness freed,
   witness and provide,
joining word and deed:
   Come and join the song,
   women, children, men.
   Jesus makes us free to live again!

Women on the hill,
   stand when men have fled;
   Christ needs loving still,
though your hope is dead.
   Come and join the song,
   women, children, men.
   Jesus makes us free to live again!

Women in the dawn,
   care and spices bring,
   earliest to mourn,
earliest to sing!
   Come and join the song,
   women, children, men.
   Jesus makes us free to live again!

© 1983, 1995 Hope Publishing Company for the USA, Canada, Australia and New Zealand and Stainer & Bell Limited for all other territories. All rights reserved.

Eight gospel glimpses, prompted by Elizabeth Moltmann-Wendel's book, *The Women Around Jesus*. Through Jesus, God invites and includes everyone, so the hymn invites women, children and men to "come and join the song." Some time after it was published, I learned that in the USA, "woman *of* the night" means prostitute. Some people stubbornly use the wrong preposition when they hear or sing this hymn. So it goes.
Metre: 5.5.5.5. Refr.
Sources in order of stanzas: Luke 2:6-7; Mark 5:24-34; John 4:7-30; Luke 7:36-50; Luke 8:1-3; John 19:25; and Luke 23:55-24:10.

Life Work

30

A man of ancient time and place,
with foreign speech and foreign face,
reveals the glory, power and grace
    of costly, unexpected love.

A rabbi, schooled in Moses' Law,
a male, amending Herod's flaw,
arouses wonder, rage and awe
    with costly, unexpected love.

By teasing word and healing deed,
a leper touched, an outcast freed,
he bears the fruit and plants the seed
    of costly, unexpected love.

The cost we barely can surmise
when, lifted up before our eyes,
the face of God we recognize
    in crucified, unfathomed love.

May faith and hope within us grow,
the way of Christ to tell and show,
and may the Spirit breathe and blow
    in costly, unexpected love.

© 1991 Hope Publishing Company for the USA, Canada, Australia and New Zealand and Stainer & Bell Limited for all other territories. All rights reserved.

March 1990, partly inspired by scholar Kenneth Bailey (Tantur Institute, Jerusalem), whose phrase, "costly, unexpected love," summarized his lecture series in Spokane, Washington, USA, in which he showed how Jesus often risked ridicule, hostility and rejection by showing God's gracious love in the "wrong place," to the "wrong people," and at the wrong time.
Long Metre (8.8.8.8.)
Matthew 3:16-18; Mark 1:40-45; John 1:38; 3:2; 3:26.

Jesus

31

Can a man be kind and caring?
    Jesus was.
Can a man who's kind and caring
be adventuresome and daring,
    bravely doing right,
    walking in the light?
Jesus did; perhaps I can:
Let me be a Jesus man.

Can a man be sad with crying?
    Jesus was.
Can a man who's sad with crying,
shed his tears, yet keep on trying,
    loving to the end,
    enemy and friend?
Jesus did; perhaps I can:
Let me be a Jesus man.

Can a man be hurt and broken?
    Jesus was.
Can a man who's hurt and broken
show his friends how God has spoken,
    giving to us then,
    power to start again?
Jesus did; perhaps I can:
Let me be a Jesus man.

Hallelujah! Hallelujah!
I will be a Jesus man.

© 1986 Hope Publishing Company for the USA, Canada, Australia and New Zealand and Stainer & Bell Limited for all other territories. All rights reserved.

June 1984, revised 1996. A song for boys and men, attempting to redefine what it means to be a 'real man,' in the light of the gospel record. Yet if Jesus can be a role model for boys and men, we must urgently ask if, and how, he can be an inspiration for women and girls. See Box Note, *Jesus - For Women and Men?* (p. 35).
Metre: 8.3.8.8.5.5.7.7.
Mark 3:1-6; Luke 7:11-15; John 11:35.

Life Work

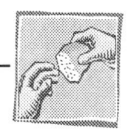

32

Here and now, if you love,
 giving mercy, making peace,
God will dignify and bless,
 saying yes, and yes, and yes,
and the makers of peace
 shall bear God's name,
and the givers of mercy be praised,
 and the hungry shall be fed,
 and the mourners shall be loved,
 and the last shall be first,
 and the lost shall be found
 in the Commonwealth of love.

Here and now, in your need,
 hungry, broken or bereaved,
God will dignify and bless,
 saying yes, and yes, and yes,
and the tears of grief shall glow with joy,
and the makers of peace
 shall bear God's name,
and the givers of mercy be praised,
 and the hungry shall be fed,
 and the mourners shall be loved,
 and the last shall be first,
 and the lost shall be found
 in the Commonwealth of love.

If your love, parched and dry,
 thirsts for justice, truth and right,
God will dignify and bless,
 saying yes, and yes, and yes,
and righteousness shall flow like a stream,
and the tears of grief shall glow with joy,
and the makers of peace
 shall bear God's name,
and the givers of mercy be praised,
 and the hungry shall be fed,
 and the mourners shall be loved,
 and the last shall be first,
 and the lost shall be found
 in the Commonwealth of love.

If your love grows more kind,
 meeting rage with gentle faith,
God will dignify and bless,
 saying yes, and yes, and yes,
and the gentle in faith shall inherit the earth,
and righteousness shall flow like a stream,
and the tears of grief shall glow with joy,
and the makers of peace
 shall bear God's name,
and the givers of mercy be praised,
 and the hungry shall be fed,
 and the mourners shall be loved,
 and the last shall be first,
 and the lost shall be found
 in the Commonwealth of love.

If you live, filled with grace,
 single-mindedly for love,
God will dignify and bless,
saying yes, and yes, and yes,
and the pure in heart shall see the living God,
and the gentle in faith shall inherit the earth,
and righteousness shall flow like a stream,
and the tears of grief shall glow with joy,
and the makers of peace
 shall bear God's name,
and the givers of mercy be praised,
 and the hungry shall be fed,
 and the mourners shall be loved,
 and the last shall be first,
 and the lost shall be found
 in the Commonwealth of love.

© 1986 Hope Publishing Company for the USA, Canada, Australia and New Zealand and Stainer & Bell Limited for all other territories. All rights reserved.

Jesus

32

If your faith brings you pain,
scarred and scorned for doing right,
God will dignify and bless,
saying yes, and yes, and yes,
and the wounds of faith shall be bathed in light,
and the pure in heart shall see the living God,
and the gentle in faith shall inherit the earth,
and righteousness shall flow like a stream,
and the tears of grief shall glow with joy,
and the makers of peace shall bear God's name,
and the givers of mercy be praised,
and the hungry shall be fed,
and the mourners shall be loved,
and the last shall be first,
and the lost shall be found
in the Commonwealth of love.

© 1986 Hope Publishing Company for the USA, Canada, Australia and New Zealand and Stainer & Bell Limited for all other territories. All rights reserved.

October 1984. The stanzas interpret Matthew's Beatitudes in contemporary terms, while the refrain keeps close to their original wording. The Beatitudes are for "here and now" (and were surely first heard as such), yet express a not-yet-realized hope. The phrase, "wounds... bathed in light," is from the New English Bible translation of Isaiah 53:11, not retained in the Revised English Bible.
Metre: Irregular   Matthew 5:1-11

33

Look at this man.
What does he say?
Has he a song for today?

Distant in time,
foreign in ways,
is he the one we should praise?

Look at this man.
What will you do
if he is looking at you?

© 1989 Hope Publishing Company for the USA, Canada, Australia and New Zealand and Stainer & Bell Limited for all other territories. All rights reserved.

February 1989, as an introit for Starfire, youth choir of Los Altos United Methodist Church, California.   Metre: 4.4.7.

Transfiguration

34

Jesus, on the mountain peak,
stands alone in glory blazing.
Let us, if we dare to speak,
   join the saints and angels praising:
      Alleluia!

Trembling at his feet we saw
Moses and Elijah speaking.
All the Prophets and the Law
   shout through them their joyful greeting:
      Alleluia!

Swift the cloud of glory came,
God, proclaiming in its thunder,
Jesus as the Son by name!
   Nations, cry aloud in wonder:
      Alleluia!

Jesus is the chosen One,
living hope of every nation,
hear and heed him, everyone;
   sing, with earth and all creation,
      Alleluia!

© 1977, 1995 Hope Publishing Company for the USA, Canada, Australia and New Zealand and Stainer & Bell Limited for all other territories. All rights reserved.

June 1962, revised 1989 and 1994. My second usable hymn, understanding the transfiguration as an experience of Jesus of Nazareth, foreshadowing his significance as Christ, the hope of all nations.   Metre: 7.8.7.8.4.   Matthew 17:1-9; Mark 9:2-8; Luke 9:28-36.

> **Jesus - for Women and Men?** "Can a man be kind and caring?- Jesus was" (31).
> If Jesus can be a role model for men, what does he mean for women? As a man, I can neither pontificate nor avoid the question. Granted that the divine could become human only in one gender, what if the Word became a woman? Her femaleness could not be a role model for me, but the stories about her might make her a challenging Saviour. For she would surely call me to take her seriously, respect her dignity, value her not only as a person but as a woman, and accept her leadership. Though women might identify with her directly, both women and men would need grace by faith to confess her as the Chosen One of God. Perhaps her first (female) apostles would know that both women and men are being remade in the image of Christ (2 Corinthians 3:18). Perhaps Jesus, who stepped out of the male role to become "*a man* who kneels, God's chosen leader, washing dirty feet," can be "to men, a model" yet also, "to women, hope; to all, enabling love" and "friend of every child" (26).

Jesus

35

I am going to Calvary.
  Would you like to come with me
  all the way and back again?
You must follow the leader then,
  come and follow the leader,
  come and follow the leader
  all the way and back again:
  come and follow-the-leader.

As I go along the road,
  I will lift a heavy load:
  I will carry a cross for you.
You will dare to carry it too
  when you follow the leader,
  when you follow the leader,
  you will dare to carry it too:
  come and follow-the-leader.

When I wear a thorny crown
  when the soldiers knock me down,
  when the people spit and shove
you will feel the power of love
  when you follow the leader,
  when you follow the leader,
  you will feel the power of love:
  come and follow-the-leader.

I am going to climb a hill
  where the soldiers wait to kill.
  Soldiers, let me pray for you.
God forgives the wrongs you do
  when you follow the leader,
  when you follow the leader;
  God forgives the wrongs you do:
  come and follow-the-leader.

I am going to stretch my hands
  reaching out to all the lands.
  When I die you'll live and learn
in the Spirit I return
  when you follow the leader,
  when you follow the leader,
  in the Spirit I return:
  come and follow the leader.

I have gone to Calvary.
  Will you travel on with me
  till the world is made anew?
There is plenty more to do
  when you follow the leader,
  when you follow the leader,
  there is plenty more to do:
  come and follow the leader.

© 1983, 1996 Hope Publishing Company for the USA, Canada, Australia and New Zealand and Stainer & Bell Limited for all other territories. All rights reserved.

June 1971, revised 1996. When my children were young a BBC Radio program *Listen With Mother*, was a daily household event. Hearing a toddler's song for a traditional melody ("I am going to Timbuctoo. Would you like to go there too, all the way and back again? You must follow the leader then"), their mother suggested the words of stanza 1, which I then extended.
Metre: Irregular
Luke 23:34; John 12:32.

Facing Death

36

Doom and danger Jesus knows,
    as with deep, determined love,
    care and courage hand in glove,
to Jerusalem he goes.

Striding onward, pressed for time,
    but alert to care and feel,
    Jesus waits to hear and heal
Bartimaeus, begging blind.

Soon Zacchaeus' life could end:
    angry crowds surround his tree.
    Jesus dares to disagree—
"I must eat with you, my friend."

On a donkey at the gate,
    Jesus, peaceable and poor,
    saying no to holy war,
knows that praise will turn to hate.

Care and courage, hand in glove,
    mark the journey to the cross,
    as in Christ God gives to us
daring, deep, determined love.

© 1993 Hope Publishing Company for the USA, Canada, Australia and New Zealand and Stainer & Bell Limited for all other territories. All rights reserved.

March 1989, from meditating on the way in which Jesus, a determined male, "set his face to go to Jerusalem" (Luke 9:51), but was nonetheless immediately available to people needing his help. To work-oriented moderns, his journey might seem full of interruptions; to Jesus, they are the journey.
Metre: 7.7 7.7.
Matthew 21:1-10; Mark 10:46; Mark 11:1-11; Luke 9:51; Luke 18:25-43; Luke 19:1-10.

Jesus

37

On the night before he died,
    to the government betrayed,
at his people's freedom meal,
    Jesus broke the bread, and said:
"Take and eat my broken self.
    Share in all I say and do.
Though I go, I shall return:
    God is making all things new."

When the meal was nearly done,
    and his blood would soon be shed,
Jesus lifted up the cup,
    "All must drink of this," he said,
"When the powers of earth prevail,
    and my blood is shed for you,
taste the sign within the wine:
    God is making all things new."

© 1995 Hope Publishing Company for the USA, Canada, Australia and New Zealand and Stainer & Bell Limited for all other territories. All rights reserved.

1994, as part of *Lift Heart and Voice - The Great Thanksgiving in Song* (page 174). Jesus' actions are understood as an acted sign in the tradition of Hebrew prophecy (see note to No. 38).
Metre: 7.7.7.7.D.   Mark 14:17-25 and parallels; 1 Corinthians 11:23-26.

38

"As Jeremiah took a jar
and smashed it on a stone
to tell, enact, and thus proclaim
how God would smash Jerusalem,
    so I am taking wine and bread
    the very night I am betrayed.

Come, eat the bread I bless and break,
and let it thus be known
that I am handed to the hate
of law, religion, and the state.
    This is my body, this is me,
    as here, tonight, I am betrayed.

Now drink the cup, and sharply taste
what I endure alone
as earth's authorities combine
to serve their bitter, deadly wine:
    this is my life-blood, drained away,
    as now, tonight, I am betrayed.

As in the breaking of a jar
the power of God was shown,
so now, at supper, I proclaim
that God will vindicate my name,
    and through my dying work for good,
    though now, tonight, I am betrayed."

© 1989, 1996 Hope Publishing Company for the USA, Canada, Australia and New Zealand and Stainer & Bell Limited for all other territories. All rights reserved.

1989, revised 1996. The original was part of a passion play, *Immanuel Today* (Music: Joan Collier Fogg) performed at Bethany Seminary (Church of the Brethren). Jesus' actions at the last supper were an acted sign in the tradition of Hebrew prophecy, whereby the prophet's action announces, explains, and dramatises God's action, indicating in this case that God will work for good, even in Jesus' betrayal, arrest, and execution. For the analysis, I am indebted to Rafael Avila, *Eucharist and Politics* (New York: Orbis Books).
Metre: 8.6.8.8.8.8.
Jeremiah 19:1-15; Mark 14:17-25 and parallels; 1 Corinthians 11:23-26.

Facing Death

39

Here hangs a man discarded,
a scarecrow hoisted high,
a nonsense pointing nowhere
to all who hurry by.

Can such a clown of sorrows
still bring a useful word
when faith and love seem phantoms
and every hope absurd?

Yet here is help and comfort
for lives by comfort bound,
when drums of dazzling progress
give strangely hollow sound:

Life, emptied of all meaning,
drained out in bleak distress,
can share in broken silence
my deepest emptiness;

And love that freely entered
the pit of life's despair,
can name our hidden darkness
and suffer with us there.

Christ, in our darkness risen,
help all who long for light
to hold the hand of promise,
till faith receives its sight.

© 1975, 1995 Hope Publishing Company for the USA, Canada, Australia and New Zealand and Stainer & Bell Limited for all other territories. All rights reserved.

June 1973, revised 1994. Prompted by Douglas John Hall's *Hope Against Hope* and Paul Tillich's *The Courage To Be*. Tillich describes three inbuilt human anxieties: fate (= calamity) and death, guilt and condemnation, and emptiness and despair. To the first and second, traditional faith says "Christ is risen: we shall live with God," and "Your sins are forgiven," but offers little to the third except, "Shape up, come and join the party." Good news may come through knowing that Christ can be with us in our desolation, having known on the cross what it means to have "life emptied of all meaning, drained out in bleak distress."
Metre: 7.6.7.6.
Mark 15:34 and parallels.

"When I Survey

40

Holy Spirit, storm of love,
  break our self-protective walls.
    Bring us out and show us why,
    nakedly upon the cross,
  open to the wind and sky,
Jesus waits and Jesus calls.

Show us, in his tortured flesh,
  earth's Creator on display,
    broken by affairs of state,
    drinking horror, pain and grief,
  arching in the winds of hate,
giving love and life away.

Show us how this dying love
  entered, bore and understood
    all our deep, unconscious drives,
    each exploiting, evil thread
  woven through our nations' lives,
all our life apart from God.

Thus convicted, claimed and called,
  freed, as Christ we freely choose,
    washed in love, reborn, re-named,
    doing justice, knowing God,
  may we witness unashamed,
confident to give good news.

News that Jesus is alive,
  as the People of the Dove,
    going out in praise and prayer,
    meet the evils of our time
  and the demons of despair
with forgiving, living love.

© 1986 Hope Publishing Company for the USA, Canada, Australia and New Zealand and Stainer & Bell Limited for all other territories. All rights reserved.

August 1985, revised 1995. One of two hymns invited (though not accepted) by the Women's Missionary Union of the Southern Baptist Convention. The hymn explores God's identification on the cross with the depths of the human condition, believing that our encounter with God in Christ through the cross is what gives us good news to share with others.
Metre: 7.7.7.7.7.7.
Mark 14:33-34(§2); Romans 6:5-11(§4); 2 Corinthians 5:21(§3); 1 Peter 2:22-25(§3).

> **Jesus - Choice and Chance.** "We sense the play of chance in Herod's anger, Peter's growth, and Pilate's troubled glance" (41). Choice and chance seem built into human life, even when choices are limited, and chance brings "pain and terror" (God the almighty fixer, who helps me win the lottery and visits 'ethnic cleansing' on Bosnian women, is an unacceptable alternative). Since Jesus was truly human, his life presumably knew both chance and choice, though hindsight, and belief in God's full involvement, shape the gospel narratives in a more lordly direction. His capacity to feel grief (John 11:35), choose to heal a leper (Luke 5:12) and be surprised into compassion (Mark 1:41), hint at chance encounters. His conversations with a Gentile woman about healing and a Samaritan woman about faith suggest that he grew and developed through interaction with others (Mark 7:24-29, John 4:1-29), as all humans necessarily do. For Jesus, as for us, other people "show us who we are" (62).

The Wondrous Cross"

41

When pain and terror strike by chance,
    with causes unexplained,
when God seems absent or asleep,
    and evil unrestrained,
we crave an all-controlling force,
    ready to rule and warn,
but find, far-shadowed by a cross,
    a child in weakness born.

We marvel at God's nakedness
    and sense the play of chance
in Herod's anger, Peter's growth,
    and Pilate's troubled glance.
Our Saviour's tempted, tested way
    never was cut and dried,
but costly, risking life and love,
    betrayed and crucified.

How deep the Wisdom of our God,
    how weak, but truly wise,
to risk, to sacrifice, to die,
    and from the grave arise,
to shed the shroud of death and fate,
    freeing our hearts for good.
We breathe the ample air of hope
    and take our chance with God.

Since Wisdom took its chance on earth,
    to show God's living way,
we'll trust that fear and force will fall,
    and Wisdom win the day.
Then, come, dear Christ, and hold us fast
    when faith and hope are torn,
and bring us, in your loving arms,
    to resurrection morn.

© 1993 Hope Publishing Company for the USA, Canada, Australia and New Zealand and Stainer & Bell Limited for all other territories. All rights reserved.

November 1991 and March 1992. The original was commissioned by First Presbyterian Church, Fort Collins, Colorado, to celebrate the release of one of their members, Dr. Thomas Sutherland, from captivity in the Lebanon.
Common Metre Double (CMD/DCM)   1 Corinthians 1:18-25

"When I Survey

42

God remembers pain:
  nail by nail, thorn by thorn,
    hunger, thirst and muscles torn.
Time may dull our griefs
  and heal our lesser wounds,
    but in eternal Love
      yesterday is now,
and pain is in the heart of God.

God remembers joy:
  touch of love, taste of food,
    all our senses know is good.
Love and life flow by
  and precious days are gone,
    but in eternal Love
      every day is now,
and joy is in the heart of God.

God remembers us:
  all we were, all we are,
    lives within our Lover's care.
Time may dull our minds
  and death will take us all,
    but in eternal Love
      every life is now:
our life is hid with Christ in God.

© 1993 Hope Publishing Company for the USA, Canada, Australia and New Zealand and Stainer & Bell Limited for all other territories. All rights reserved.

Easter Sunday, 1989. In God, nothing is forgotten: joy, pain, the experience of being human, and us.
Metre: 5.6.7.5.6.6.5.8.   Colossians 3:3-4

God - and Evil Radical evil is so horrific that faith becomes "speechless in a world that suffers" (116, 118). How does God deal with evil? Scripture and tradition offer a vocabulary steeped in the language of battle, so much so that it is hard to speak of the matter without saying that God will "overcome," "triumph," and "conquer." Though combat-language can satisfy the longing that justice be conclusively done, and can speak helpfully provided that love's aim and method are articulated and kept in the foreground, it is a dangerous vocabulary, perennially perverted from "spiritual battles" to power-plays, manipulation and force of arms: from holy love to holy war. We need to mint new metaphors, put them in circulation, and test their validity as currency. So I have pictured God outrunning and outlasting evil, "dancing ahead of evil, kissing Satan's face" (2), or as exhausting evil in love's embrace (145 and 162). God's grace mends the broken threads of life (145,169). The risen Christ forever eludes the people and systems that crucified the Chosen One, and, "arising over earthly powers...has begun to catch them in a web of love and weave them into one" (10). Or we may hope that the Spirit of God - Spirit of Jesus is able to incorporate "peoples and histories, beauty and pain," and even "wickedness," into a transformed and rebirthed creation (169).

The Wondrous Cross"

43

Dying love has been my birth,
    undeserved and undisguised;
Christ declares me full of worth,
    valued, loved, accepted, prized!

Love that bore and understood
    all my emptiness and sin,
recreates me new and good,
    healed, and beautiful within.

Let this love my love release,
    hopeful through defeat or loss,
peaceful, as I work for peace,
    faithful, though I bear the cross.

All are worthy, full of worth,
    loved, whoever would despise.
Tell and show it here on earth!
    Shout hosanna to the skies!

© 1983, 1995 Hope Publishing Company for the USA, Canada, Australia and New Zealand and Stainer & Bell Limited for all other territories. All rights reserved.

Good Friday 1983, revised 1993. Provoked by a Maundy Thursday sermon which intended to announce God's grace but actually kept telling us how worthless we are. The first stanza was written during the sermon, the rest later. The revision makes the order of themes more logical.
Metre: 7.7.7.7.
John 3:1-16 and 16:20-22.

44

Dear Christ, uplifted from the earth,
    your arms stretched out above
through every culture, every birth,
    to draw an answering love.

Still east and west your love extends
    and always, near and far,
you call and claim us as your friends
    and love us as we are.

Where age and gender, class and race,
    divide us to our shame,
you see a person and a face,
    a neighbour with a name.

May we, accepted as we are,
    yet called in grace to grow,
reach out to others, near and far
    your healing love to show.

© 1973, 1996 Hope Publishing Company for the USA, Canada, Australia and New Zealand and Stainer & Bell Limited for all other territories. All rights reserved.

October 1970, revised 1995. Prompted by a long-forgotten tension in the congregation I served, probably connected with the 1960s generation gap. Since hymns should not be used for preaching or polemic, I shelved the original utterance, moderated it, and pruned it from six stanzas to four.
Common Metre
John 12:32; Romans 15:7.

Easter Vigil

45

Joyful is the dark,
holy, hidden God,
rolling cloud of night beyond all naming:
   Majesty in darkness,
   Energy of love,
Word-in-Flesh, the mystery proclaiming.

Joyful is the dark
Spirit of the deep,
winging wildly o'er the world's creation,
   silken sheen of midnight,
   plumage black and bright,
swooping with the beauty of a raven.

Joyful is the dark,
shadowed stable floor;
angels flicker, God on earth confessing,
   as with exultation,
   Mary, giving birth,
hails the infant cry of need and blessing.

Joyful is the dark
coolness of the tomb,
waiting for the wonder of the morning;
   never was that midnight
   touched by dread and gloom:
darkness was the cradle of the dawning.

Joyful is the dark
depth of love divine,
roaring, looming thundercloud of glory,
   holy, haunting beauty,
   living, loving God.
Hallelujah! Sing and tell the story!

© 1989 Hope Publishing Company for the USA, Canada, Australia and New Zealand and Stainer & Bell Limited for all other territories. All rights reserved.

February 1986, prompted by "Bring Many Names" (No. 173), whose "joyful darkness far beyond our seeing" suggested the first line. Main sources were *The Dark and the Light In the Imagery of God* (Tony Brown: unpublished) and *Darkness* (Philip Seddon, Grove Books, Bramcote, England, 1983).
Metre: 10.10.11.10.
Genesis 1:2; Exodus 20:18-21; 1 Kings 8:10-13; Psalm 18:8-12.

Darkness Into Dawn

46

The waiting night is slowly changing.
A greyness glimmers in the east.
The fields appear, and formless shadows
take shape as trees, a house, a road.
> *Christ, in our darkness, be our hidden light.*
> *Show us a way.*
> *Help us to walk together.*

The growing light is strong and shining.
The morning clouds are tipped with gold,
and in the towns with silent houses
the street lamps fade into the dawn.
> *Christ, in our darkness, be our growing light.*
> *Give us your peace.*
> *Wake us to hope together.*

The east is red, its waking glory
cannot be hidden or delayed.
It draws the gaze of hurried travellers,
and celebrates the coming day.
> *Christ, let your dying draw our wondering eyes.*
> *Exultant love,*
> *bring all the peoples together.*

The morning sun breaks into vision.
A rim of fire is on the hills.
A child, entranced, sits at her window,
and men, half-smiling, shield their eyes.
> *Christ, lift our spirits while we wait for dawn.*
> *Sing in our hearts,*
> *bring us to resurrection.*

© 1983, 1996 Hope Publishing Company for the USA, Canada, Australia and New Zealand and Stainer & Bell Limited for all other territories. All rights reserved.

Easter 1973, from an overnight sponsored walk for world hunger (§1) and an early morning walk to Colchester Station, Essex, England (§§ 2-4). Revised 1995.
Metre: Irregular

Easter Vigil

47

As in a clear dawn, spreading from the east,
and with a glow of hidden fire,
>   the light comes, older than the earth,
>   but new every morning,
so in a stable, gazing at a child,
the shepherds meet the Word in flesh,
>   and Love dawns, older than the sky,
>   but new every morning.   Alleluia!

As in a grey dawn, from a hidden sun,
diffused, and growing unobserved,
>   the light comes, older than the earth,
>   but new every morning,
so in a garden, tired, and numb with grief,
the women find an empty tomb,
>   and Hope dawns, older than the sky,
>   but new every morning.   Alleluia!

As on a cool dawn, glowing through the fog,
then bright, uncurtained by the wind,
>   the light comes, older than the earth,
>   but new every morning,
so in a market, touched with sudden fire,
believers babble other tongues,
>   and Joy dawns, older than the sky,
>   but new every morning.   Alleluia!

© 1994 Hope Publishing Company for the USA, Canada, Australia and New Zealand and Stainer & Bell Limited for all other territories. All rights reserved.

January 1994, commissioned to celebrate 25 years of creative excellence by Jerry (Gerald) Crawford (Minister of Music, First Presbyterian Church, Birmingham, Michigan), one of whose favourite texts is Lamentations 3:22-23, which gives the key phrase, "new every morning."
Metre: 10.8.8.6.D. with Alleluias
Lamentations 3:22-23; Mark 16:1-8; Luke 2:8-20; Acts 2:1-13.

> **Darkness and Light.** Tony Brown's paper, *The Dark and the Light* (see No. 45) highlights the racist assumptions that equate *darkness* with *blackness* and *blackness* with *evil*. If we pray, "wash me, and I shall be *whiter* than snow" (Psalm 51:7 NRSV), we accept a dubious translation choice which tacitly supports the inaccurate label, "white," for Caucasian skin. "*Brighter* than snow" is non-racist and more accurate, and *paleface* is arguably a better label. I have been glad to draw on the positive meanings of "darkness" in the Bible and Christian tradition, by speaking of God as "joyful darkness far beyond our seeing" (173), "warm and loving darkness" (2), and as the joyful, dark, depth of love divine (45).

Darkness Into Dawn

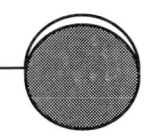

48

A dancer's body leaps and falls,
  and as the move succeeds or fails,
    she cannot hide behind her pride
  but openly, herself reveals.

No mask to hide behind
  for Mary's child.
  Her baby's naked needs
    have neither modesty nor tact:
    God isn't putting on an act.
    No script to hide behind,
    but in the street
  Christ's open, jostled love
  can heal a woman in the crowd
and show that touching is allowed.

A dancer's body leaps and falls,
  and as the move succeeds or fails,
  she cannot hide behind her pride
but openly, herself reveals.

No drum to hide behind,
  no hero's sword
  and patriotic war,
    for what you get is what you've heard:
    a healer's parabolic word.
    No crown to hide behind
    at Pilate's bar.
  Christ's body, tired and bruised,
  will be the only truth that sings
  (no angel army in the wings).

A dancer's body leaps and falls,
  and as the move succeeds or fails,
  she cannot hide behind her pride
but openly, herself reveals.

  No clothes to hide behind
  upon the cross.
    God's nailed and naked dance
    in pain is learning to be still,
    and all its promises fulfil.
    No tomb to hide behind,
    but in the dawn,
    a body, filled with light,
    will dance among us as we grieve
  and gasp, and soaringly believe.

  A dancer's body leaps and falls,
    and as the move succeeds or fails,
    she cannot hide behind her pride
  but openly, herself reveals.

© 1989 Hope Publishing Company for the USA, Canada, Australia and New Zealand and Stainer & Bell Limited for all other territories. All rights reserved.

April 1988. In a workshop at Princeton Theological Seminary, Judith Rock demonstrated a falling movement, and said that while some artists have things to hide behind (the preacher behind the pulpit, the actor behind the role), a dancer has no hiding place: what you see is what you get. The refrain came a few hours later, and I wrote the stanzas overnight. Kathy Wonson Eddy then composed the tune, and the work was premiered on the closing day.
Metre: 6.4.6.8.8.Refr.   Mark 5:24-34; John 6:15; John 18:33 - 19:16.

Easter Joy

49

Christ is risen! Shout Hosanna!
    Celebrate this day of days!
Christ is risen! Hush in wonder:
    all creation is amazed.
In the desert all-surrounding,
    see, a spreading tree has grown.
Healing leaves of grace abounding
    bring a taste of love unknown.

Christ is risen! Raise your spirits
    from the caverns of despair.
Walk with gladness in the morning.
    See what love can do and dare.
Drink the wine of resurrection,
    not a servant, but a friend.
Jesus is our strong companion.
    Joy and peace shall never end.

Christ is risen! Earth and heaven
    nevermore shall be the same.
Break the bread of new creation
    where the world is still in pain.
Tell its grim, demonic chorus:
    "Christ is risen! Get you gone!"
God the First and Last is with us.
    Sing Hosanna everyone!

© 1986 Hope Publishing Company for the USA, Canada, Australia and New Zealand and Stainer & Bell Limited for all other territories. All rights reserved.

September 1984. An attempt to express the inexpressible. John 15:15; Revelation 22:2,13.
Metre: 8.7.8.7.D. Trochaic

> **Easter Joy - Action for Justice.** "Faith, moving onward from the cross, in Easter light, knows that whatever may happen, Jesus is risen" (54). Christian peace and justice action finds its wellspring, not in moral zeal or guilty conscience, but in the resurrection. The more we trust and know that Christ is risen, the more we can elude despair and endure disappointment, as "Christ, unjustly killed, arises over governments and powers, and gives us peaceful strength to do what we can do, and see it through" (129). In the eucharist (communion), the risen Christ presides at the one table where everyone has enough, no-one has too much, everyone is fed, and no-one has to pay (98), as we "taste and tell how all the world should be" (99).

Christ Is Risen!

50

Jesus is good news to all the poor,
  hungry, scorned, oppressed or unemployed:
    "God will make a world that gives you more:
      food, and hope, and life to be enjoyed."

Power and money, having much to lose,
  crucified the love that shook their thrones.
    Jesus, raised by God, repeats the news,
      Apathy and death are overthrown.

Jesus shouts the gospel from the poor:
"Love will make a world that's good and free.
  Leave your gods of money, pomp, and power,
    Join the struggle, hope, and follow me."

51

Christ crucified now is alive.
  Gates of freedom open wide.
    Gravestones shatter and despair takes flight
    as the godforsaken is bathed in light.

    Love conquers Law. Grace now has grown
      flowers to crack its earth and stone:
        Guilt dissolves and walls are broken down.
        Sinners welcome sinners and the lost are found.

        Justice and Peace walk hand in hand.
          Jesus brings a new command:
            Love your oppressors, and resist them too,
            Set them free to celebrate God's hope with you.

            Red in the west rises the sun;
              Love turns all creation upside down.
                Hills and mountains skip like lambs
                    and the clouds and continents are clapping their hands.

Nos. 50 and 51 © 1983 Hope Publishing Company for the USA, Canada, Australia and New Zealand and Stainer & Bell Limited for all other territories. All rights reserved.

No. 50 - July 1981. The sovereignty of God's partnership-love is good news to all who long for food, dignity, and freedom. It cannot be reduced to a private matter, yet challenges the best any human society can be.   Metre: 9.9.9.9.   Matthew 6:24, 33.
No. 51 - June 1974. Christian words to a Chinese revolutionary anthem, THE EAST IS RED. Metre: Irregular   Psalm 118:19(§1, line 2); Isaiah 53:11(§1 line 4: NEB only); Psalm 85:10 (§3 line 1); Matthew 5:43-44(§3); Acts 17:6(§4, line 2); Psalm 114:4-6(§4 lines 3-4).

Easter Joy

52

Christ is alive! Let Christians sing.
  The cross stands empty to the sky.
Let streets and homes with praises ring.
  Love, drowned in death, shall never die.

Christ is alive! No longer bound
  to distant years in Palestine,
but saving, healing, here and now,
  and touching every place and time.

In every insult, rift and war,
  where colour, scorn or wealth divide,
Christ suffers still, yet loves the more,
  and lives, where even hope has died.

Women and men, in age and youth,
  can feel the Spirit, hear the call,
and find the way, the life, the truth,
  revealed in Jesus, freed for all.

Christ is alive, and comes to bring
  good news to this and every age,
till earth and sky and ocean ring
  with joy, with justice, love and praise.

© 1969, 1995 Hope Publishing Company for the USA, Canada, Australia and New Zealand and Stainer & Bell Limited for all other territories. All rights reserved.

April 1968, revised 1978, 1989, 1993. Ten days after the assassination of Dr. Martin Luther King Jr., the congregation I served as Minister, Hockley and Hawkwell Congregational [now United Reformed] Church, Essex, met to celebrate Easter. I tried to express an Easter hope out of that terrible event, in words which could be more widely applied, and wrote "Christ is alive!" because our available hymns spoke of Easter as a glorious event long ago, far away, and high above. Revisions keep the original theme (the risen Christ shares yet outlasts our suffering, making Easter good news for all), while searching for better language than the command-and-control vocabulary of the original. The 1993 revision added the stanza, "Women and men, in age and youth etc.", affirming that the life and love of God are "revealed in Jesus, freed for all."
Long Metre
Luke 12:50 and Romans 6:3-4 ("drowned in death"); Acts 2:17; John 14:6; Colossians 1:24.

Christ Is Risen!

53

Sing my song backwards, from end to beginning,
Friday to Monday, from dying to birth.
Nothing is altered, but hope changes everything:
sing "Resurrection!" and "Peace upon Earth!"

Whisper a hope through the fear in Gethsemane,
horror and emptiness darker than night;
visit the wounds, and the failure of Calvary:
sing "Resurrection!" and bathe them in light.

Gather the bones and the sinews of memory—
healings and parables, laughter and strife,
joy with the outcasts and love for the enemy—
breathe "Resurrection!" and dance them to life.

Stretch out a rainbow from cross to nativity.
Deck out the stable with shepherds and kings,
angels and miracles, glory and poetry—
Sing my song backwards, till all the world sings!

© 1983, 1995 Hope Publishing Company for the USA, Canada, Australia and New Zealand and Stainer & Bell Limited for all other territories. All rights reserved.

December 1974, revised 1994. When the disciples met Christ, risen from the dead and alive among them, their understanding of Jesus' life was transformed. The four gospels culminate a process of remembering which probably began with the passion narratives, added teachings and encounters, and in some cases ended with birth narratives, whose "angels and miracles, glory and poetry" are only possible in the light of Easter Day. Hence, "Sing my song backwards." On Christmas night the angels do not sing, till Christ is crucified and risen.
Metre: Irregular
Mark 15:32-33; Luke 2:14.

Easter Joy

54

Faith, moving onward
from the cross, in Easter light,
knows that whatever may happen,
    Jesus is risen,
    key to the promises of God.

    Tyrants and experts
    plan a future cut and dried.
    Faith, moving onward, surmises
        hopeful surprises,
        gleams of the promises of God.

        Though terror rages
        and oppression blocks their way,
        hope knows the poor will awaken
            and thrones be shaken,
            trusting the promises of God.

            When hopeful action,
            running risks and taking sides,
            burns all our bridges behind us,
                Christ longs to find us
                seeking the promises of God.

                Hope keeps in vision,
                as the dust and ashes fall,
                love's final transfiguration
                    of all creation,
                    filled with the promises of God.

© 1982, 1995 Hope Publishing Company for the USA, Canada, Australia and New Zealand and Stainer & Bell Limited for all other territories. All rights reserved.

1982, revised 1994. Originally written for the UK annual ecumenical *One World Week*, when churches focus on global issues. Christian hope is neither optimism nor simple expectation, but the future-focused consequence of faith in Jesus Christ: hence, "faith moving onward ... knows that Jesus is risen etc."
Metre: 5.7.8.5.8.

Christ Is Risen!

55

A woman in a world of men
    was chosen to receive
the news of Christ alive again,
    though men would not believe.

A witness telling what she knew,
    her faith, her worth denied,
was first to greet and love anew
    the living Crucified.

The hands whose touch had made her well,
    with wounds by love made good,
she treasured, kissed, then ran to tell
    of Christ alive in God.

Faith finds, in spirits given worth,
    a fertile habitat:
in resurrection, as at birth,
    God sings Magnificat.

A woman's faith has testified;
then following her lead,
let all rejoice: Christ crucified
    is risen now indeed!

© 1989 Hope Publishing Company for the USA, Canada, Australia and New Zealand and Stainer & Bell Limited for all other territories. All rights reserved.

March 1988. The women around Jesus, especially Mary of Magdala, were the first witnesses to the Resurrection, their testimony in one account dismissed as "nonsense" (Luke 24:11) in a society where women were subordinate to men, likely to be scorned because female, and where in consequence a woman's testimony was probably invalid in law. Their resurrection testimony, the first preaching of the gospel, is therefore God's "Magnificat" (see Luke 1:51-53) overturning the established order, while calling all to rejoice that Christ is risen. A simple, short version can be made by using stanzas 2, 3 and 5.
Common Metre

The Risen Christ

56

Jesus is with God,
    endlessly alive.
All he did and said and suffered,
all he hoped and all he offered
    beats with shimmering wings
    in the heart of things.

Jesus is with God
    where the victims cry
from the crosses of oppression,
praying for our intercession:
    "Leave your nets, and see!
    Christians, follow me!"

Jesus stands with God
by an open door,
calling us to pray and follow
through the struggles of tomorrow,
    sowing hopeful seeds
    where the Spirit leads.

57

Here am I,
    where underneath the bridges
    in our winter cities
    homeless people sleep.
Here am I,
    where in decaying houses
    little children shiver,
    crying at the cold.
Where are you?

Here am I,
    with people in the line-up,
    anxious for a handout,
    aching for a job.
Here am I,
    where pensioners and strikers
    sing and march together,
    wanting something new.
Where are you?

Here am I,
    where two or three are gathered,
    ready to be altered,
    sharing wine and bread.
Here am I,
    where those who hear the preaching
    change their way of living,
    find the way to life.
Where are you?

© 1986 (No. 56) and 1983, 1995 (No. 57) Hope Publishing Company for the USA, Canada, Australia and New Zealand and Stainer & Bell Limited for all other territories. All rights reserved.

No. 56 - July 1984. Portraits of Christ at God's right hand in heaven may now suggest remoteness, but intend to show Christ's universal presence reaching all: hence this reinterpretation.
    Metre: 5.5.8.8.5.5.   Matthew 25:31-45; Ephesians 1:20-23; Colossians 3:1-4;
                               Hebrews 1:1-4; Revelation 3:8.
No. 57 - October 1982, revised 1994. Written for SHELTER IN SCOTLAND, and best used as a spoken or sung solo, in which Christ calls us to discipleship, rather than as a congregational song.
    Metre: 3.7.6.5.D.3.   Matthew 25:31-45

Alive Among Us

58

A body, broken on a cross,
with watching women's helpless grief,
and men in heedless, headlong flight,
through fear, despair or disbelief —
> in this, though still we find it strange,
> are life, and hope, and power to change.

A people weaponless and weak,
not many wealthy, great or wise,
but women, labourers and slaves,
absurd to Greek and Roman eyes,
> their Caesar's rages could forgive,
> out-die, out-suffer, and out-live.

And still today, abroad, at home,
from suburb or from shanty-town,
the Spirit's new, surprising word,
in ours or other faiths, or none,
> our sad routines will disarrange
> with gospel-hope of power to change.

When disillusion chains our feet
and might and money turn to dust,
when exile, desert, or defeat
have left us nothing else to trust,
> at last our spirit understands
> the strength of peaceful, nail-scarred hands.

A nation drifting in decline
can turn to just and loving ways,
and people empty, bruised, ashamed,
can find rebirth to joy and praise,
> and churches, wakened, can exchange
> a huddled death for power to change.

© 1989 Hope Publishing Company for the USA, Canada, Australia and New Zealand and Stainer & Bell Limited for all other territories. All rights reserved.

1986. Commissioned by the Overseas Division of the Methodist Church (UK) for its 1986-87 theme, *Power to Change*.
Metre: 8.8.8.8.8.8. Luke 23:49; 1 Corinthians 1:26-31.

Praising Christ Today

59

Jesus, as we tell your story,
still you come, alive among us,
risen from the past,
Christ, the first and last. Alleluia!

Welcome Door,
    entry into safety,
    open as we knock,
    seeking home and refuge,
      then as we are ready,
      open us to life,
      threshold of beginnings.
Welcome Guest,
    hosting us at table,
    take us by surprise,
    running from the party,
      searching street and alley
      calling out with joy,
      "Everyone is welcome!"

Wind of Change,
    singing gale of freedom,
    stir our drowsy hope,
    shaking greedy comfort,
      waking the downtrodden,
      stirring holy dreams
      of emancipation;
Worker-Friend,
    faithful in the struggle,
    showing us our strength,
    counsellor and leader,
      healer and survivor,
      grip us with your truth,
      passionate for justice.

Light of Love,
    dawning in our darkness,
    be our noonday sun,
    showing us our shadows
      and the far horizons,
      blazing high above,
      watching and observing;
Travel-Guide,
    still you go before us,
    checking out the trail,
    looking for the landmarks,
      coming back to meet us,
      saying, "Come and eat,
      I will make the supper."

Rock of Care,
    massive as the mountains,
    ground our every hope,
    in your deep formation,
      age by age preserving
      layers of the past,
      all the human story;
Teacher-Christ,
    calling us together,
    catch us with a word,
    metaphor, or story,
      helping us discover
      wisdom for today,
      we are yours for ever.

Jesus, as we tell your story
still you come, alive among us,
risen from the past,
Christ, the first and last. Alleluia!

© 1996 Hope Publishing Company for the USA, Canada, Australia and New Zealand and Stainer & Bell Limited for all other territories. All rights reserved.

March 1996, commissioned for the 150th anniversary of The Park Church, Elmira, New York, blending scriptural and contemporary titles and themes.
Metre: 3.6.5.6.6.5.6.D.Refr.   Matthew 28:20; Luke 14:15-24; John 10:7-9; Acts 2:1-2.

Becoming Whose We Are

A Covenant People, Worshipping and Working

The Church of Christ, in every age,
beset by change, but Spirit led,
must claim and test its heritage,
and keep on rising from the dead.

Fred Pratt Green (b. 1903)

© 1971 Hope Publishing Company for the USA and Canada,
and Stainer & Bell Limited for all other territories. All rights reserved.

Belonging To Christ

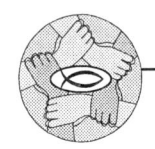

60

Water, splashing hands and face,
    tells of God's refreshing grace.
Shared with gladness, wine and bread
    show a people freed and fed.
Touching us through common things,
healing love the Spirit brings.
    Thus God's covenant is known.
    Alleluia! Welcome home!

Long ago, with shouts of praise
    telling God's amazing ways,
slaves, escaping through the sea,
    hailed the power that set them free:
love, by law and promise sealed,
through the centuries revealed.
    In this story we belong.
    Alleluia! Join the song!

Tell how Jesus lived and led.
    Treasure all he did and said:
teacher, healer, Spirit-filled,
    peasant-prophet, captured, killed.
From his life the Spirit soars,
all of history explores,
    reaching us and seeking all.
    Alleluia! Hear the call!

Grateful, faithful, come today.
    Promise now in Christ to stay,
caring, growing into health,
    finding worth and sharing wealth,
patiently, in age and youth,
seeking justice, peace and truth.
    Sing, with hearts and voices raised,
    Alleluia! God be praised!

© 1994 Hope Publishing Company for the USA, Canada, Australia and New Zealand and Stainer & Bell Limited for all other territories. All rights reserved.

August 1994, commissioned for the 175th anniversary of Covenant Presbyterian Church, Springfield, Ohio, USA. The church's name suggested the theme.
Metre: 7.7.7.7.D.   Exodus 15:1-5

And To Each Other

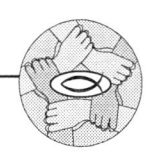

61

In water we grow,
    secure in the womb,
        and speechlessly know
            love's safety and room.
            Baptizing and blessing
        we publish for good
        the freeing, caressing
safe keeping of God.

In water we wash:
    the dirt of each day,
        its trouble and rush
            are carried away.
            In Christ re-created
        by love's cleansing art,
        self-will and self-hatred
dissolve and depart.

In water we dive,
    and cannot draw breath,
        then surface alive,
            rebounding from death.
            Our old self goes under,
        in Christ dead and drowned.
        We rise, washed in wonder,
by love clad and crowned.

In water we dwell,
    for by its deep flow
        through bloodstream and cell,
            we live, think, and grow.
            Praise God, love outflowing,
        whose well of new birth
        baptizes our knowing,
and waters the earth.

© 1993 Hope Publishing Company for the USA, Canada, Australia and New Zealand and Stainer & Dell Limited for all other territories. All rights reserved.

May 1989. Statements of conviction about Christian baptism. Calvin says somewhere that human reason is unreliable without God's grace, hence "baptizes our knowing."
Metre: 5.5.5.5.6.5.6.5.
Acts 2:38-39 and 22:16; Romans 6:3-10; Colossians 2:12; 1 Peter 3:21.

Belonging to Christ

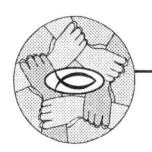

62

We are not our own. Earth forms us,
human leaves on nature's growing vine,
   fruit of many generations,
      seeds of life divine.

      We are not alone. Earth names us:
         past and present, peoples near and far,
           family and friends and strangers
           show us who we are.

           Through a human life God finds us;
           dying, living, love is fully known,
           and in bread and wine reminds us:
           we are not our own.

         Therefore let us make thanksgiving,
         and with justice, willing and aware,
         give to earth, and all things living,
         liturgies of care.

      And if love's encounters lead us
      on a way uncertain and unknown,
   all the saints with prayer surround us:
We are not alone.

   Let us be a house of welcome,
   living stone upholding living stone,
gladly showing all our neighbours
we are not our own!

© 1989 Hope Publishing Company for the USA, Canada, Australia and New Zealand and Stainer & Bell Limited for all other territories. All rights reserved.

September 1987, for the tenth anniversary of the Liturgical Studies Program at Drew University School of Theology, New Jersey. As always when a hymn is commissioned, I asked what themes were important, blended concerns of my own, and began work. The writing included one false start, numerous revisions, and successful completion only when I saw the possibility of structuring it chiasmically, like an arch seen sideways, with the central themes forming the keystone, and the opening and closing stanzas repeating "we are not our own" and "we are not alone."
Metre: 8.9.8.5.
1 Corinthians 6:19-20; Hebrews 12:1-2; 1 Peter 2:4-5.

And To Each Other

63

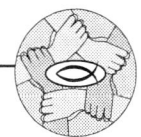

We are your people,
Spirit of grace,
   you dare to make us
   to all our neighbours,
Christ's living voice, hands and face.

Joined in community,
treasured and fed,
   may we discover
   gifts in each other,
willing to lead and be led.

Rich in diversity,
help us to live
   closer than neighbours,
   open to strangers,
able to clash and forgive.

Glad of tradition,
help us to see
   in all life's changing,
   where you are leading,
where our best efforts should be.

Give, as we venture
justice and care
   (peaceful, resisting,
   waiting or risking)
wisdom to know when and where.

Spirit, unite us,
make us, by grace,
   willing and ready,
   Christ's living body,
loving the whole human race.

64

Love alone unites us,
wakens and invites us.
   Nothing else can root and ground us.
Habits of compliance,
dictates and defiance,
   soon dispirit and confound us.
     If by law
     we keep score,
       pride will soon divide us.
Love alone shall guide us!

Christ alone shall lead us,
love that kneels to feed us.
   No-one else can safely rule us.
Power can ruin pastors,
servants turn to masters,
   even saintliness can fool us.
     Worldly games
     love big names,
       tyrants and crowd-pleasers.
Christ alone shall lead us!

Grace alone sustains us,
washes and ordains us.
   Nothing else can work salvation.
Wealth and growth in numbers,
zeal in helping others,
   lacking grace, become temptation.
     May our faith
     feel God's breath,
       freeing, pentecostal:
Grace alone is gospel.

© 1975, 1995 (No. 63) and 1989 (No. 64) Hope Publishing Company for the USA, Canada, Australia and New Zealand and Stainer & Bell Limited for all other territories. All rights reserved.

No. 63 - August 1973, revised 1994.   Metre: Irregular   1 Corinthians 12:4-11
No. 64   March 1988.   Metre: 6.6.8.D.6.6.6.
Luke 22:24-27; John 13:3-5, 17:20-21, and 20:22; 1 Corinthians 13:5(REB); Ephesians 2:8; Colossians 1:18; 1 John 4:7-12.

Finding Friends

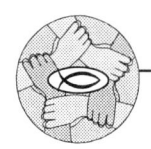

65

-1-
Where shall Wisdom be found? -
　in the welcoming ear
of a spirit that's patiently able to hear,
　and can offer at will
an awakening word,
or the skill to be still.

-2-
Where shall Wisdom be found? -
　in the teachable tongue
of the spirit that loves what the Saviour has done,
　and can beckon us on
with a poem of hope,
and a scriptural song.

Wisdom is bread, made in community,
kneaded, baked and shared.
Wisdom is water, hidden in the rock:
let the well go deep,
let the spring run clear
and the river flow on.

-3-
Where shall Wisdom be found? -
　in the journeying mind
that can stir us to seek and allow us to find,
　and will study to know
the intelligent word
that will free us to grow.

-4-
Where shall Wisdom be found? -
　in the passionate heart
ever worthy of trust, never acting a part,
　that can break or be bruised,
but will never despair,
and will never abuse.

Wisdom is bread, made in community,
kneaded, baked and shared.
Wisdom is water, hidden in the rock:
let the well go deep,
let the spring run clear
and the river flow on.

Where shall Wisdom be found? -
　in the Spirited soul
that will gaily expand our parochial goal,
　till our spirits, uncurled,
open gladly to God, reaching out to the world.

Wisdom is bread, made in community,
kneaded, baked and shared.
Wisdom is water, hidden in the rock:
let the well go deep,
let the spring run clear
and the river flow on.

© 1993 Hope Publishing Company for the USA, Canada, Australia and New Zealand and Stainer & Bell Limited for all other territories. All rights reserved.

February 1993, for Chicago, United and Eden Theological Seminaries of the United Church of Christ, USA.　　Metre: 6.6.12.6.12. Refr.
Numbers 20:10-11; Job 28:12; Isaiah 50:4-5.

To Serve And Lead

66

By contact with the Crucified,
we all are gathered, called, and named,
in faith, by water ratified,
reborn, uplifted, and ordained;
    yet when, in Christ, we name our needs
        for guidance, leadership, and care,
            the Spirit's blessing far exceeds
                what our unaided faith could dare.

For when, in Christ, we serve and lead,
appointed, called, and clothed with grace,
we make no claim, and have no need
of sacred power, or special place:
    the Spirit's breath, the Church's faith
        will help us go a second mile
            and give us unexpected strength
                to love, resist, and reconcile.

The Spirit gives, the Spirit moves,
surprising some, and touching all,
and for our Ministers reserves
one awesome, glad, prophetic role:
    by trial and error, cursed or blessed,
        acclaimed, rejected, heard, ignored,
            to point us every day to Christ,
                the Way, the Wisdom, and the Word.

© 1986, 1996 Hope Publishing Company for the USA, Canada, Australia and New Zealand and Stainer & Bell Limited for all other territories. All rights reserved.

October 1983, revised 1996 Written for the Merseyside Province of the United Reformed Church (UK), to express a Reformed understanding of Christian leadership, ministry, and ordination.
Long Metre Double (DLM/LMD)
Matthew 5:41; John 3:5-8; Ephesians 4:1-4, 11-16; Colossians 2:12.

Finding Friends

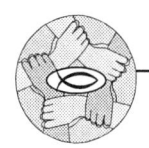

67

Come, celebrate the call of God
    that wakens and renews,
and chooses from us, for our good,
    the bringers of good news.
The Spirit's blessing all ordains
    to show what God has done,
yet brings to focus and contains
    the many in the one.

A chosen one today replies,
    and fit and ready stands.
Her calling now we recognise
    with prayer and loving hands.
A servant leader, truthful friend,
    we gladly will receive,
to stir and comfort, shake and mend,
    be glad with us, and grieve.

Great Spirit, give *her* word and breath
    in Christ to live and speak,
and shield against the powers of death
    the outcast and the weak,
her flag of faith, above defeats,
    in heaven's breeze unfurled,
as all *her* deepest gladness meets
    the hunger of the world.

* for *her*, read *him* as appropriate

© 1993 Hope Publishing Company for the USA, Canada, Australia and New Zealand and Stainer & Bell Limited for all other territories. All rights reserved.

No. 67 - September 1989. Commissioned by Than and Jennifer Ward for the ordination of their daughter, Alida Ward Schuchert, at Greenfield Hill Congregational Church, Connecticut.
Metre: CMD

No. 68 - October 1991. Commissioned by St. Andrew's Presbyterian Church, Thunder Bay, Ontario, Canada, to celebrate the 25th Anniversary of the Presbyterian Church in Canada's acceptance of women in ordained ministry. In ancient tradition, Mary of Magdala is called *apostola apostolorum*, "apostle to the apostles."
Metre: 8.7.8.7.D. Iambic
Mark 14:3-9; Luke 24:1-11; John 20:11-18; Acts 2:18; 1 Corinthians 12:4-11; Galatians 3:27-28; Ephesians 2:14.

To Serve And Lead

68

A prophet-woman broke a jar,
    by Love's divine appointing.
With rare perfume she filled the room,
    presiding and anointing.
A prophet-woman broke a jar,
    the sneers of scorn defying.
With rare perfume she filled the room,
    preparing Christ for dying.

A faithful woman left a tomb
    by Love's divine commission.
She saw, she heard, she preached the Word,
    arising from submission.
A faithful woman left a tomb,
    with resurrection gospel.
She saw, she heard, she preached the Word,
    apostle to apostles.

Though woman-wisdom, woman-truth,
    for centuries were hidden,
unsung, unwritten and unheard,
    derided and forbidden,
the Spirit's breath, the Spirit's fire,
    on free and slave descending,
can tumble our dividing walls,
    our shame and sadness mending.

The Spirit knows, the Spirit calls,
    by Love's divine ordaining,
the friends we need, to serve and lead,
    their powers and gifts unchaining.
The Spirit knows, the Spirit calls,
    from women, men and children,
the friends we need, to serve and lead.
    Rejoice, and make them welcome!

© 1993 Hope Publishing Company for the USA, Canada, Australia and New Zealand and Stainer & Bell Limited for all other territories. All rights reserved.

See explanatory note on facing page

Finding Friends

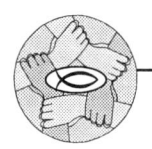

69

Give thanks for music-making art,
    and praise the Spirit's choice
of members called and set apart
    with instrument and voice.
With work and wisdom, skills hard-won,
    life-giving and life-long,
they celebrate what God has done,
    and lead the people's song.

Through years of training they accrue
    the skills of mind and hand,
which hours of practice must renew,
    enliven, and expand.
With Spirit-grace they tune our hopes;
    to Christ their hearts belong;
for love of God must guide the arts
    that lead the people's song.

With music, moving on through time
    in sequences of sound,
we show and tell God's story-line
    of how the lost are found:
the old, unfolding covenant
    of justice righting wrong,
resounds through word and sacrament,
    and leads the people's song.

Then let us reach for excellence
    to sing and symphonise
for God, our utmost audience,
    with joy our highest prize.
When kindly skill our spirit lifts
    and makes the humble strong,
give thanks, and praise the graceful gifts
    that lead the people's song.

God, give us music to express
    and richly interweave
our yearning with our thankfulness,
    and sing what we believe,
till, glorious in the realms of grace,
    with new creation's throng,
our Saviour meets us face to face
    and leads the people's song.

© 1993 Hope Publishing Company for the USA, Canada, Australia and New Zealand and Stainer & Bell Limited for all other territories. All rights reserved.

May 1992. Commissioned by Choir IV, Immanuel United Church of Christ, Shillington, Pennsylvania, in honour of J. Richard Smoker, Minister of Music, who celebrated his 20th anniversary there in June 1992. The writing was informed by his particular gifts, and by Paul Westermeyer's excellent book, *The Church Musician* (Harper).
Common Metre Double (DCM/CMD)   1 Corinthians 13:12; 1 John 3:2.

To Serve And Lead

70

All saints? How can it be?
   Can it be me,
   holy and good,
   walking with God?
How can we say that we're all saints?
   O that we could!

All saints! — Crucified love
   sings from above
   what it will do
   making us new,
naming and claiming us "all saints,"
   till it comes true.

Some Saints touch the divine,
   and as they shine,
   candles at night,
   holy and bright,
gladden the spirits of all saints,
   giving us light.

All saints stumble and fall.
   God, loving all,
   knowing our shame,
   longs to reclaim:
standing or falling we're all saints.
   Treasure the name!

Come, saints, crowds who have gone
   beckon us on,
   hindrances shed,
   joy in our tread,
one in the Spirit with all saints,
   looking ahead.

71

In Christ, our humble head,
we meet, and long to be
a loving people, wisely led,
forgiving, strong, and free.

Our walls of soaring stone,
and tales of old renown,
can send us out and spur us on,
or drag and weigh us down.

Yet saints of former years
did not live in the past,
but shared their present joy and tears
with Christ, the First and Last.

Then let us look ahead,
expecting God will do
through Christ, arisen from the dead,
things greater, good and new.

© 1989 (No. 70) and 1994 (No. 71) Hope Publishing Company for the USA, Canada, Australia and New Zealand and Stainer & Bell Limited for all other territories. All rights reserved.

No. 70 - September 1988, for the Centenary of the Anglican Parish of All Saints, Hunter's Hill, near Sydney, during a six-week visit to Australia which it co-sponsored. After exploring the varied meanings of the word, "saint," with the Rector, Clive Harcourt-Norton, the first stanza came to mind as I was walking round All Saints Church, and the others followed fairly rapidly.
   Metre: 6.4.4.4.8.4.   Romans 1:7; 1 Corinthians 1:2; 1 John 3:2; Hebrews 12:1-2.
No. 71 - August 1994, for the consecration of Michael Doe as (Anglican) Bishop of Swindon, UK. Stanza 3 recalls my doctoral supervisor, George Caird, who once said that the great saints of the past did not live in the past, but in their present, looking towards God's future.
   Short Metre (6.6.8.6.)   John 14:12; Revelation 22:13.

Looking Back

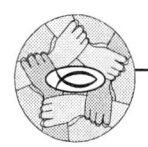

72

Look back and see the apostles' road,
the quarry where our faith was hewn,
the tree from which the church has grown:
look back, and meet the living God.

Look out, and love the world we know,
and ask what can be done and said
for freedom, dignity and bread,
with Christ, who meets us as we go.

Look on, and in the Spirit say
that Jesus lives, and gives us breath,
through change, uncertainty and death,
and travels with us, come what may.

73

Source of All, Sustaining Spirit,
    Living Christ, the First and Last,
thankful, joyful, we inherit
    boundless treasure from the past.
Pioneering, persevering,
    countless saints have shown the way.
We, like them, to Christ adhering,
    praise your boundless love today.

Reaching out to all in Jesus,
    still you seek the world to win,
saving people, powers and systems
    out of aimlessness and sin.
Bid our praise flow into service,
    and where hatreds crucify,
keep us peaceful, truthful, hopeful
    as to Christ we testify.

Christ, who knows our scattered stories,
    gently weaves us into one,
till the covenants that bind us,
    set us free and lead us on.
Living God, Eternal Spirit,
    be our judge, our joy, our friend,
till we meet and move together
    through your realm that has no end.

© 1986 (No. 72) and 1996 (No. 73) Hope Publishing Company for the USA, Canada, Australia and New Zealand and Stainer & Bell Limited for all other territories. All rights reserved.

No. 72 - September 1984, for the centenary of Marston Road United Reformed Church, Oxford, where I was a member and student pastor.
    Long Metre   Isaiah 51:1

No. 73 - February 1996. An alternate centennial hymn for First Congregational Church, Bellevue, Washington, USA, written when the first offering ("We meet as friends at table" - No. 96) did not meet their need for a celebratory hymn.
    Metre: 8.7.8.7.D. Trochaic

And Moving On

74

A cloud of witnesses around us,
    a thousand echoes from the past,
proclaim the One who freed and found us,
    and leads us on, from first to last.
      For such a gift, let all uplift
      a thousand alleluias.

A carnival of faiths and cultures
    parading through our settled praise,
with jangled rhythms, songs and dances,
    expresses Love's expansive ways.
      Christ is our song. To God belong
      a thousand alleluias.

A crowd, that clamours pain and anger,
    prevents us from nostalgic pride;
the cries of poverty and hunger
    recall us to our Saviour's side.
      There we entrust, to God most just,
      a thousand alleluias.

A throng of future shapes and shadows,
    a world that may, or may not be,
names us the servants and the stewards
    of all the Spirit longs to see.
      In awe we bend, and onward send
      a thousand alleluias.

A rainbow-host of milling children,
    God's varied image, from all lands,
awakes again our founding vision,
    that onward, urgently expands.
      Give all, give more. Let love outpour
      a thousand alleluias.

© 1992 Hope Publishing Company for the USA, Canada, Australia and New Zealand and Stainer & Bell Limited for all other territories. All rights reserved.

September 1992, for the Centennial of the Scaritt-Bennett Center, Nashville, Tennessee.
Metre: 9.8.9.8.8.8.7.
Matthew 25:3-45; Hebrews 12:1.

Coming Together

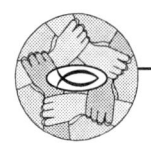

75

Painting many pictures
in the hall of faith,
    seeking God we gather,
    happily, or grieving,
    doubting or believing,
and piece together praise.

Weaving many values
in a gown of truth,
    born of love, we gather,
    patient in our hearing,
    daring in our sharing,
to piece together praise.

Sewing many stories
in a quilt of love,
    friends of God, we gather,
    variably able,
    at a common table,
and piece together praise.

Shining many visions
on the screen of hope,
    one in Christ, we gather,
    seeking new directions,
    joining our perceptions,
to piece together praise.

Blending many longings
in a song of peace,
    Spirit-led, we gather,
    growing and forgiving,
    loving all things living,
and piece together praise.

© 1995 Hope Publishing Company for the USA, Canada, Australia and New Zealand and Stainer & Bell Limited for all other territories. All rights reserved.

March 1995. Commissioned by the *Shalom Pieces* Conference of the Fellowship of United Methodists in Worship Arts, Tacoma, Washington, July 1995. The hymn follows the conference theme, depicting the varied gifts God pieces together into unity.
Metre: 6.5.6.6.6.6.   1 Corinthians 12:4-13

Why, How, and When

76

Holy Weaver, deftly intertwining
    and combining
threads and colours old and new,
from our fragments make one vestment fit for you,
    beautiful and true.

Though our strands be twisted, torn and fraying,
    grace amazing
all untangles and rewinds.
Nail-imprinted love has tinted new designs,
    bright with crimson lines.

Holy Weaver, twine your Church's vision
    into mission,
till with joy in every place,
seeker, sceptic, in our fabric clearly trace
    patterns of your grace.

© 1989 Hope Publishing Company for the USA, Canada, Australia and New Zealand and Stainer & Bell Limited for all other territories. All rights reserved.

March 1988. Third prizewinner in a hymn competition celebrating the newly-formed Evangelical Lutheran Church in America. Entries had to be for tunes in the *Lutheran Book of Worship*. Having got "Holy Weaver" as the opening line, I found an apparently compatible Czech tune, PAN BUH, in the metrical index, sight-read it in C major, and wrote the text for it. I later found that PAN BUH is sombrely in the minor, so re-thought the melody in the major, naming it for Milan Opocensky, General Secretary of the World Alliance of Reformed Churches.   Metre: 10.4.7.11.5.

Worship Order. Hymns 77-110 are placed in the framework of Sunday worship in my tradition ("Reformed" which in my case means Congregational and Presbyterian). They belong here, partly because of their content, but mainly because public worship (liturgy) is the centre and hub of life for "a covenant people, worshipping and working." The order is: *Gathering* (it takes longer to become a worshipping community than it does to physically assemble), followed by *Cleansing and Deliverance*, though I am often more ready for this after *Hearing the Living Word* (seeking and hopefully being met by God through the Bible story and its interpretation). Our response to God's gracious love includes declaring our faith and offering our whole selves to God (*Trust and Commitment*), arising from thanksgiving (*Joy*), to which I add a neglected category, *Lament*, where we need to do what the Psalmists did and Jewish faith still does: grieve, argue, and wrestle with God over the pain, evil and suffering in our lives and in our world. Then comes communion (*Christ's Freedom Meal*), for me a staple part of worship, which my tradition wishes it had the nerve to do more often than it does. Though appropriate after communion, *Reaching Out In Prayer* usually comes earlier. It is placed here because it provides space for hymn-poems on mission, service and evangelism, which lead naturally to *Going Out In Praise*.

Meeting for Worship

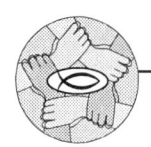

77

Against the clock, within this bounded place,
we show unbounded love, out-soaring time and space,
with breath and body, eyes and voices, hands and face.
What foolishness!
Yet stay awhile, and pray.
Perhaps today,
our slow and creaking show
will be the means of grace.

Come and review the acts of God
   for the healing of pain
     in the drama of love.
With mind and heart review the part
that you played before,
   and admit who you really are
   as you hear what you'll be
     in the drama of love.
In the Sunday Show the play is real:
this senseless song, this foolish thing,
   is the truest thing we know.
	Come and rehearse the acts of God
	   for the ending of wrong
	     in the drama of love.
	Give mind and heart to learn your part
	so you play it well,
	   and pretend you already are
	   what you'll be and become
	     in the drama of love.
	In the Sunday Show the play is real:
	this senseless song, this foolish thing,
	   is the truest thing we know.

Come and perform the acts of God
   for the dying of death
     in the drama of love.
With mind and heart we'll live the part;
when we play it well
   its as if we already are
   what we'll be and become
     in the drama of love.
In the Sunday Show the play is real:
this senseless song, this foolish thing,
   is the truest thing we know:

So on with the show!

© 1996 Hope Publishing Company for the USA, Canada, Australia and New Zealand and Stainer & Bell Limited for all other territories. All rights reserved.

"Against the Clock" is previously unpublished. "Come and Review" is a shortened version of *The Sunday Show*, a song lyric written in August 1989 for Starfire (Youth Choir), Los Altos United Methodist Church, California.

Gathering

78

Made one in Christ, we gather
   with Christians near and far.
      Our week begins with worship,
      recalling whose we are,
      for Sunday is the Birth Day
      from which our hopes derive,
   the Easter Day, the First Day,
when Christ returns alive.

From Monday into Tuesday,
   wherever you may be,
      remember Jesus teaching
      and saying, "Follow me"
      with love, befriending, healing,
      that makes our spirits thrive,
   and grounds the joy of Sunday
when Christ returns alive.

Take stock of life on Wednesday,
   and measure every aim
      by Jesus' faithful journey
      towards Jerusalem.
      Our anxious urge to prosper,
      succeed, and long survive,
   fades in the glow of Sunday
when Christ returns alive.

On Thursday night, at supper,
   remember while you eat
      how Jesus left the table
      and knelt to wash our feet.
      Lift up your hearts! Be thankful!
      Let broken bread revive
   the triumph-song of Sunday
when Christ returns alive.

Recall on Friday evening,
   when Jesus' work was done,
      the wisdom, love and courage
      by which our hope was won.
      The hour of death and sadness
      can never quite contrive
   to steal the joy of Sunday
when Christ returns alive.

On Saturday, be willing
   to taste the in-between,
      suspended in the stillness
      of things unheard, unseen.
      Break into song at midnight
      and bid the dawn arrive
   to wake the world for Sunday
when Christ returns alive.

© 1996 Hope Publishing Company for the USA, Canada, Australia and New Zealand and Stainer & Bell Limited for all other territories. All rights reserved.

February 1996, a hymn for Lent, commissioned by First Presbyterian Church, Hastings, Nebraska. Lent is a period of forty days, commemorating Jesus' testing time in the desert, as he prayed and struggled with his calling and mission. From ancient times, Christians have observed Lent as a forty day period of preparation for Easter, following Jesus' life-journey with prayer, self-denial and reflection. Sundays do not form part of those forty days, because each Sunday celebrates Christ's resurrection. Hence, this hymn, following Jesus' life-journey through each day of the week, then returning to Sunday as the mini-festival of Easter. The poem can be a spiritual journey through the working week, and also through Holy Week.
Metre: 7.6.7.6.D. Iambic   Mark 16:2 and parallels; Acts 20:7; 1 Corinthians 16:2.

Meeting For Worship

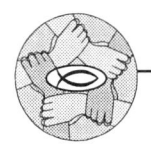

79

How great the mystery of faith,
  how deep the purposes of God,
in birth and ageing, life and death,
  unveiled, yet never understood!

Attracted by life's deepest claim
  we wait, assembled in this place,
with needs and hopes we cannot name,
  athirst for healing, truth and grace.

The best that we can do and say,
  the utmost care of skill and art,
are sweepers of the Spirit's way
  to reach the depths of every heart

Come, walk among us, Holy Friend,
  as all are gathered and prepared,
that scattered lives may meet and mend
  through open Word and table shared.

© 1989 Hope Publishing Company for the USA, Canada, Australia and New Zealand and Stainer & Bell Limited for all other territories. All rights reserved.

October 1988, for Southport Christian Church, Indianapolis. When people come to church from separate lives and experiences, it takes time to become a community of faith. The opening line recalls 1 Timothy 3:16, which would be an appropriate call to worship.
Long Metre   Luke 15:8-10; 1 Timothy 3:16.

"Sin" - A word best put in quotes because so widely misunderstood. Our personal acts of "broken trust and chosen wrong" (84) are part of it, but so are conditioned responses [the "deadly game" of "patterned wrong" (82)], and projection on others of the fear and pain within ourselves, as we "fill our world with sheep and goats and feed our self-esteem by doing others down" (90, also 126). People of my class and culture often hide from God by focusing on sin as individual wrongdoing, fanning the embers of guilt by over-estimating personal responsibility and under-estimating the social forces that sweep us along (84), which include "cruel, quiet, systemic greed" (162, also 73) and the way in which even "bland routine and good intent" can "hurt and hinder, starve and kill the outcast and the innocent" (121). On a personal level, we worship false gods by idolizing partially conditioned needs like "controlling, feeling high, and having more, submissive hiding, winning, keeping score, the tribe, the trend, and privacy in walls" (3, also 149). To avoid misunderstanding, I rarely use the word "sin," but grieve over, lament, and confess human bondage, exile, hiding, and rebellion, each of which has both systemic and personal dimensions.

Gathering

80

How good to thank our God
and speak our Saviour's name,
with flute and trumpet, heart and voice,
God's wonders to acclaim:
Sing praises, sing praises,
with psalms and hymns and songs!

Yet streams of praise go foul,
or run into the sand,
if justice cannot run its course
and water all the land:
Do justice with kindness,
and sing our Saviour's song!

When wealth's uncaring ways
our neighbour's hopes destroy,
the house of prayer that bears God's name
is dead, though filled with joy:
Do justice with kindness,
and sing our Saviour's song!

Yet Christ has shown the way
of love and praise combined,
and treads the path of peace on earth
with justice intertwined:
Sing praises, sing praises,
with psalms and hymns and songs!

Our praises cannot wait
till word and deed are done.
The Spirit fills us through and through
with all that God has done:
Sing praises, sing praises,
with psalms and hymns and songs!

Then let us walk in love—
By love our faith is shown.
Unloving, we are far from God.
In loving, God is known:
Through justice, with kindness
we'll sing our Saviour's song!

© 1993 Hope Publishing Company for the USA, Canada, Australia and New Zealand and Stainer & Bell Limited for all other territories. All rights reserved.

September 1990, to celebrate the publication of the *Presbyterian Hymnal* (USA). Throughout the Bible, the "prophetic" tradition cries out against worship and ritual divorced from the practice of justice, while the "priestly" tradition feels compelled to pour out praise for God's greatness and goodness. This hymn counterpoints and interweaves these two traditions.
Short Metre with Refrain
Scripture by stanza: §1- Psalm 92:1-3; §2 - Amos 5:23-24 and Micah 6:8; §3 - Jeremiah 7:1-11; §4 - Psalm 85:10; §5 - Ephesians 5:19; §6 - 1 John 4:7-8.

Meeting For Worship

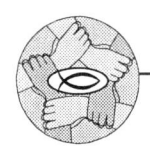

81

By purpose and by chance
    our company has grown,
and sweet is each advance
    if Christ is seen and known.
Let all who love God's loving ways
    not stand aloof
    but raise the roof
with sounds of hope and songs of praise!

We'll bang no boastful drum,
    nor fill the air with pride,
for Christ, who makes us one,
    for everyone has died,
and fills us full of power and worth
    to tell and share
    God's yearning care
for earth, and all who live on earth.

Great Spirit, roam and reach,
    till we, who worship bring,
are touched by what we teach
    and shaped by what we sing.
Disturbing Friend, yet welcome Guest,
    be seen and heard
    through table, word,
and people outcast and oppressed.

By purpose and by chance,
    as time and seasons move,
we join the Spirit's dance
    and find the feast of love.
Christ welcomes all, without reserve.
    Lift heart and voice,
    in God rejoice!
We meet to praise, and leave to serve.

© 1993 Hope Publishing Company for the USA, Canada, Australia and New Zealand and Stainer & Bell Limited for all other territories. All rights reserved.

October 1989. Commissioned to dedicate the new Sanctuary of Glen Mar United Methodist Church, Maryland.
Metre: 6.6.6.6.8.4.4.8.   1 Corinthians 1:29-31

Cleansing and Deliverance

82

Come, Holy Breath,
>to seek and know me,
>to reach and show me
how I can walk in better ways
>alive with praise
>for Christ alone.

When I have failed,
>I want a new start,
>I want a clean heart
and Holy Breath to change my ways
>as I appraise
>how I have failed.

Each time I fall,
>I start a new game
>with foolhardy claim
of better faith, then start to play
>the same old way,
>and so I fall.

Who can reach and rescue me
>*from this deadly game?*
Who can touch me, turn me around,
>*and take away the shame?*
Christ of God, Christ my love,
>*you gave yourself, your all,*
Before we cared, before we knew,
>*you bent to break our fall,*
Before we knew the countless ways
>*our lives would do you wrong,*
you saw them all, and bore the pain,
>*to sing our freedom song.*

Only your love,
>that kneels to serve me,
>can heal and nerve me
to see and shift my patterned wrong,
>and sing my song
>for you alone.

Come, Holy Breath,
>to seek and know me,
>to reach and show me
how I can walk in better ways
>alive with praise
>for Christ alone.

© 1993 Hope Publishing Company for the USA, Canada, Australia and New Zealand and Stainer & Bell Limited for all other territories. All rights reserved.

November 1989. Written on my own journey, and first performed by *Sister Spirit*, a United Methodist clergywomen quartet. One of its founder members, Susan Heafield, composed the tune, and we have since become partners-in-marriage.
Song Lyric   Romans 5:8 and 7:14-8:5.

Meeting For Worship

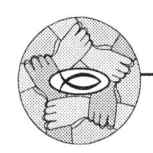

83

Dust and ashes touch our face,
mark our failure and our falling.
   Holy Spirit, come,
   walk with us tomorrow,
   take us as disciples,
washed and wakened by your calling.
     Take us by the hand and lead us,
     lead us through the desert sands,
     bring us living water,
     Holy Spirit, come.

Dust and ashes soil our hands -
greed of market, pride of nation.
   Holy Spirit, come,
   walk with us tomorrow
   as we pray and struggle
through the meshes of oppression.
     Take us by the hand and lead us,
     lead us through the desert sands,
     bring us living water,
     Holy Spirit, come.

Dust and ashes choke our tongue
in the wasteland of depression.
   Holy Spirit, come,
   walk with us tomorrow
   through all gloom and grieving
to the paths of resurrection.
     Take us by the hand and lead us,
     lead us through the desert sands,
     bring us living water,
     Holy Spirit, come.

© 1989 Hope Publishing Company for the USA, Canada, Australia and New Zealand and Stainer & Bell Limited for all other territories. All rights reserved.

February 1986, for the choir of the United Church, Hyde Park, Chicago. Written with Ash Wednesday in mind, the hymn explores personal and social dimensions of sin and new life, believing that the Holy Spirit is with us throughout the year, not only at Pentecost.
Metre: 7.8.5.6.6.8. Refr.
Genesis 3:19 and 18:27; Job 42:6; Isaiah 58:5-9; Jonah 2:5-9; John 4:13-14.

Cleansing and Deliverance

84

Great God, your love has called us here,
as we, by love for love were made.
Your living likeness still we bear,
though marred, dishonoured, disobeyed.
    We come, with all our heart and mind
    your call to hear, your love to find.

We come with self-inflicted pains
of broken trust and chosen wrong,
half-free, half-bound by inner chains,
by social forces swept along,
    by powers and systems close confined,
    yet seeking hope for humankind.

Great God, in Christ you call our name
and then receive us as your own,
not through some merit, right or claim,
but by your gracious love alone.
    We strain to glimpse your mercy seat
    and find you kneeling at our feet.

Then take the towel, and break the bread,
and humble us, and call us friends.
Suffer and serve till all are fed,
and show how grandly love intends
    to work till all creation sings,
    to fill all worlds, to crown all things.

Great God, in Christ you set us free
your life to live, your joy to share.
Give us your Spirit's liberty
to turn from guilt and dull despair
    and offer all that faith can do
    while love is making all things new.

© 1975, 1995 Hope Publishing Company for the USA, Canada, Australia and New Zealand and Stainer & Bell Limited for all other territories. All rights reserved.

April 1973, revised 1982, 1989. A revisioning (not replacement) of the central themes of Charles Wesley's hymn, "And Can It Be That I Should Gain," widening the perspective to include deliverance from sin as conditioned responses and entrapment in socio-economic structures.
Metre: 8.8.8.8.8.8.
Genesis 1:27; Isaiah 43:1-2; John 13:1-17; Romans 3:21-26; 2 Corinthians 3:17 and 5:10.

Meeting For Worship

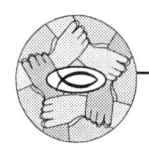

85

Sing praises old and new,
    past and present join in one.
Old covenants renew:
    new commitments have begun.
God's soaring purpose spans
all ages, lives and lands.
    Christ's open, wounded hands
    past and present join in one.

    Word, from the heart of God,
        costly, unexpected grace,
    Love, making all things good,
        Light of all the human race,
    Hail, Wisdom, deep and vast,
    shining in Israel's past,
        raising the least and last:
        costly, unexpected grace!

    Great Spirit, make us wise,
        doors of promise open wide.
    Though evil's deadly lies
        truth and goodness set aside,
    faith never stands alone,
    hope rolls away the stone,
        love makes your presence known,
        doors of promise open wide.

People of hope, be strong!
    Love is making all things new.
Lift our united song,
    show what faith can dream and do!
Come, Presence ever near,
revive us, year by year,
    sing through our joy and fear,
    Love is making all things new!

© 1993 Hope Publishing Company for the USA, Canada, Australia and New Zealand and Stainer & Bell Limited for all other territories. All rights reserved.

June 1991. Commissioned for the 120th Anniversary of Lake Charles United Methodist Church, Louisiana.
Metre: 6.7.6.7.6.6.6.7.   Mark 16:2-4

Hearing The Living Word

86

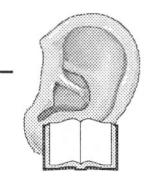

Deep in the shadows of the past,
    far out from settled lands,
some nomads travelled with their God
    across the desert sands.
The dawning hope of humankind
    by them was sensed and shown:
a promise calling them ahead,
    a future yet unknown.

While others bowed to changeless gods
    they met a mystery,
invisible, without a name:
    "I AM WHAT I WILL BE";
and by their tents, around their fires,
    in story, song and law,
they praised, remembered, handed on
    a past that promised more.

From Exodus to Pentecost
    the promise changed and grew,
while some, remembering the past,
    recorded what they knew,
or with their letters and laments,
    their prophecy and praise,
recovered, kindled and expressed
    new hope for changing days.

For all the writings that survived,
    for leaders long ago,
who sifted, copied, and preserved
    the Bible that we know,
give thanks, and find its story yet
    our promise, strength and call,
the model of emerging faith,
    alive with hope for all.

© 1975, 1995 Hope Publishing Company for the USA, Canada, Australia and New Zealand and Stainer & Bell Limited for all other territories. All rights reserved.

September 1973, revised 1994, to tell the story of the Bible in a manner acceptable to different understandings of its authority and inspiration. The idea of the Bible as the classic model of Christian faith is from James Barr, *The Bible in the Modern World*, SCM Press, London, 1973. For "I AM WHAT I WILL BE" see Exodus 3:13-15, where the Hebrew denotes an incomplete action. Double Common Metre (DCM/CMD)

Meeting For Worship

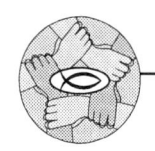

87

Outgoing God,
    your promise is an open door
    that all may enter and explore,
therein to know
    safe-haven, food, and room to grow.
        Then make your church an open space,
        a healing and belonging place.

Outspoken Love,
    your story in an open book
    reveals you to the searching look;
your word revives
    with telling-power that changes lives.
        Then give your church an open mind
        to freely speak the truth we find.

Undying Joy,
    you break the shackles that enslave,
    and drive a highway through the grave,
and at its start
    the cross reveals your open heart.
        Upon that highway we will raise
        our song of open-hearted praise.

Ongoing Life,
    you bid us live with open ears
    to cries of pain, and children's tears.
Give open hands
    to all our praying and our plans.
        Keep us, in sunlight and in storm,
        a people ready for reform.

© 1992 Hope Publishing Company for the USA, Canada, Australia and New Zealand and Stainer & Bell Limited for all other territories. All rights reserved.

August 1992. Commissioned for the 50th Anniversary of Trinity Presbyterian Church, Nashville, Tennessee.
Metre: 4.8.8.4.8.8.8.
Isaiah 43:19-21; Revelation 3:8.

Hearing The Living Word

88

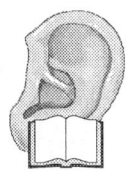

A Stranger, knocking on a door
that opens only from inside,
our withered spirits can restore
    if only we will open wide
        our hearts, ourselves, and give the key
            to love that longs to set us free.

A Shepherd, dying for the sheep,
will gather others to the fold,
with love unstinting, wide and deep
    and tales of faith as yet untold.
        Each lamb, embraced, shall taste and know
            safe pasture, sun, and room to grow.

A Saviour, risen from the dead,
with marks of pain in hands and feet,
is known to us in breaking bread,
    and draws us closer when we meet:
        majestic love most humbly bends
            to raise us up, and make us friends.

The Spirit makes an open door
and calls us, gathered here today,
to praise the past that's gone before,
    then go along our pilgrim way:
        With Christ alive, and at our side,
            we'll take the future in our stride.

© 1993 Hope Publishing Company for the USA, Canada, Australia and New Zealand and Stainer & Bell Limited for all other territories. All rights reserved.

April 1990. Commissioned for the centennial celebration of St. Paul's United Methodist Church, Tacoma, Washington, using images from the church's stained glass windows.
Metre: 8.8.8.8.8.8.
Luke 24:30-40; John 10:11-16; 13:3-5, 15.15; 20: 24-29; Revelation 3:20.

Meeting For Worship

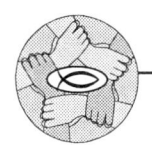

89

Joy has blossomed out of sadness.
   Call our neighbours, near and far.
Bring to God, with grateful gladness,
   all we have and all we are.
God, who grieved with us at midnight,
turns our shadows into sunlight.
   Praise our Maker, Friend and Helper,
   healing Tree and guiding Star.

Christ our Truth, in whom we gather,
   founding Rock of all we share,
build our hearts and lives together
   in a house of praise and prayer,
open, joyful, safe, and spacious,
living proof that God is gracious,
   meeting-place of friends and strangers,
   home of hope, with room to spare.

Healing Spirit, flowing through us,
   daily make your presence known.
Challenge, comfort, and renew us;
   we are Christ's, and not our own.
At our doors the world is waiting.
Lead us out, anticipating
   in our caring, work and striving,
   faith to live by grace alone.

© 1994 Hope Publishing Company for the USA, Canada, Australia and New Zealand and Stainer & Bell Limited for all other territories. All rights reserved.

October 1994, commissioned for the dedication of the redesigned and rebuilt Trinity Evangelical Lutheran Church, Lynnwood, Washington. The church had been destroyed in August 1992, in a series of arson attacks on buildings in the area. Pastor and congregation showed their forgiveness to the arsonist, whose family contributed to the new sanctuary.
Metre: 8.7.8.7.8.8.8.7.

> **Guilt - or Lament?** A reviewer found No. 91 "preachy," and assumed I was trying to make him feel guilty for a past he didn't find problematic (On "preachiness" see Box Note, p. 104). I suggest that we should lament the evils of colonialism, racism, sexism and other -isms, and that lament is both fundamental to Christian identity and a more accurate response than guilt. Telling the story of God, in history, Judaism, Jesus, and the church, is an essential part of Christian identity. Worship and theology are inconceivable without it, because God's self-disclosure to us comes in story (narrative) form. But the obverse of that gracious, saving story is the painful, evil tragedy of the human story, collective as well as personal. Guilt is appropriate where there is personal responsibility, but in lament we express sorrow at the historic and current systemic evils from which we suffer or benefit, but for which we are not individually "guilty." So I invite you to lament Christian anti-Judaism (90), the way in which woman-wisdom and woman-truth has so long been "unsung, unwritten and unheard, derided and forbidden" (68), the horrors of our history (118), and the expansion of Christendom in the Americas, "proclaiming love and taking land" (92, also 91). On "lament" see also Box Note, p. 71.

Joy and Lament

90

God, thank you for the Jews,
   your chosen people, full of grace.
Through Covenant and Law
   they knew you first, the Holy One.
In prophecy and praise,
they wrestled with your love
through centuries of tested faith,
to be a light to all the world.
    Hosanna!
    Hallelujah!

God, thank you for the Jews
   who first revealed to us your Name:
for Peter, Martha, Paul,
   for John, and Mary Magdalen,
who prayed, "Your Kingdom Come,"
in synagogue and home,
and found you as they knew and loved
a Rabbi out of Nazareth.
    Hosanna!
    Hallelujah!

God, thank you for the Jews.
   Redeem your church's ancient crime.
Believing Christ had come,
   we cursed them as forever wrong,
through centuries of hate
that paved the devil's way
to Auschwitz, and the Holocaust.
How could your Christians be so blind?
    Kyrie eleison!
    Christe eleison!
    Kyrie eleison!

God, thank you for the Jews.
   Their sorrow shows our common sin.
With sad, demonic pride,
   we fill our world with sheep and goats,
and feed our self-esteem
by doing others down,
applauding "us" and cursing "them,"
like crowds who mock the crucified.
    Kyrie eleison!
    Christe eleison!
    Kyrie eleison!

God, thank you for the Jews.
   We celebrate their living faith.
Help us, who long to mend
   our ancient parting of the ways,
to recognize their claim,
and utter Jesus' name,
not in polemic, but in praise,
till all our hopes are made complete.
    Hallelujah!
    Amen!

© 1986, 1996 Hope Publishing Company for the USA, Canada, Australia and New Zealand and Stainer & Bell Limited for all other territories. All rights reserved.

February 1984, revised 1995. Written after a meeting of the Oxford Council for Christians and Jews, where I struggled with the absurdity of giving "A Reformed View of the Holocaust." "Hosanna," "Hallelujah," and "Amen" are Hebrew acclamations, common to Jews and Christians. Stanzas 3 and 4 are Christian lament, using the Greek petitions from early Christian liturgies, "Lord have mercy, Christ have mercy, Lord have mercy."
Metre: 6.8.6.8.6.6.8.8. Refr.   Deuteronomy 14:2; Isaiah 49:5-6; Matthew 25:31-33.

Meeting For Worship

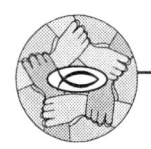

91

Once, from a European shore,
    strong nations reached around the earth,
    to bid for slaves with bales of cloth,
and plunder, conquer and explore.
Recall how some, upon that tide,
    with faith and failings like our own,
    set out to make the gospel known,
that Christ for all the world had died.

Remember how, from tangled strands
    of terror, honour, greed and love,
    a single world God's Spirit wove
from earth's long-separated lands,
and as our fractured world must face
    the pain and hope of being one,
    give thanks, that Christ is named and known
in every culture, every place.

While many idolise or crave
    their nation's glory, might or gain,
    and hoarded wealth, unheeded pain,
divide, dishonour and enslave,
we answer to the Spirit's call,
    by faith to heal, resist, abate
    oppression, poverty and hate,
and break each new dividing wall.

Christ, open every heart and mind
    to show what still your Church can be:
    a source of hope and unity,
a prototype for humankind.
Help us to honour, heed and serve
    the global friends your love has made.
    Give us a hope that does not fade,
to build a world of peace and love.

© 1983, 1995 Hope Publishing Company for the USA, Canada, Australia and New Zealand and Stainer & Bell Limited for all other territories. All rights reserved.

November 1976, revised 1994. An attempt to speak truthfully and hopefully of the ambiguities of western missionary expansion and the world-wide Church of Jesus Christ. See commentary on "The Gospel Came With Foreign Tongue," No. 92.
Double Long Metre (LMD/DLM)   Ephesians 2:14-15

Joy and Lament

92

The gospel came with foreign tongue,
disrupting all the ancient ways,
beside the merchant and the gun,
in search of profit, souls and slaves.

With God we weep, lament, confess
how holy zeal and bloodied hand
reached out to kill and dispossess,
proclaiming love and taking land.

How hard, today, to meet and share
our needs, suspicions, hopes and fears,
when some have ease, and food to spare,
while others walk a trail of tears!

• • • • • • • • • • • • • • • • • • •

In hope we come, by grace reborn,
as clashing stories still collide,
to listen, pray and travel on,
companions of the Crucified.

We tell our varied memories,
assembled in our global room,
that Christ may wash our histories,
as threads for Love's eternal loom.

We pray, as in a dream come true,
to hear the world again declare
"These Christians are divinely new:
they truly love, and freely share."

© 1983, 1995 Hope Publishing Company for the USA, Canada, Australia and New Zealand and Stainer & Bell Limited for all other territories. All rights reserved.

November 1976, rewritten 1994. The "trail of tears" names the forced migration of Cherokee peoples to Oklahoma from their Appalachian homeland in the winter of 1838-39, an American example of "ethnic cleansing," in which thousands died. The final couplet recalls how Aristides told the Roman Emperor Hadrian that Christians would fast for several days to give their poorer members food, adding, "This is really a new kind of person. There is something divine in them." (Tissa Balasurlya, *The Eucharist and Human Liberation*, 1979, pp. 26 27). To prevent the transition between stanzas 3 and 4 being glib, ease it with instrumental music, poems, or prayers.
Long Metre

Meeting For Worship

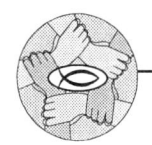

93

Come, build the Church - not heaps of stone
in safe, immobile, measured walls,
but friends of Jesus, Spirit-blown,
and fit to travel where he calls.

Come, occupy with glad dissent
where death and evil fence the ground,
and pitch a Resurrection-Tent
where peace is lived, and love is found.

Exposed upon the open ground
to screams of war in East and West,
our ears will catch a deeper sound:
the weeping of the world's oppressed.

In wearied face, or frightened child,
in all they know, and need to say,
the living Christ shall stand revealed.
Come, let us follow and obey!

94

Christ loves the Church, with grace beyond all measure.
We bear his name, for all the world to see.
He will not let us go or let us be,
but chooses earthen vessels for his treasure.

Christ bears the Church, corrupted or conforming,
obsessed with trifles, blessing greed and war.
His love outwits us, spinning gold from straw,
through saints and prophets, praying and reforming.

Christ feeds the Church, and fills us with a vision,
through praise and preaching, wine and broken bread,
of sharing people, doing what they've said,
who win the world's respect, or opposition.

Christ needs the Church, to live and tell his story,
so praise his love, and marvel at his trust,
till, bathed in light, awakened from the dust,
we walk with God, alive in grace and glory.

Nos. 93 and 94 © 1986 Hope Publishing Company for the USA, Canada, Australia and New Zealand and Stainer & Bell Limited for all other territories. All rights reserved.

No. 93 - October 1983, for a gathering of the Presbyterian Church (USA).
    Long Metre   Exodus 33:7
No. 94 - July 1985. Commissioned by High Street United Methodist Church, Muncie, Indiana, for its 150th Anniversary.
    Metre: 11.10.10.11.   2 Corinthians 4:7

Trust and Commitment

95

When anyone is in Christ,
there is a new creation:
the old is dead and gone.
Behold, the new has come.

Old evasions end,   Ancient curses fade:
and no-one hides, or runs away;   the ring of power is melted down,
the chain of blame is broken,   the sword becomes a ploughshare,
and men and women meet as friends.   and men are freed to laugh and love.

When anyone is in Christ,
there is a new creation:
the old is dead and gone.
Behold, the new has come.

Old subjections fall: Dominations die:
the captives break the prison door;   The prince is kneeling at our feet,
the young and old see visions,   the edge is at the centre,
and women preach and prophesy.   and little children lead us all.

When anyone is in Christ,
there is a new creation:
the old is dead and gone.
Behold, the new has come.

© 1993 Hope Publishing Company for the USA, Canada, Australia and New Zealand and Stainer & Bell Limited for all other territories. All rights reserved.

December 1993, for Than and Jennifer Ward, with love. Just before Christmas, my composer friend Hal Hopson told me he could find few choral works responding to the curse-stories of Genesis 3:1-24, which form part of a widely used service of Christmas lessons and carols. I wrote this poem in response, from a conviction that Christ transforms and re-births all our relationships, and Hal set it to music.
Metre: 5.8.7.8. Refr.
Genesis 3:1-24; Isaiah 11:6; Micah 4:3; Acts 2:17-18; 2 Corinthians 5:17.

Meeting For Worship

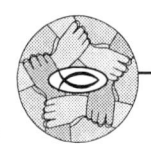

96

We meet as friends at table,
    to listen, and be heard,
united by the Spirit,
    attentive to the Word.
Through prayer and conversation
    we tune our varied views
to Christ, whose love has made us
    the bearers of good news.

With food and drink for sharing
    the table soon is spread.
The freedom-meal of Jesus
    is crowned with wine and bread,
and all, without exception,
    may eat, and speak, and stay,
for this is Christ's own table
    where none are turned away.

We share our lives and longings,
    and when the meal is done
we pray as friends at table
    and promise to be one.
To Christ, and to each other,
    we cheerfully belong:
apart, our hope is fruitless;
    together, we are strong.

Fulfilled, and glad to follow
    wherever Christ may lead,
we journey from the table
    to love a world in need
with patience, truth and kindness,
    that justice may increase
and all may sit at table
    in freedom, joy, and peace.

© 1996 Hope Publishing Company for the USA, Canada, Australia and New Zealand and Stainer & Bell Limited for all other territories. All rights reserved.

January 1996. Commissioned for the Centennial Celebration of First Congregational Church (UCC), Bellevue, Washington, and modelled on a United Church of Christ document, *Toward the 21st Century*, in which the UCC hopes to be an "attentive"(§ 1), "inclusive"(§ 2), "supportive"(§ 3) and "responsive" church (§ 4).   Double Common Metre   John 6:37

Christ's Freedom Meal

97

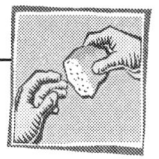

I come with joy, a child of God,
    forgiven, loved and free,
the life of Jesus to recall,
    in love laid down for me.

I come with Christians far and near
    to find, as all are fed,
the new community of love
    in Christ's communion bread.

As Christ breaks bread, and bids us share,
    each proud division ends.
The love that made us, makes us one,
    and strangers now are friends.

The Spirit of the risen Christ,
    unseen, but ever near,
is in such friendship better known,
    alive among us here.

Together met, together bound
    by all that God has done,
we'll go with joy, to give the world
    the love that makes us one.

© 1971, 1995 Hope Publishing Company for the USA, Canada, Australia and New Zealand and Stainer & Bell Limited for all other territories. All rights reserved.

July 1968, revised 1977, 1993. Originally written for Hockley and Hawkwell United Reformed (then Congregational) Church, Essex, to conclude a sermon-series about communion, the hymn moves from the individual ("I come") to the collective ("we'll go"). Stanza 4 describes Christ's "real presence" in the faith community and in the communion meal.
Common Metre

Meeting For Worship

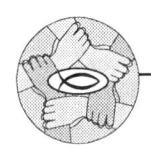

98

At the table of the world,
some have plenty, some have none.
At the table of our God,
all are plentifully fed.
Blow among us, Spirit of God,
fill us with your courage and care!
Hurricane and Breath,
take us on a journey of love!

At the table of the world,
some have honour, some have scorn.
At the table of our God,
all are welcomed and acclaimed.
Blow among us, Spirit of God,
fill us with your courage and care!
Hurricane and Breath,
take us on a journey of love!

Set the table of our God
in the Church and in the world,
till the children, fed and loved,
taste and see that life is good.
Blow among us, Spirit of God,
fill us with your courage and care!
Hurricane and Breath,
take us on a journey of love!

© 1989 Hope Publishing Company for the USA, Canada, Australia and New Zealand and Stainer & Bell Limited for all other territories. All rights reserved.

July 1987. The Eucharist / Lord's Supper's inbuilt themes of sharing and community have been spiritualised and obscured by most Christian traditions. The text draws on the insights of Bolivian writer Rafael Avila and Sri Lankan theologian, Tissa Balasuriya.
Metre: 7.7.7.7. Refr.

Justice, Peace and Love. From Martin Luther King I learned to distinguish the negative peace which is the absence of tension from the positive peace which is the presence of justice, a theme elaborated in "Say 'No' to peace" (122). The communion sevice models what a just commnity is like (see 98, above), and excludes the notion of love as condescending charity. Many expressions of Christian love assume that "we" (who have much to give), generously give it to "them" (who have little or nothing), and that "they" are then grateful to "us." Hence the prayer that "if I love my neighbour out of my knowledge, leisure, power or wealth," the Holy Spirit may help me to "understand the shame and anger of helplessness that hates *my power to help*," and that when acts of kindness enable the oppressed group or dependent person to rise from subordination and despair, I may respond faithfully "when the cry for justice requires of me the changes that I fear" (131). Doing justice-with-love includes hearing and honouring the opressed (130, 133), treating children with respect (141), giving thanks for "the wisdom, strength and kindness of those we kneel to serve" (102), accepting our mortality so that we can do justice to the claims of the coming generation (156), and making space for foreigners and strangers (125).

Christ's Freedom Meal

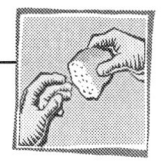

*We bring - you take,
and bless, and break,
and all are fed
with wine and bread.*

The night you were betrayed, good friend and Lord,
you ate with friends your people's freedom-meal
and gave them bread, and shared a cup of wine,
to show how you would give yourself for all.

Beside the sea, at dawn, you came again,
when all the world declared you dead and gone,
and cooked your friends a meal of bread and fish,
to show your glory, endlessly alive.

Now, every time we share the bread and wine,
and all are fed, and no-one is despised,
we taste and tell how all the world should be
and sing of fairness, freedom, love and peace.

We bring ourselves, and offer all we have.
We bring our caring for our town and land.
We bring our hope that every child be fed.
We taste eternal life, and dwell in love.

*We bring - you take,
and bless, and break,
and all are fed
with wine and bread.*

© 1989, 1996 Hope Publishing Company for the USA, Canada, Australia and New Zealand and Stainer & Bell Limited for all other territories. All rights reserved.

June 1987, revised 1995. The original was for Brighthelm United Reformed Church, Brighton, Sussex, England, inspired by its loaves-and-fishes sculpture by John Skelton, which proclaims Brighthelm's mission to its seaside town. The text was revised with helpful suggestions from Betty Pulkingham, whose tune HOST was composed for it in early 1995.
Metre: Irregular   John 21:9-13

Meeting For Worship

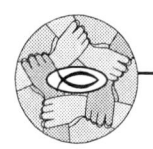

100

"You are my body!" Joy and wonder!
    Assembled in our Saviour's name,
our scattered spirits gladly gather
    the Way of Jesus to proclaim.
Come, Spirit, weave us into one,
to show and tell what God has done.

"This is my body!" Simple Glory! —
    cup of wine, a loaf of bread
feed us, and join us to the story
    of Christ, arisen from the dead,
whose Life, forever flowing free,
enlivens all: O taste and see!

At one in Christ, around the table
    where all may eat, and nothing pay,
where all are honoured and enabled,
    and none are scorned or turned away,
we prophesy, with broken bread,
a world where every child is fed.

We are your body! One in Spirit,
    dear Christ, with all your church, we pray
your body-language to inherit.
    Come, lead us in your Truthful way!
To seek for what is fair and right
shall be our duty and delight!

© 1993 Hope Publishing Company for the USA, Canada, Australia and New Zealand and Stainer & Bell Limited for all other territories. All rights reserved.

November 1993, for the Centennial Celebration of Warner Memorial Presbyterian Church, Kensington, Maryland, USA.
Metre: 9.8.9.8.8.8.   1 Corinthians 12:12-13; Colossians 1:18.

Christ's Freedom Meal

101

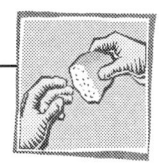

There's a spirit in the air,
  telling Christians everywhere:
    "Praise the love that Christ revealed,
    living, working in our world!"

  Lose your shyness, find your tongue,
  tell the world what God has done:
  God in Christ has come to stay.
  Live tomorrow's life today!

When believers break the bread,
  when a hungry child is fed,
    praise the love that Christ revealed,
    living, working, in our world.

  Still the Spirit gives us light,
  seeing wrong and setting right:
  God in Christ has come to stay.
  Live tomorrow's life today!

When a stranger's not alone,
  where the homeless find a home,
    praise the love that Christ revealed,
    living, working, in our world.

  May the Spirit fill our praise,
  guide our thoughts and change our ways.
  God in Christ has come to stay.
  Live tomorrow's life today!

There's a Spirit in the air,
  calling people everywhere:
    Praise the love that Christ revealed,
    living, working, in our world.

© 1969, 1995 Hope Publishing Company for the USA, Canada, Australia and New Zealand and Stainer & Bell Limited for all other territories. All rights reserved.

May 1969, revised 1987/89, to celebrate the Spirit of God / Spirit of Jesus, "living, working in our world." The alternating refrains are modelled on Isaac Watts' hymn, "Give to Our God Immortal Praise."   Metre: 7.7.7.7.

Meeting For Worship

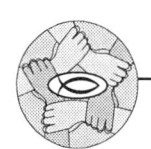

102

To Christ our hearts now given,
   we join in joyful praise,
and pray, in all our living,
   to grow in loving ways.
The freeing grace that found us,
God's healing, winning call,
   in freedom now has bound us
   to love, and give our all.

From many tribes and places,
   with thankful songs we come
to blend our gifts and graces,
   and pray and work as one.
We vow, whate'er betide us,
in love and truth to stay,
   for Christ moves on beside us,
   and guides us on our way.

Wherever we may venture
   to witness, heal and care,
the Spirit of our Saviour
   has long been lodging there.
Then let us give with gladness,
not claiming to deserve
   the wisdom, strength and kindness
   of those we kneel to serve.

The freeing grace that found us,
   the love that makes us one,
is ranging far beyond us,
   and bids us travel on
to share God's great salvation,
defend our neighbour's worth,
   dismantle domination,
   and heal our aching earth.

© 1995 Hope Publishing Company for the USA, Canada, Australia and New Zealand and Stainer & Bell Limited for all other territories. All rights reserved.

June 1995. Commissioned by the Ministry of Worship at Westminster Presbyterian Church, Lincoln, Nebraska, for a joint mission-and-service visit from that church and a church in Lohmen, Germany, to Daugavpils, Lithuania. The hymn was written for a tune in the *Presbyterian Hymnal*, USA (WIE LIEBLICH IST DER MAIEN), which was also familiar to the Lohmen congregation.
Metre: 7.6.7.6.D. Iambic

Mission - Who has the gospel? The church of Jesus Christ is world wide, and finds expression in a kaleidoscopic variety of cultures. In the mostly North American congregations with whom I work, I sense that patronising conceptions of "us" having the gospel and giving it to "them" are being displaced by a growing understanding of partnership in mission. So I welcome opportunities to express the conviction that "wherever we may venture to witness, heal and care, the Spirit of our Saviour has long been lodging there" (102), and was not surprised that the people for whom I wrote it were glad to have this theology put into words they could sing. Taking a step further, it is helpful to remind ourselves that Christians among the poorest of the poor "pray that we may hear and live the gospel that they long to give" (104). Though we should "offer Christ" to everyone, we should also be aware that Christ's "fulness far exceeds our local view," with the result that those to whom we offer Christ are likely to claim their own part in God's mission and "bring Christ to us, the same, yet strangely new" (105).

Reaching Out In Prayer
103

Far and wide the gospel travels,
    healing wounds and righting wrongs.
Fear and hate its touch unravels;
    praise unites ten thousand tongues:
        Alleluia! Alleluia! Alleluia!

Reaching deep, the Spirit, searching,
    tends, in every faith and place,
hopes of one, new world emerging,
    freeing all the human race:
        Alleluia! Alleluia! Alleluia!

Though our hearts may limp and stumble,
    bruised by terror, greed and loss,
faith has seen their empires crumble,
    mocked and cancelled by the cross:
        Alleluia! Alleluia! Alleluia!

Joined by grace, in Christ communing,
    freed and fed by bread and wine,
thousands meet, their vision tuning
    to the Spirit's grand design:
        Alleluia! Alleluia! Alleluia!

Raise your voices, clear your vision,
    turn your longing into song.
Praise can change our heart's condition:
    let our praise be full and strong:
        Alleluia! Alleluia! Alleluia!

© 1993 Hope Publishing Company for the USA, Canada, Australia and New Zealand and Stainer & Bell Limited for all other territories. All rights reserved.

September 1993. Commissioned for the 10th anniversary of the Chancel Choir of West Side Presbyterian Church, Ridgewood, New Jersey.
Metre: 8.7.8.7. with Alleluias   Colossians 2:13-14

Meeting For Worship

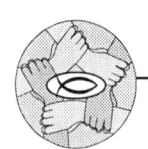

104

In Great Calcutta Christ is known.
   Soweto thunders with his voice.
   In Salvador his friends rejoice.
He rises in the Spirit's power
   among the poorest of the earth,
   and calls the nations to rebirth.

The suffering churches sing his grace
   and pray that we may hear and live
   the gospel that they long to give.
Beset by hunger, fear and death,
   their hopes miraculously thrive:
   they know that Jesus is alive!

And all the powers that wreck and rule
   must lose their glamour, strength and skill
   to dazzle minds or crush the will.
The waking hopes of God's oppressed
   will not be beaten, bowed and awed:
   they tell the world that Christ is Lord.

Where money glitters in our streets,
   applauding honour and success,
   their prophets come, in ragged dress.
In them we hear our Saviour's voice,
   like them discarded and despised,
   who calls the weak to save the wise.

They bring a promise old, yet new,
   of food and freedom for the slave,
   and joyous life beyond the grave.
"Repent, and Christ will set you free,"
   their faithful missionaries cry,
   and call us through the needle's eye.

Christ Jesus, love us through and through,
   until our wakened hearts receive
   your glorious gospel, and believe.
From barrio,* bustee,* and slum,
   with Asian and Hispanic voice,
   our Saviour comes! Sing and rejoice!

* Spanish and Hindi for shanty towns.

© 1986 Hope Publishing Company for the USA, Canada, Australia and New Zealand and Stainer & Bell Limited for all other territories. All rights reserved.

August 1985. Inspired, in part by Sri Lankan theologian Tissa Balasuriya's plea, in his book, *Planetary Theology*, for Asian Churches to send missionaries to the West. The theme had been on my mind for some time, but I had to wait till it was fully part of me and could be sung and prayed. Metre: 8.8.8.D.
Matthew 6:24(§4) and 19:24(§5); 1 Corinthians 1:26-29(§1 and §4); 2 Corinthians 1:2-7; 4:7-12(§2); Colossians 2:14-15(§3); Revelation 11:15(§3).

Reaching Out In Prayer

105

We offer Christ
    to all the world around us,
born into faith, released from pride and shame;
embraced by love, we show how love has found us;
at peace with God, we speak our Saviour's name.

We offer Christ
    from all our best traditions,
by grace alone, amazed and strangely warmed,
created equal, stirred by freedom-visions,
self-critical, prepared to be reformed.

We offer Christ
    the barrier-bestrider,
whose fulness far exceeds our local view,
whose Spirit, breathing deep in every culture,
brings Christ to us, the same, yet strangely new.

We offer Christ
    and, God-beloved, our Saviour
now offers us, born of the Spirit's kiss,
to love creation and creation's Lover,
with skill, compassion, justice, care and peace.

© 1989 Hope Publishing Company for the USA, Canada, Australia and New Zealand and Stainer & Bell Limited for all other territories. All rights reserved.

July 1986. Commissioned by St. Paul's United Methodist Church, Orangeburg, South Carolina, for its 150th Anniversary. The first line derives from John Wesley's advice to Thomas Coke, as the latter departed for America: "Offer them Christ." The second stanza recalls John Wesley's conversion (his heart "strangely warmed") and the Reformation themes of being set right with God by grace, through faith, in a church which must be (in the Latin phrase), "ecclesia semper reformanda" (continuously being reformed).
Metre: 11.10.11.10. Iambic

Meeting For Worship
106

"Go forth in faith, from kindred, home and custom.
Leave the old gods":— what easy words to say!
How hard to move, with Abraham's decision,
break free, and risk a new uncertain way.

How hard to trek from ease in Pharaoh's palace,
from boardroom power, or popular acclaim,
to bear discomfort, ridicule, or malice,
with earth's discarded people, in God's name.

Yet when we laugh at hope, like Sarah, grieving
that nothing changes, nothing can be done,
we bear, like her a promise past conceiving,
of justice, joy, shalom, and kingdom-come.

Within the womb of every best tradition
the Spirit moves, and cannot be ignored.
We feel the kicking of our inner vision
and sing, "My soul shall glorify the Lord!"

The voices from the past re-echo round us.
Take courage from the faith of many friends.
Go forth in faith, and look ahead to Jesus,
on whom, from start to finish, faith depends.

With faith newborn, and passionate for justice,
together now, we'll travel out from home,
to sacrifice the peace of calm uprightness,
and struggle for the city of Shalom.

© 1989 Hope Publishing Company for the USA, Canada, Australia and New Zealand and Stainer & Bell Limited for all other territories. All rights reserved.

February 1986, commissioned by the Annual Conference of the Church of the Brethren (USA), at whose seminary I was Scholar in Residence in late 1985, and based on Hebrews 11:1-12:2, the Conference theme.
Metre: 11.10.11.10. Iambic

Going Out In Praise

107

Ever-journeying Friend,
    from beginning to end,
our travel-horizon
    you daily extend.
When we stumble or hide,
    your compassion is wide.
You heal us, you find us,
    you counsel and guide.
    Spirit of God, Companion for good,
        bring us together in praise.
        Awake us, and shake us, and lead us on,
    a journeying people forever.

Living Partner most wise,
    from the grave you arise,
and give us the business
    of God's enterprise.
By your gracious bequest,
    love and life you invest.
In wonder we answer
    and offer our best.
    Crucified Christ, Compassion of God,
        keep us together in praise.
        Redeem us, and feed us, and lead us on,
    a love-giving people forever.

Hidden Parent of Light,
    ever faithful and right,
most holy, most humble,
    our trust you invite.
All the wonders of space
    you unfold and embrace;
conceiving, creating,
    our thoughts you outpace.
    Founder of Life, all-giving, all-good,
        lead us together in praise.
        Be near us, to cheer us, and call us home,
    a thanks-giving people forever.

© 1993 Hope Publishing Company for the USA, Canada, Australia and New Zealand and Stainer & Bell Limited for all other territories. All rights reserved.

December 1991. Commissioned by First Congregational Church, Crystal Lake, Illinois, to celebrate its sesquicentennial (150th) year.   Metre: 6.6.6.5.D.Refr.

Meeting For Worship

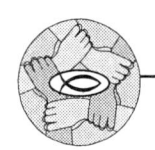

108

Sing together on our journey!
Sing with joy, Alleluia!
    Share, as we proceed,
    canticle and creed,
and with faith and fervour strong
spin our stories into song:
sing with joy, Alleluia!

Pray together on our journey!
Pray in love, Alleluia!
    Say the Name you praise
    not in hurtful ways
as a hammer or a sword,
but as life for all outpoured;
pray in love, Alleluia!

Seek together on our journey!
Seek the truth, Alleluia!
    In the Spirit grow,
    trusting we will know,
where to look and when to leap,
reaching high, and digging deep;
seek the truth, Alleluia!

Walk together on our journey!
Walk in peace, Alleluia!
    With the Crucified
    risen at our side,
let us listen and befriend,
quick to mediate and mend;
walk in peace, Alleluia!

Dance together on our journey!
Dance with hope, Alleluia!
    Follow with your feet
    freedom's thrilling beat,
with endurance amply shod,
doing justice, knowing God:
Dance with hope, Alleluia!

Sing together on our journey!
Sing with joy, Alleluia!
    Stewards of the earth,
    given second birth,
to our Maker we belong,
praise the Source of every song,
sing with joy, Alleluia!

© 1992 Hope Publishing Company for the USA, Canada, Australia and New Zealand and Stainer & Bell Limited for all other territories. All rights reserved.

November 1992. Commissioned by the Boston Theological Institute, to express what unites its diverse members, who include Roman Catholic, Unitarian, "mainstream" and "evangelical" seminaries and colleges. The hymn suggests that theology is a communal enterprise, active as well as reflective, a matter of seeking more than stating. Communal song and dance can be literally part of it, but stand also as metaphors for the intellectual process (as do "walking together" and "seeking together"), modelling modes of reasoning which can be as precise and rigorous as argument, without becoming combative.
Metre: 8.7.5.5.7.7.7.

Going Out In Praise

109

"Peace is my parting gift to you.

Go in Peace:
  not as the world gives;
  not in pretending;
  not in submitting;
  not in possessing;
    not in the glory of winning,
    the fever of getting.

For Peace is my parting gift to you.

  Go in Peace:
    as the makers of peace;
    as the shakers of wrong;
    as the people of God,
    singing a peacable song.
  Go in Peace."

110

May the Sending One sing in you,
May the Seeking One walk with you,
May the Greeting One stand by you,
  in your gladness and in your grieving.

May the Gifted One relieve you,
May the Given One retrieve you,
May the Giving One receive you,
  In your falling and your restoring.

May the Binding One unite you,
May the One Belov'd invite you,
May the Loving One delight you,
  Three-in-One, joy in life unending.

Nos. 109 and 110 © 1989 Hope Publishing Company for the USA, Canada, Australia and New Zealand and Stainer & Bell Limited for all other territories. All rights reserved.

No. 109 - February 1989. A poem written as an anthem text; John Horman's setting is published by Sacred Music Press, Dayton, Ohio, USA.   Matthew 5:6-9; John 14:27.
No. 110 - March 1989, while visiting composer Mikkel Thompson, for music he had written. The three blessings are in Celtic style, each trinitarian in itself.   Metre: 8.8.8.9.

What kind of theology?

What kind of theology does a hymn-text do, and in what sense is this collection a theological work?

Poetic Lyrics

Most items in *Piece Together Praise* follow the form of the English *hymn*: they are verse lyrics, mostly in rhyme, in unvarying sequential strophes, meaning that each stanza has the same shape and form as its predecessor. The exceptions are a few song lyrics and free-verse poems.

Few hymns reach the depth of Robert Frost, Wilfrid Owen, and Dylan Thomas. Yet most hymns can be read and heard as *poetry*, able to articulate thoughts and visions, as other poems do.

Community Speech

As poetry, hymns are statements by the writer, but as hymns, they are *community speech* - written for and from within an actual or presumed congregation, in the hope that, somewhere, faith communities will want to speak or sing them in their public worship of God.

Though cast in hymn form, I know that some of these items are more appropriate as solo speech or song. But mostly, I hope that somewhere, a faith community will want to speak or sing them.

Viewpoint

Every hymn presents a *viewpoint*. Some hymns appeal widely. Others get limited use, because their viewpoint is less widely acceptable.

If you disagree with a hymn's viewpoint, you may call it "preachy," but the label is justified only if the writer is standing outside a presumed congregation, not simply because the presumed congregation's viewpoint differs from your own.

Hindsight sometimes shows me where I've been preachy, as in "Christian people, sleekly fed, Christian comforts can afford" (189), whose language put me outside the "Christian people" I hoped would sing the hymn.

Metaphor

As poetry, hymns and hymn collections cannot do *systematic theology*, namely, discuss different viewpoints and develop a reasoned exposition of Christian faith. Yet hymns can state their viewpoint memorably, and with metaphor explore themes hard to put briefly in conceptual form. To test this suggestion, ask how the significance of a life lasting only eight years (157), described metaphorically as a melody given eternal harmonies and variations, would be expressed in more abstract, conceptual forms.

Collegial Community

Though a hymn collection may be quite *comprehensive*, it cannot be *complete*: hymn-poets not only share the common limitations of being gendered, class-bound, time-bound etc. (which the revision-process partially reveals even to the writer), but write within a *collegial community* whose work complements their own: so that when someone else says something well, we say "Amen," not try to duplicate or outdo it.

So this collection, and hymns in general, can be described as doing *lyric theology* (using the hymn form of lyric verse and poetic methods especially metaphor) *in the form of community speech and song*.

Living in the World God Loves

Creation, Suffering, Peace and Justice

Forth in thy name, O Lord, I go,
my daily labour to pursue,
thee, only thee, resolved to know
in all I think, or speak, or do.

Charles Wesley (1707-1788)

Living With God

111

Thank you, God, for water, soil and air,
large gifts supporting everything that lives.
    Forgive our spoiling and abuse of them.
    Help us renew the face of the earth.

Thank you, God, for minerals and ores,
the basis of all building, wealth and speed.
    Forgive our reckless plundering and waste.
    Help us renew the face of the earth.

Thank you, God, for priceless energy,
stored in each atom, gathered from the sun.
    Forgive our greed and carelessness of power.
    Help us renew the face of the earth.

Thank you, God, for weaving nature's life
into a seamless robe, a fragile whole.
    Forgive our haste, that tampers unaware.
    Help us renew the face of the earth.

Thank you, God, for making planet earth
a home for us, and ages yet unborn.
    Help us to share, consider, save and store.
    Come and renew the face of the earth.

© 1975 Hope Publishing Company for the USA, Canada, Australia and New Zealand and Stainer & Bell Limited for all other territories. All rights reserved.

September 1973, revised 1983. Originally written for *New Church Praise*, a hymnal supplement produced by the United Reformed Church of Great Britain. Sources of inspiration included Barry Commoner's book, *The Closing Circle* (an early discussion of ecology) and NASA photographs of the earth from space, enrobed in its biosphere of "water, soil, and air."
Metre: 9.10.10.9.
John 19:23

Cherishing The Earth

112

Come, cradle all the future generations,
and guard their right to live upon this earth,
    lest human deeds, by stealth or conflagration,
    snuff out all life, and put an end to birth.

Come, contemplate the sadness of extinction:
a wasted earth, with empty sky and sea,
    no mourners to lament its desolation,
    no voice, no words, no thought, no eyes to see.

We cannot stifle knowledge or invention.
The ways divide, the choice forever clear:
    to drift, and be delivered to destruction,
    or wake and work, till trust out-matches fear.

The precious seed of life is in our keeping,
yet if we plant it, and fulfil our trust,
    tomorrow's sun will rise on joy and weeping,
    and shine upon the unjust and the just.

Our calling is to live our human story
of good and bad, achievement, love and loss,
    then hand it on to future shame or glory,
    lit by our hope, and leavened by the cross.

    Come, let us guard the gateway to existence,
    that thousands yet may stand where we have stood,
        give thanks for life and, praising our persistence,
        enjoy this lovely earth, and call it good.

© 1983 Hope Publishing Company for the USA, Canada, Australia and New Zealand and Stainer & Bell Limited for all other territories. All rights reserved.

January 1983, revised 1993. Inspired by Jonathan Schell's book, *The Fate of the Earth*, a profound reflection on the fact that, by ecological collapse, nuclear catastrophe, biological warfare, genetic tampering, or otherwise, the human race can henceforth destroy itself, and possibly all life on earth. We need to express these realities in prayer and lament, hence this hymn.
Metre: 11.10.11.10. Iambic   Genesis 1:31; Matthew 5:45.

Living With God

113

Water in the snow:
the mountains sparkle white;
the muffled trees bow low,
burdened with light.

Water in the rain:
the wheat is growing tall;
the fields are packed with grain –
plenty for all.

Water in the ground:
where earth is cracked and dry,
down deep the well has found
ample supply.

Water from the stream:
the tap runs fresh and clear;
the clothes, now washed and clean,
blow in the air.

Water fills the dam:
it tumbles with a roar,
and makes the turbines hum,
throbbing with power.

Water in the sea:
the trawling nets unfurl;
the oyster in the deep
treasures its pearl.

Water gives us life,
and beauty, power and food—
Praise God, whose life and love
make all things good.

114

Praise God for the harvest of orchard and field,
praise God for the people who gather their yield,
the long hours of labour, the skills of a team,
the patience of science, the power of machine.

Praise God for the harvest that comes from afar,
from market and harbour, the sea and the shore:
foods packed and transported, and gathered and grown
by God-given neighbours, unseen and unknown.

Praise God for the harvest that's quarried and mined,
selected and smelted, or shaped and refined:
for oil and for iron, for copper and coal,
praise God, who in love has provided them all.

Praise God for the harvest of science and skill,
the urge to discover, create, and fulfil:
for plans and inventions that promise to gain
a future more hopeful, a world more humane.

Praise God for the harvest of mercy and love
from leaders and peoples who struggle and serve
with patience and kindness, that all may be led
to freedom and justice, and all may be fed.

No. 113 ("Water in the snow") - September 1969, revised 1995. Metre: 5.6.6.4.
No. 114 ("Praise God for the harvest") - April 1968 (revised 1978, 1995). The original appeared in the UK Baptist Supplement, *Praise for Today*, and was revised because of its sexist language ("Pray God that man's harvest by men may be shared"!) and over-optimism about nuclear power. Metre: 11.11.11.11.

© 1972 (No. 113) and 1974, 1996 (No. 114) Hope Publishing Company for the USA, Canada, Australia and New Zealand and Stainer & Bell Limited for all other territories. All rights reserved.

Cherishing The Earth

115

We plough and sow with tractors
    and bale the new-mown hay.
We reap the fields with combines
    to bring our harvest day,
yet all the skill of science,
    the life of root and seed,
the air and earth and water,
    are gifts to meet our need.
    All creation's wonders
        are born from Love alone,
    Lift heart and voice, in God rejoice,
        and bring the harvest home.

The Owner and Creator
    of planets near and far,
gives us the earth to cherish,
    and life to make or mar,
with wondrous power to increase
    and share our daily bread,
that friends might welcome strangers
    and every child be fed.
    All creation's wonders
        are born from Love alone,
    Lift heart and voice, in God rejoice,
        and bring the harvest home.

Creator, Friend and Partner,
    Companion of our days,
how wide, how deep, your wisdom,
    how wonderful your ways!
Help us, in glad thanksgiving
    for all you freely give,
to love you in our neighbour,
    and by the way we live.
    All creation's wonders
        are born from Love alone,
    Lift heart and voice, in God rejoice,
        and bring the harvest home.

© 1983 Hope Publishing Company for the USA, Canada, Australia and New Zealand and Stainer & Bell Limited for all other territories. All rights reserved.

September 1969, revised 1993. Because God's love is global, faith names the joys and inequalities of food production in a global economy.   Metre: 7.6.7.6.D. Refr.

Living With God

116

Speechless in a world that suffers,
   seeking hope, in prayer we come,
sick with warfare, rape, and murder,
   crying out, or stricken, dumb.
Are you loving? Are you listening?
Hear our hearts, crying,
Why, Oh Why, Oh Why, Oh Why?
   Will you help, or pass us by?

Did your love, unseen and holy,
   seeking human love and trust,
give a law and keep a treaty,
   though your people turned unjust?
Did you tend them through affliction,
loving still, judging,
grieving, weeping, feeling loss,
   in a foretaste of the cross?

Could a loving, wise Creator,
   seeing evil unresolved,
stay aloof, a silent ruler,
   calm, unchanging, uninvolved?
Could a heart that heard the Saviour,
near despair, crying,
"Why, oh why, am I alone?"
   sit unmoved, as cold as stone?

Hour by hour, as life advances,
   as eternally you trace
all our choices, all the chances,
   howling evil, healing grace,
far beyond our understanding,
do you know, weighing
every if and why and where,
   joy and grief beyond compare?

Living in a world that suffers,
   pain and evil fret our mind.
Reason ends with broken answers.
   Let us pray, and hope to find,
through each other, joined together,
Christ alive, caring,
bearing evil, giving joy
   that the world cannot destroy.

In the grief, by fear undaunted,
   telling truth through tearful songs,
in the burst of loving anger,
   giving strength to tackle wrongs,
in a neighbour, in a stranger,
show your love, living,
glowing, warming, gleaming bright,
   like a candle in the night.

© 1995 Hope Publishing Company for the USA, Canada, Australia and New Zealand and Stainer & Bell Limited for all other territories. All rights reserved.

September 1995. Commissioned by the 1995 Chi-Rho Lecture Series, Eugene, Oregon, where Dorothee Sölle lectured on, "After the Shoah: Half a Century Later - Theological Reflections on Remembrance, Pain and Hope." Stanzas 2 and 3 may be read over quiet organ improvisation or sung as solos. I am indebted to Elizabeth Johnson, *She Who Is* (SCM Press, London, and Crossroad Books, New York), Chapter 12.
Metre: 8.7.8.7.8.5.7.7.   Mark 15:34 and parallels.

Facing Pain And Evil

117

How deep our Maker's grief
when love is pushed aside,
and life destroyed by false belief,
and children crucified!

Tomorrow may explain
the how and what and why;
today we drink the cup of pain
and vent our grieving cry.

• • • • • • • • • •

Yet as we weep and pray,
and share our pain and loss,
a Stranger meets us on our way,
interpreting the cross.

The hidden Christ declares
God's living way, and ours.
The Spirit, sighing through our prayers,
refreshes and empowers.

Let love's lament dissolve
aloofness and despair,
and resurrect our best resolve
to comfort, pray, and care.

© 1993 Hope Publishing Company for the USA, Canada, Australia and New Zealand and Stainer & Bell Limited for all other territories. All rights reserved.

20 April 1993, after the death of children, women and men in the Branch Davidian compound at Waco, Texas, and dedicated to the people of Dunblane, Scotland, following the children's massacre in March 1996. To prevent the move from stanza 2 to stanza 3 seeming glib or abrupt, divide the reading or singing with an instrumental interlude, or scripture readings and prayers.
Short Metre   Luke 24:13-35

Living With God

118

The horrors of our history
  are vast, beyond belief.
We greet each new atrocity
  with bafflement, or grief,
yet all the evil energies
  that haunt the human race,
come, not from alien galaxies,
  but from our inner space,
  and terror, pain and genocide
  intrude on every prayer,
  with shades that whisper,
    "Where is God?
      If only God were there!"

By torture, war and poverty,
  by flame and firing squad,
for glory, flag and destiny,
  and with a prayer to God,
God's image finds a thousand ways
  to torment, and to kill
and asks how love can justify
  such terrible freewill:
  for every cry of suffering
  will drive us back to prayer,
  as thousands clamour,
    "Where is God?
      If only God were there!"

Yet if, like some robotic race,
  though warm with flesh and blood,
our happy self, with smiling face,
  was programmed to be good,
and had no freedom, seeing wrong,
  to seek it, or say no,
our praise would be a puppet-song,
  and love, and empty show.
  Our pain and terror mark the cost
  of every faithful prayer
  that chooses justice,
    love, and trust,
      and hopes that God is there.

And God is not an analyst,
  observing gain and loss,
but loves us to the uttermost
  and suffers on a cross:
for love comes, not like Heads of State,
  in power and glamour known,
but as a loser, desolate,
  in anguish, and alone:
  the cross, revealed in Easter light,
  will nourish every prayer
  when faith discovers,
    "There is God,
      and all of God is there!"

© 1983 Hope Publishing Company for the USA, Canada, Australia and New Zealand and Stainer & Bell Limited for all other territories. All rights reserved.

September 1982, revised 1994. Originally, "the horrors of our century," amended because it will probably ring true in the next millennium. The hymn deals with terrible realities, yet Christian faith needs to think, pray, and lament about them, publicly, before God and the world.
Metre: CMT (8.6.8.6. Triple)
Matthew 27:32-56.

Facing Pain And Evil

The fruits of knowledge, plucked and prized,
   have scattered wide their seed:
we are as gods, with open eyes,
   for shame or glory freed,
and share, as midwives to our God,
   the work of giving birth
to faith's fulfilment, mercy's child:
   new heavens and new earth.
Come blow, great wind of Pentecost:
*   let all the churches dare*
to bear the horrors,
*   heal the wounds,*
*   and show that God is there!*

119

God, give us freedom to lament
and sing an honest, aching song,
when faith is twined with discontent,
and all is empty, wrecked and wrong.

Give us the candour to complain
when pain attacks without reprieve
and evil rages unrestrained
while you are absent, or on leave.

As faith and understanding show
how love could gamble to create
by letting be and letting go,
we tremble at the risks you take.

The stakes are infinitely high,
when love, its purpose to achieve,
must leave the Word in Flesh to die,
while God is absent, or on leave.

    We'll walk beside you, come what may,
    to you our hopes and hearts belong,
    and when we've nothing else to say,
    we'll sing an honest, aching song.

© 1993 Hope Publishing Company for the USA, Canada, Australia and New Zealand and Stainer & Bell Limited for all other territories. All rights reserved.

July 1989, at the Presbyterian Association of Musicians' Conference in New Wilmington, Pennsylvania, which focused on Psalmody. The hymn was written (with *Let All Creation Dance*, No. 167) as part of my lecture commitment to the Conference. The final line of stanzas 2 and 4 is from a TV documentary about Simon Wiesenthal, the "Nazi Hunter." In his teens, he was imprisoned in a Nazi death camp; the film shows him walking through the camp, crying, "God is on leave."
Long Metre   Psalm 88; Matthew 27:32-56.

Living With God

120

Weep for the dead. Let tears and silence tell
of blood and battle, horror and renown.
The years diminish, but do not dispel
the pain of lives destroyed, and life laid down.

Silent the dead. Remembering, we stand
silent as they, for words cannot esteem
causes of war, the love of native land,
all that they were, and all they might have been.

Raising our flag, we stand with muffled drum,
judged by the colours of God's love and loss,
recalling, as we pray, "Your kingdom come,"
a purple robe, and blood upon a cross.

Summoned by love that leaves no room for pride,
we pray that every continent and isle,
wounded by war, war's hate may lay aside,
and find a way to heal and reconcile.

Weep for the dead, from all the ills of earth.
Stand by the cross that bids all hatred cease.
March to the drums of dignity and worth.
Salute the King of Love, the Prince of Peace.

© 1989 Hope Publishing Company for the USA, Canada, Australia and New Zealand and Stainer & Bell Limited for all other territories. All rights reserved.

August 1987, revised 1988. Written at the request of the Chaplain to the Norwich Branch (UK) of the Royal British Legion, to provide new words for their beloved tune, O VALIANT HEARTS. My aim was to speak truthfully about patriotism, peace, and war. The hymn is dedicated to my parents, Arthur and Mabel Wren, to thank them for the love for people, distrust of national pride, and care for justice and universal human dignity, which they have lived and modelled for me.
Metre: 10.10.10.10. Iambic
Isaiah 9:6-7 and 11:6-11.

Facing Pain And Evil

121

Not only acts of evil will,
but bland routine and good intent,
can hurt and hinder, starve and kill
the outcast and the innocent.
    In such a world, and in God's name,
    we seek a gospel to proclaim.

Our normal, ordinary ways
of doing business, getting more,
entrap the poorest in a maze
of hunger, debt, disease and war.
    In Christ we would make good our claim,
    and find a gospel to proclaim.

The heart that's born again from God
will pray and work to understand
the ills that sabotage the good
in trade and credit, wealth and land,
    and will not turn aside its aim,
    a smaller gospel to proclaim.

The beauty, bondage, joy and fear
of every person ever born
are always in God's eye and ear,
as near as breath, as sharp as thorn,
    and we are born again to share
    that fierce, impassioned, healing care.

And so, in Christ, we drink our fill
of daring, deep, determined love,
and practise to unite the skill
of wily snake and peaceful dove,
    as, loving earth in Jesus' name,
    we live the gospel we proclaim.

© 1989 Hope Publishing Company for the USA, Canada, Australia and New Zealand and Stainer & Bell Limited for all other territories. All rights reserved.

March 1988, prompted by a documentary on "third world" debt. In 1974, oil producing states raised prices, to get a better return on their finite resource; they invested their unspendable earnings in Euro-American banks; the banks, needing to re-invest these huge sums, offered them to third world governments badly hit by the rising price of oil. Despite some unwise decisions, the process seemed reasonable till rising interest rates and worsening terms of trade astronomically increased the debts. Third world governments then squeezed the poorest even harder, at the behest of financial institutions controlled by the world's richest nations. Thus, strictly and literally, the opening stanzas of this poem, which longs for a "full gospel" of structural as well as personal evangelism.
Metre: 8.8.8.8.8.8.   Matthew 10:16; John 3:3-5 and 19:2.

Living With God

122

Say "No" to peace,
   if what they mean by peace
      is the quiet misery of hunger,
         the frozen stillness of fear,
            the silence of broken spirits,
               the unborn hopes of the oppressed.

    Tell them that peace
      is the shouting of children at play,
    the babble of tongues set free,
    the thunder of dancing feet,
and a father's voice singing.

Peace is a tree,
growing from the soil of justice,
watered by the rain of love.

Say "No" to peace,
   if what they mean by peace
      is a rampart of gleaming missiles,
         the arming of distant wars,
            money at ease in its castle,
               and grateful poor at the gate.

    Tell them that peace
    is the hauling down of flags,
    the forging of guns into ploughs,
    the giving of fields to the landless,
and hunger a fading dream.

Peace is a song,
playing to the pipes of freedom,
swinging to sound of love.

© 1986 Hope Publishing Company for the USA, Canada, Australia and New Zealand and Stainer & Bell Limited for all other territories. All rights reserved.

April 1984, expanded 1985. Originally a poster for BOTHER, the OXFAM (UK) youth magazine, which I edited at the time. The poem expresses a Jewish-Christian understanding of peace (Shalom) as interpersonal harmony characterized by the presence of God's equalizing justice.
Metre: Irregular   Micah 4:3

Seeking Peace With Justice

123

Love is the only hope
  for peace on earth.
Love isn't quick to take offence
  at other nations,
but listens and decides
  with careful patience.
Love is realistic, love isn't blind.
Love is determined, caring and kind.
Spirit of Jesus, friend and forgiver,
near us for ever, fill us with love.

Love is the only hope
  for peace at home.
Love doesn't need to sneer and shout
  at friends and strangers,
but gladly lets them be,
  and calls them neighbours.
Love is realistic, love isn't blind.
Love is determined, caring and kind.
Spirit of Jesus, friend and forgiver,
near us for ever, fill us with love.

Love is the only hope
  for peace of mind.
Nothing that's going on today,
  or in the future,
can tear us from the love
  of Christ our Saviour.
Love is realistic, love isn't blind.
Love is determined, caring and kind.
Spirit of Jesus, friend and forgiver,
near us for ever, fill us with love.

124

I love this land:
its people, towns and scenery,
for good and ill, are part of me,
gift of the goodness of God.

I give this land
the life that Christ would live in me
with stranger, friend or enemy,
serving the Spirit of God.

I love this world,
where foreigners can give to me
their marvellous diversity,
made in the image of God.

I give to Christ
my first and highest loyalty,
till all our flags together fly,
cheering the coming of God.

Nos. 123 & 124 © 1986 Hope Publishing Company for the USA, Canada, Australia and New Zealand and Stainer & Bell Limited for all other territories. All rights reserved.

No. 123 - 1985. A reflection on 1 Corinthians 13 and Romans 8:38-39, provoked by comments from Britain's Defence Secretary that anti-nuclear protesters were "naive and reckless," and that the nuclear arms race represented realism. In a world where humanity can self-destruct, a love "not quick to take offence" (1 Corinthians 13:5, REB) has more claim to be "realistic." See also 1 Corinthians 13:7 ("nothing love cannot face" - REB), which implies seeing things as they really are.
    Metre: 10.8.56.5. Refr.   1 Corinthians 13; Romans 8:38-39.
No. 134 - Pentecost 1983. Written for *Patriotism and Peace*, a study pack on nuclear weapons which I prepared for the Oxford Diocese of the Church of England.   Metre: 4.8.8.7.

Living With God

125

Break the bread of belonging,
welcome the stranger in the land,
we have each been a stranger,
we can try to understand.
Break the bread of belonging,
fear of the foreigner still blows strong;
make a space for the strangers:
give them the right to belong.

Travelling, travelling over the world,
   people can be out of place,
dashing for freedom, looking for work,
   needing a friendly face:

Some have fled from terror by night,
   hiding from bullets by day,
weary and hungry, in fear of their life,
   seeking a safe place to stay:

Some are far from the people they love,
   driven by family need,
tired and exploited, doing their job,
   thinking of children to feed:

Travelling, travelling over the world,
   no-one should be out of place.
What would we say, then, if we were alone,
   needing a friendly face?

Break the bread of belonging,
welcome the stranger in the land,
we have each been a stranger,
we can try to understand.
Break the bread of belonging,
fear of the foreigner still blows strong;
make a space for the strangers:
give them the right to belong.

© 1986 Hope Publishing Company for the USA, Canada, Australia and New Zealand and Stainer & Bell Limited for all other territories. All rights reserved.

February 1984, for worship materials I prepared for Christian Aid, world development agency for the British Churches, on their focus theme of "exile and migration."
Metre: 8.7.8.6. Refr.
Deuteronomy 24:14-22

Seeking Peace With Justice

126

A child, a woman and a man
are people dear and close to me:
a name, a smile, a voice I know,
a hand I touch, a face I see,
   yet more than I can see and know,
     my Saviour knows, and fully loves
     that very woman, child and man.

A child, a woman and a man
are people in a foreign land,
whose word I doubt, whose hopes I fear,
whose ways I cannot understand,
   and yet I need to feel and know
     how Christ, my Saviour, knows and loves
     that very woman, child and man.

For if I somehow shift the blame
for all my fear and guilt within,
the foreigners I cannot love
will be the scapegoats for my sin,
   as they look evil, I feel good,
     and in the name of Christ destroy
     the work of Christ, and feel no shame.

Yet Christ was hated and reviled,
and branded as the enemy —
a scapegoat who endured the cross
in love for all, and love for me,
   and when I meet you, Lamb of God,
     I find myself: convicted, loved,
     forgiven, healed, and reconciled.

     Enlarge our vision, as you can,
     until we see, confess, condemn,
     more than the evil others do,
     the evils we might do to them.
        Renew and cleanse our inmost heart,
        till we are looking through your eyes
        at every woman, child and man.

© 1986 Hope Publishing Company for the USA, Canada, Australia and New Zealand and Stainer & Bell Limited for all other territories. All rights reserved.

February 1985, revised 1996, inspired by *21 Theses for Christians in a Nuclear Age*, prepared by a Dominican monk for Oxford Christians for Peace, one of which reads: "The evils that Christians should fear most are not what their enemies might do to them, but what they might do to their enemies."
Metre: 8.8.8.8.8.8.8.
Leviticus 16:20-22 ("scapegoat"); Psalm 51:10; Ezekiel 11:19-20; Matthew 5:7-9; John 1:29; 1 Peter 2:21-24.

Living With God

127

God of Jeremiah, grieving with an aching heart
for an empire, unbelieving as it falls apart,
when your thunder goes unheard, we will tend the prophet's word
    and in season, out of season, we will sing your song.

When our wound is left to fester, though the pain goes deep,
when we've sown a hundred whirlwinds, but have yet to reap,
when the platitudes of peace only make our fears increase,
    with a poem and a story we will sing your song.

When the palace looks at poverty with scornful eyes,
when the scroll of truth is shredded by a leader's lies,
when the glory of the cross is a propaganda gloss,
    in the square and in the senate we will sing your song.

We will break the jar of plenty by the gates of gold,
we will buy a field of promise when the farm is sold,
at the ending of the dream, in the death of false esteem,
    at the bank and in the market we will sing your song.

We will praise the grainy granite of the Law's demands,
and the Life-creating, Lover-God with wounded hands;
we will spin your storyline to an empire in decline,
    and in exile or in honour we will sing your song.

© 1993 Hope Publishing Company for the USA, Canada, Australia and New Zealand and Stainer & Bell Limited for all other territories. All rights reserved.

July 1989, at Princeton Theological Seminary, with gratitude to Walter Brueggemann for his Summer School lectures on Jeremiah.
Metre: 13.13.14.13.
Jeremiah 6:14; 8:18-9:1; 19:1-3 and 10-12; 29:4-14; 32:6-15; 36, esp. v. 23; Hosea 8:7; 2 Timothy 4:2 KJV.

Seeking Peace With Justice
128

Prophets give us hope.
They thirst for truth and right,
and feel the pain of all discarded people,
crushed, ignored, oppressed.
They give and get no rest,
but stand against the powers-that-be
as signposts of integrity,
to point the way, and give us light.

Prophets give us truth.
They come too close to home,
and show our wordy faith where love would take us,
if we dared to go.
We do not want to know,
yet still they call us to decide,
to banish them, or take their side,
and set our sights on Christ alone.

Prophets give us life.
Alone yet not apart,
their quirks and failings make them very human,
sinners, yet forgiven.
They are the Spirit's leaven,
that makes our aspirations rise,
then gives, unknowing as it dies,
a taste of hope, a singing heart.

© 1983 Hope Publishing Company for the USA, Canada, Australia and New Zealand and Stainer & Bell Limited for all other territories. All rights reserved.

February 1983, and dedicated to Beyers and Ilse Naudé, pilgrims, movers and shakers in the South African freedom struggle.
Metre: 5.6.11.5.6.8.8.8.
Amos 7:10-17; Matthew 5:6; 6:39 and 13:33.

Living With God

129

This we can do for justice and for peace:
   be still, with time to pray
     and heed the prayers that other people say.
This we can do, for Christ has borne the cross,
revealing God, whose gracious, winning love
   awakes a deep desire
     to do what we can do, and see it through.

This we can do for justice and for peace:
   reach out, and gladly give,
     that others too may eat, and laugh, and live.
This we can do, for Christ, with wine and bread,
brings food and love to satisfy us all,
   and lifts our thankful hearts
     to do what we can do, and see it through.

This we can do for justice and for peace:
   sing out, and shed our fear,
     when angry foes abuse and domineer.
This we can do, for Christ, unjustly killed,
arises over governments and powers,
   and gives us peaceful strength
     to do what we can do, and see it through.

This we can do for justice and for peace:
   press on, and keep in view,
     a dream of peace on earth, and all things new.
This we can do, for Christ, alive in God,
from God's tomorrow touches us with hope,
   and gives us faith renewed,
     to do what we can do, and see it through.

© 1975, 1995 Hope Publishing Company for the USA, Canada, Australia and New Zealand and Stainer & Bell Limited for all other territories. All rights reserved.

October 1972, rewritten 1994. The original was for a study pack of the same title, for British aid-and-development agencies. The rewrite more firmly grounds our work for peace and justice in the life, death, and risen presence of Christ.
Metre: 10.6.10.10.10.6.10.   Colossians 2:14-15

Seeking Peace With Justice
130

Great soaring Spirit,
sweeping in uncharted flight
beyond the bounds of time and space.
God's breath of love,
you fill the outflung galaxies,
and move through earth's long centuries
with aching, mending, dancing grace.

Great eagle Spirit,
crying from the tallest crags
to all discarded, all distressed,
glad gusting love,
come, scatter trivialities,
and raise envisioned ministries
to hear and honour earth's oppressed.

Great nesting Spirit,
sheltering with mighty wings
your chattering, demanding brood,
deep, restless love,
come, stir us, show us how to fly,
till, heading for tomorrow's sky,
we soar together, God-renewed.

© 1989 Hope Publishing Company for the USA, Canada, Australia and New Zealand and Stainer & Bell Limited for all other territories. All rights reserved.

August 1986. Commissioned by McKendrie United Methodist Church, Nashville, Tennessee, for its 200th Anniversary (1787-1987).
Metre: 12.8.12.8.8.8.
Genesis 1:2; Deuteronomy 32:11-13; Isaiah 40:31; Luke 13:34.

Living With God

131

Spirit of Jesus, if I love my neighbour
   out of my knowledge, leisure, power or wealth,
     help me to understand the shame and anger
         of helplessness that hates my power to help.

And if, when I have answered need with kindness,
   my neighbour rises, wakened from despair,
     keep me from flinching when the cry for justice
         requires of me the changes that I fear.

If I am hugging safety or possessions,
   uncurl my spirit, as your love prevails,
     to join my neighbours, work for liberation,
         and find my freedom at the mark of nails.

132

Lead us in paths of truth.
Let love our light provide.
In work or leisure, age or youth,
let justice be our guide.

© 1983 (No. 131) and 1993 (No. 132) Hope Publishing Company for the USA, Canada, Australia and New Zealand and Stainer & Bell Limited for all other territories. All rights reserved.

No. 131 - 1973, revised 1995, 1996. Inspired by my study tour of South Africa, January-March 1973, and by the "pilgrimage of confession" of nine white South African Christians, who walked from Grahamstown to Cape Town in December 1972, reversing the direction of the Afrikaaner "Great Trek," to draw attention to the suffering caused by apartheid's migrant labour laws. One of the pilgrims received a greeting card with the words, "the justice some (men) seek is the change others fear," which partially prompted the hymn.
    Metre: 11.10.11.10. Iambic   Mark 10:17-22; Acts 2:43-45.
No. 132 - 1991. A short response for personal devotion or repeated use in a litany or series of scripture readings.
    Short Metre

Seeking Peace With Justice

133

We want to love
antagonists and enemies,
giving blessings,
meaning what we say:
    Deep, cool, well of peace,
    wine of mercy at the feast,
Holy Spirit, come!

We want to serve
with confident humility,
facing trouble,
never losing heart:
    Green, strong, living oak,
    seed and root and flower of hope,
Holy Spirit, come!

We want to work,
renewed with peaceful energy,
seeking justice,
heeding the oppressed:
    Fire bright, blazing light,
    flame of justice, truth and right,
Holy Spirit, come!

We want to care,
forgiving with sincerity,
shedding evil,
clinging to the good:
    Great, wild, eagle-dove,
    storm and breath and song of love,
Holy Spirit, come!

© 1986 Hope Publishing Company for the USA, Canada, Australia and New Zealand and Stainer & Bell Limited for all other territories. All rights reserved.

October 1984, revised 1994, and based on Romans 12:9-17, following the New English Bible translation.
Metre: 4.8.4.5.5.7.5.

"Embracing All Our Destiny"
134

Great Lover, calling us to share
your joy in all created things
from atom-dance to eagles' wings,
we come and go, to praise and care.

Though sure of resurrection-grace,
we ache for all earth's troubled lands
and hold the planet in our hands,
a fragile, unprotected place.

Your questing Spirit longs to gain
no simple fishing-ground for souls,
but as life's story onward rolls,
a world more joyful and humane.

As midwives who assist at birth,
we give our uttermost, yet grieve
lest folly, greed or hate should leave
a spoiled, aborted, barren earth.

Self-giving Lover, since you dare
to join us in our history,
embracing all our destiny,
we'll come and go with praise and care.

© 1989 Hope Publishing Company for the USA, Canada, Australia and New Zealand and Stainer & Bell Limited for all other territories. All rights reserved.

July 1986, at a Frontier Seminar which I taught at San Francisco Theological Seminary, aided by Gordon Kaufman's book, *Theology for a Nuclear Age* (Philadelphia: The Westminster Press / Manchester: Manchester University Press, 1985), whose twin concepts of God as engaged in human history to *humanise* and *question* us, suggested the metaphor of God as the *Questioning Lover* of all humankind.
Long Metre

Seasons of Life

Birth, Childhood, Love, Trials, Mortality, Hope

Through all the changing scenes of life,
in trouble and in joy,
the praises of my God shall still
my heart and tongue employ.

Nahum Tate (1652-1715)
and Nicholas Brady (1659-1726)

Our Human Story

135

Thank you, God,
for times of growing:
   ending of childhood,
   birth of a child.
From generation to generation
you spin the thread, and life goes on —
   And the seasons shift, and life moves on,
     and the wheel goes turning, turning,
       for God is young, and God is old,
         and the song of love goes singing on.

Thank you, God,
for times of wonder:
   grandchildren's laughter,
   grandparents' love.
From generation to generation
you spin the thread, and life goes on —
   And the seasons shift, and life moves on,
     and the wheel goes turning, turning,
       for God is young, and God is old,
         and the song of love goes singing on.

Thank you God,
for times of ending:
   sleeping and parting,
   saying goodbye.
From generation to generation
you spin the thread, and life goes on —
   And the seasons shift, and life moves on,
     and the wheel goes turning, turning,
       for God is young, and God is old,
         and the song of love goes singing on.

© 1996 Hope Publishing Company for the USA, Canada, Australia and New Zealand and Stainer & Bell Limited for all other territories. All rights reserved.

July 1989 for Arlo Duba, who inspired it.
Metre: 8.5.4.10.8. Refr.

From Generation to Generation

136

How can we name a love
that wakens heart and mind,
indwelling all we know
   or think or do
   or seek or find?
Within our daily world,
in every human face,
   Love's echoes sound
   and God is found,
hid in the commonplace.

If we awoke to life
upheld by loving care
that asked no great reward
   but firm, assured,
   was simply there,
we can, with parents' names,
describe, and thus adore,
   love unconfined,
   our Father kind,
our Mother strong and sure.

When people share a task,
and strength and skills unite
in projects old or new,
   to make or do
   with shared delight,
our Friend and Partner's will
is better understood,
   that all should share,
   create, and care,
and know that life is good.

So in a hundred names,
each day we all can meet
a presence, sensed and shown
   at work, at home,
   or in the street.
Yet names and titles all
shine in a brighter sun:
   In Christ alone
   is love full grown
and life and hope begun.

© 1975, 1995 Hope Publishing Company for the USA, Canada, Australia and New Zealand and Stainer & Bell Limited for all other territories. All rights reserved.

September 1973, revised 1987, 1994. An early attempt to break away from the hegemony of male-authority images of God, partly prompted by Peter Berger's book, *A Rumour of Angels*. Short Metre Double

---

Finality (Eschatology). Ancient cosmologies held that God made heaven and earth in the beginning, and would later or sooner end them, after which the dead would be raised and brought to judgement with eternal happiness in God for believers. Though science currently sees our universe beginning with a bang, it's end is billions of years after the likely end of life on earth, a radically different scenario from biblical pictures of God's direct intervention. While I find scientific cosmology inspiring and fascinating, it is unwise to peg theology to the latest theories. Yet we need to speak of finality, even if we must speak paradoxically, e.g. of "a time, *time-less yet final*, in a world new-born, where all is weighed, accounted for, made good" (160). Our final hope must see God acting consistently (utterly gracious to every human being, not suddenly vindictive), and be able to motivate us here and now, inspiring us to "passionately care" for peace, justice, healing and spreading the good news of Christ "here on earth" (163), till, "pain and anger past, evil exhausted, love supreme at last, alive in God, we sing an unsurpassed alleluia" (161).

Our Human Story

137

Wonder of wonders,
life is beginning,
fragile as blossom,
    strong as the earth.
Shaped in a person,
love has new meaning.
Parents and people
    sing at the birth.

Now with rejoicing
make celebration:
joy full of promise,
    laughter through tears.
Naming and blessing,
bring dedication,
humble in purpose
    over the years.

Wisdom of ages,
new every morning,
Mother and Father,
    Partner and Friend,
freeing, forgiving,
lift all our loving
into your presence,
    joy without end.

138

Born into love,
    royal, you crown us,
    infant you claim us,
    and as we hold you,
    name and enfold you,
    no words can tell
    all we would give you.

Grow and be whole,
offer your vision;
daily be certain
God sees within you
insight and value;
follow your star
till Christ receives you.

© 1983 (No. 137) and 1993 (No. 138) Hope Publishing Company for the USA, Canada, Australia and New Zealand and Stainer & Bell Limited for all other territories. All rights reserved.

No. 137 - December 1974, revised 1994. Written for friends, Jackie and Dave Lyus, for the dedication of their first-born, Matthew, at their (Baptist) Church, and intended to be suitable for infant baptism, infant dedication, and services of "naming and blessing."
    Metre: 5.5.5.4.D.
No. 138 - September 1988, as a gift to Brianna Semran, born August 1988, and named after me by her parents, Ron and Gerry Semran. The poem is an acrostic on her name, reading BRIANNA GODGIFT.   Metre: 4.5.5.5.5.4.5.

Birth And Childhood

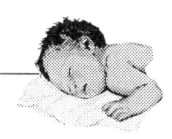

139

The light of God is shining bright
in every girl of woman born,
and in her fingers and her face
are heaven's glory, power and grace,
  so when she's walking,
    running, leaping,
      sitting and thinking,
    talking, sleeping,
      don't ever treat a girl with scorn,
  but look and see the face of God
in every girl of woman born.

The light of God is shining bright
in every boy of woman born,
and his fingers and his face
are heaven's glory, power and grace,
  so when he's walking,
    running, leaping,
      sitting and thinking,
    talking, sleeping,
      don't ever treat a boy with scorn,
  but look and see the face of God
in every boy of woman born.

140

I'll try, my love, to love you
  when you're good or bad
    or happy or sad
      or right or wrong
        and this shall be my song;
          and I need you to love me
            when I'm good or bad
            or happy or sad
            or right or wrong
            for I know all along...
                that Jesus came to love us
                  when we're good or bad
                  or happy or sad
                  or right or wrong
                    and love can make us strong.

© 1989 (No. 139) and 1983 (No. 140) Hope Publishing Company for the USA, Canada, Australia and New Zealand and Stainer & Bell Limited for all other territories. All rights reserved.

No. 139 - March, 1988. Visiting a United Methodist church in North Dakota, whose worship included the baptism of two children, brother and sister, I chose "Wonder of wonders" (No.137), not knowing that they were well past infancy. Hence, "The light of God." The hymn was first sung in Nunawading Uniting Church, near Melbourne, Australia in September, 1988.
Metre: 8.8.8.8.9.9.8.8.8.

No. 140 - January 1973, for my two children (then aged 6 and 4) as I prepared for an eight-week study-tour of Southern Africa. The words formed part of a bedside book written for them to remember me by.   Metre: 7.5 5.4.6.

Our Human Story
141

Listen...Listen...Listen...
This is a poem,
from all of us,
to all of you.

When children pray,
    please do not say, "How nice!"
Remember — Jesus cares,
    and listens to our prayers.

When children speak,
    please do not say, "How sweet,"
and pat us on the head.
    Remember what we've said.

And when we sing,
    please do not say, "How cute —
It is so nice to hear
    the children do their thing."

Look in our eyes.
    We may be angels in disguise.

Our singing voice
    may be God's choice.

We don't want you to miss
    the Holy Spirit's kiss.

The things that children say and do
may be God's way
of calling you.

© 1994 Hope Publishing Company for the USA, Canada, Australia and New Zealand and Stainer & Bell Limited for all other territories. All rights reserved.

July 1993. A poem written for the Children's Choir at the Presbyterian Association of Musicians' Westminster Conference, New Wilmington, Pennsylvania. Ann Wilson's delightful anthem setting is published in the USA by Selah Publishing Company.

Birth And Childhood
142

The gifts of God, by sin abused,
    can damage and destroy,
yet give us all, when kindly used,
    the power of giving joy.

By loving hands, and offered food,
    our selfhood comes alive,
and needs a thousand gifts of good
    to grow, and to survive.

Deceiving love can move by stealth
    to snare, or to control,
but love that gives its very self
    can heal, and make us whole.

In Jesus, thought and word and deed
    are open, true and good,
and love is given, found and freed,
    when flesh is nailed on wood.

    The Lamb of God brings worth and wealth
        to body, mind and soul,
    for love that gives God's very self,
        can heal, and make us whole.

© 1993 Hope Publishing Company for the USA, Canada, Australia and New Zealand and Stainer & Bell Limited for all other territories. All rights reserved.

April 1990. Love is what makes us fully human; without it, we are damaged and incomplete.
Common Metre   Revelation 7:16-17

> **Can God Grow?** In the universe as we know it, "order turns with chance, unfolding space and time" (167). Christian faith developed in a world where change most visibly meant decay and death, and since God could neither decay nor die, divinity had to mean absolute unchangeability. The belief in God as untouchable and unchangeable persists in everyday theology. By contrast, the Bible shows God changing direction in response to human intervention (e.g. Genesis 18:22-33, Exodus 3:20-33) and human response (e.g. Jonah 3:10), a belief not incompatible with modern discoveries of randomness and chance in the universe. If God, as it were, spins the wheel of creation, "giving it randomness," can we say that God is "willing to be surprised" (2) and in some sense able to grow? For us, growth can mean both enrichment and improvement. While God cannot "improve" by becoming more wise, more loving, or more faithful, it seems reasonable to suppose that God's love and faithfulness (because they are genuine) bring delight, joy and enrichment to the Living One, as the universe grows, and sentient creatures discover, invent, create, act kindly, love justice, and hopefully find God. Though the Holy One effortlessly knows every possible thing that might happen (spanning an inconceivably vast vortex shimmering with all conceivable possibilities), divine love surely encompasses the divine equivalent of what we know as "good surprises" (173). Therefore, it seems reasonable to depict divine energy as "young, growing God, eager, on the move" (173). In doing so, I take my cue also from the story of the burning bush (Exodus 3) where God's "name" (v.14) includes both faithfulness and incompleteness, "moving, endlessly becoming" (7).

Our Human Story

143

-1-
True friends
  like us to tell
    our joys and our fears
and need us to hear
  their plans and ideas.
    Jesus says,
      travel with me
        and we'll be friends
          for ever.

-2-
True friends
  show that they care
    when life gets us down.
they never play boss
  or push us around.
    Jesus says,
      travel with me
        and we'll be friends
          for ever.

-3-
True friends
  say what they think
    (and sometimes it hurts),
but stay on our side
  when we're at our worst.
    Jesus says,
      travel with me
        and we'll be friends
          for ever.

-4-
True friends
  don't make us pay
    for all that they give;
they even will die
  so others can live.
    Jesus says,
      travel with me
        and we'll be friends
          for ever.

© 1986 Hope Publishing Company for the USA, Canada, Australia and New Zealand and Stainer & Bell Limited for all other territories. All rights reserved.

October 1984, based on John 15:12-15, exploring the implications of Jesus calling us "not servants but friends."
Metre: 2.4.5.5.5. Refr.

Friendship and Love
144

Life is great! So sing about it,
as we can and as we should—
shops and buses, towns and people,
village, farmland, field and wood.
Life is great and life is given.
Life is lovely, free and good.

Life is great! - whatever happens,
snow or sunshine, joy or pain,
hardship, grief or disillusion,
suffering that I can't explain.
Life is great if someone loves me,
holds my hand and calls my name.

Love is great! — the love of lovers,
whispered words and longing eyes;
love that gazes at the cradle
where a child of loving lies;
love that lasts when youth has faded,
bends with age, but never dies.

Love is giving and receiving —
boy and girl, or friend with friend.
Love is bearing and forgiving
all the hurts that hate can send.
Love's the greatest way of living:
hoping, trusting to the end.

Great is God, who lived among us:
truth in Jesus seen and done,
healing, teaching, hate resisting,
loving where we scoff and shun,
dying, rising, joy surprising
reaching out to everyone.

© 1974 Hope Publishing Company for the USA, Canada, Australia and New Zealand and Stainer & Bell Limited for all other territories. All rights reserved.

March 1970, revised 1995. Written for a youth service to which no young people came, then submitted to a TV hymn contest where it wasn't sung. Though all kinds of loving have their source in God, God is not intrusive, and is accepted only by faith. So God's love in Christ is anonymous (though not absent) in stanzas 1-4. Stanza 1, line 2 echoes the classic eucharistic prayer, and stanza 4 paraphrases 1 Corinthians Chapter 13.
Metre: 8.7.8.7.8.7.

Our Human Story

145

God, the All-Holy,
Maker and Mother,
gladly we gather,
    bringing in prayer
old hurts for healing,
new hopes for holding,
giving, receiving,
    loving and care.

Spirit, All-Seeing,
knitting and blending
joy in desiring,
    friendship and ease,
make our belonging
loyal and lasting,
so that our pledging
    freshens and frees.

Christ, All-Completing,
Nature enfolding,
evil exhausting
    in love's embrace,
weaving and mending,
make every ending
God's new beginning
    glowing with grace.

© 1989 Hope Publishing Company for the USA, Canada, Australia and New Zealand and Stainer & Bell Limited for all other territories. All rights reserved.

September 1988, as a gesture of affection for Pitt Street Uniting Church, Sydney, Australia.
Metre: 5.5.5.4.D.
Colossians 1:17

Friendship and Love

146

When love is found
    and hope comes home,
sing and be glad
    that two are one.
When love explodes
    and fills the sky,
praise God, and share
    our Maker's joy.

When God has flowered
    in trust and care,
build both each day,
    that love may dare
to reach beyond
    home's warmth and light,
to serve and strive
    for truth and right.

When love is tried
    as loved-ones change,
hold still to hope,
    though all seems strange,
till ease returns
    and love grows wise
through listening ears
    and opened eyes.

When love is torn,
    and trust betrayed,
pray strength to love
    till torments fade,
till lovers keep
    no score of wrong,
but hear through pain
    love's Easter song.

Praise God for love,
    praise God for life,
in age or youth,
    in calm or strife.
Lift up your hearts!
    Let love be fed
through death and life
    in broken bread.

© 1983 Hope Publishing Company for the USA, Canada, Australia and New Zealand and Stainer & Bell Limited for all other territories. All rights reserved.

April 1978, revised 1992 (I am indebted to Rebecca Pugh Brown for 5/4: "calm or strife"). My brother Keith was uniting in marriage with Sandra Matthews in Bombay, India, and an English friend, Gill Todd, was marrying a Sri-Lankan, Percy Fernando, in Scotland. I couldn't go to either wedding, so wrote this for both, to an old folk tune, "O Waly Waly" ("The river is wide"), easily accompanied on guitar. The metre is 4.4.4.4.D, not Long Metre (8.8.8.8.). Writing in short lines gives simplicity and directness - you can't use many long words in a 4-syllable line.
Metre: 4.4.4.4.D.
1 Corinthians 13:6, REB (§4).

Our Human Story

147

LOVE   makes a bridge
     from heart to heart, and hand to hand.
LOVE   finds a way,
     when laws are blind, and freedom banned.

LOVE   breaks the walls
     of language, gender, class and age.
LOVE   gives us wings
     to slip the bars of every cage.

LOVE   lifts the hopes
     that force and fear have beaten down.
LOVE   breaks the chains
     and gives us strength to stand our ground.

LOVE   rings the bells
     of wanted birth and wedding day.
LOVE   guides the hands
     that promise more than words can say.

LOVE   makes a bridge
     that winds may shake, yet not destroy.
LOVE   carries faith
     through life and death, to endless joy.

148

Go now in peace; though friends must part,
  your presence lives in every heart.
  Your gifts to us no words can tell:
go now in peace, in Christ go well.

Go now in hope, and hopeful stay,
  though shadowed valleys hide your way;
  through good and evil, joy and pain,
with God, in Spirit, you remain.

Go now in faith, through time and chance,
  until we join the wedding dance
  as partners of the Three-in-One,
where all is ended and begun.

© 1983 (No. 147) and 1993 (No. 148) Hope Publishing Company for the USA, Canada, Australia and New Zealand and Stainer & Bell Limited for all other territories. All rights reserved. For notes, see opposite

Struggle and Growth

149

All-perceiving Lover,
    sensing each disguise,
kindly you uncover
    bruised and aching eyes.
Wake us into wonder
    at your dawning day.
Halt us with your thunder
    on our stubborn way.

Armoured with our work-load,
    in unfeeling walls,
reaching for your love-road
    as the Spirit calls,
guide us as we fumble
    for the open air.
Show us, though we stumble,
    how to feel and care.

Let no gift lie fallow
    in self-bruising blight,
hiding in the shadow
    of another's light.
Let your new commission
    touch our every choice,
free from false submission
    as we find our voice.

Ever-singing Lover,
    good and guiding Star,
helping us discover
    who we really are,
Life-creating Wisdom,
    always you amaze!
Fit us for your freedom.
    Fill us with your praise!

© 1989 Hope Publishing Company for the USA, Canada, Australia and New Zealand and Stainer & Bell Limited for all other territories. All rights reserved.

No. 147 - October 1980. A joyful song, but written in 30 minutes of anger, on hearing that British immigration officials had tried to deport the German fiancé of an English friend as they returned to Britain from a student Christian conference in Geneva. He was allowed to stay, and their wedding took place a few months later.   Metre: 4.0.4.0.

No. 148 - June 1990/July 1991. Developed from several occasions when a leaving blessing was needed, and written for the tune, TALLIS CANON, easily sung unaccompanied, and/or as a round.   Long Metre   Psalm 23:4

No. 149 - January 1987, prompted by Acts 23:12-23, written en route to Yale University, where I preached on that text at Berkeley Divinity School on the Feast of the "Conversion" of St Paul (See Box Note below). Stanzas 2 and 3 explore how we hide from God, whether it be within the castle of the self, or behind another person whom we make all-important in our life
    Metre: 6.5.6.5.D.   Acts 26:12-23

Was Paul Converted? "All-Perceiving Lover" was written for the Feast of the "Conversion" of St. Paul. I would not now speak in that way. As Krister Stendahl points out, "conversion" is a loaded word, suggesting a change from being Jewish, Buddhist, etc. to being Christian (*Paul Among Jews and Gentiles*, Fortress Press 1976, pp. 1-23). Here is an example of how language habits can shape and distort our thinking. To speak of Paul's experience as "conversion" is (a) anachronistic - there wasn't a full-fledged Christianity to be converted to; (b) anti-Jewish, reading back later divisions and later anti-Judaism into the text; and (c) inaccurate, since Paul speaks of his experience as God's call to him, a Jew, to proclaim Jesus, a Jew, as Christ (Messiah) to the Gentiles.

Our Human Story

150

How shall I sing to God
when life is filled with gladness,
    loving and birth,
    wonder and worth?
I'll sing from the heart,
    thankfully receiving,
    joyful in believing.
This is my song, I'll sing it with love.

How shall I sing to God
when life is filled with bleakness,
    empty and chill,
    breaking my will?
I'll sing through my pain,
    angrily or aching,
    crying or complaining.
This is my song, I'll sing it with love.

How shall I sing to God
and tell my Saviour's story:
    passover bread,
    life from the dead?
I'll sing with my life,
    witnessing and giving,
    risking and forgiving.
This is my song, I'll sing it with love.

© 1986 Hope Publishing Company for the USA, Canada, Australia and New Zealand and Stainer & Bell Limited for all other territories. All rights reserved.

February 1985, echoing the psalmist's determination to praise God at all times (Psalm 34:1) and Tate and Brady's paraphrase, "Through all the changing scenes of life" (see p.127).
Metre: 6.7.4.4.5.6.6.9.

Struggle and Growth

151

When on life a darkness falls,
   when the mist flows chilling,
paths and signposts lost in doubt,
   loveless, unfulfilling,
reach us, Jesus, from your cross,
   though we feel forsaken;
keep us through the aching night
   till new dawns awaken.

When the dreams and vows of youth
   painfully accuse us,
stab our conscience, steal our worth,
   Christ will not refuse us:
peace the world cannot provide,
   daily resurrection,
strong companion at our side
   for each new direction.

Come and meet him, Friend and Lord,
   through the gospel story:
open door to life and peace,
   window into glory.
All who seek him, soon are found,
   made his close relation:
Christ our pathway, Christ our home,
   Christ our sure foundation!

© 1986 Hope Publishing Company for the USA, Canada, Australia and New Zealand and Stainer & Bell Limited for all other territories. All rights reserved.

July 1983. At the (USA-Canada) Hymn Society conference, on my first visit to the United States, Don Hustad led a festival of gospel music. Moved by an early American tune, DROOPING SOULS, I wrote these words for it, trying to frame contemporary needs in the idioms of the gospel-song tradition. The hymn was sung at the conference by a friend, Cort Bender.
Metre: 7.6.7.6.D. Trochaic
Job 19:8; John 10:7-9; 14:6 and 14:27; 1 Corinthians 3:11.

Our Human Story

152

When illness meets denial and rejection,
    when friends recoil, and faces turn to stone,
Christ of our Sorrows, raise us from dejection,
    to travel on, assailed but not alone.

Forgive your Church's searing, numbing silence,
    unholy huddles, muddles and delays.
Forgive our zeal to hide the fear that drives us
    with harsh, unloving words, unhealing ways.

Help us resist, refuse all vengeful naming
    of lepers, plagues, and punishment for sin,
with love's determined power to banish blaming,
    shed light and truth, and heal the hurt within.

Show us our hidden strength and human limits.
    Free us from guilt, self-hatred and despair,
to celebrate, as flesh-embodied spirits,
    our body's beauty, and our Maker's care.

Give us, amid our passion and persistence,
    the peace that wishful thinking cannot fake.
Link us in loving circles of resistance,
    with love of life that death can never break.

Through summer joys, and winters of dejection,
    help us, by faith, to travel, weep and sing,
with hearts that reap the fruit of resurrection,
    and hands that bear the loving touch of spring.

© 1993 Hope Publishing Company for the USA, Canada, Australia and New Zealand and Stainer & Bell Limited for all other territories. All rights reserved.

April 1993. Commissioned on behalf of the AIDS Ministry of Grace and Holy Trinity Cathedral, Kansas City, Missouri, and completed with thanks to John and Charmaine Fowler and Etta Mae and Fritz Mutti. In memoriam: Andrew Oren and Dan Vowell. It was hard to write this, and hear the stories that prompted it. Shirley Murray has written a better hymn on this theme, "When our lives know sudden shadow" (*Supplement 1996*, Hope Publishing Company).
Metre: 11.10.11.10. Iambic   Isaiah 53:4

Pain and Heartbreak

153

Grief of ending,
  wordless sorrow,
    pain of parting,
      dry or weeping,
        on our lips and in our bodies,
Loving God, to you we offer.

Times remembered,
  joy discovered,
    love and friendship,
      voice and gesture,
        precious, lovely, one and only,
Giving God, we tell and treasure.

Word of promise,
  lift our singing,
    blending grieving
      with believing.
        in your hands is all completed,
Lasting God, our hope and measure.

Christ among us,
  Spirit-breathing,
    safe companion,
      in your keeping
        death is birth to resurrection,
Living God, our joy forever.

154

When grief is raw,
  and music goes unheard,
    and thought is numb,
we have no polished phrases to recite.
In Christ we come
to hear the old familiar words:
    "I am the resurrection. I am life."

God, give us time
  for gratitude and tears,
    and make us free
to grieve, remember, honour and delight.
Let love be strong
to bear regrets and banish fears:
    "I am the resurrection. I am life."

The height and breadth
  of all that love prepares
    soar out of time,
beyond our speculation and our sight.
The cross remains
to ground the promise that it bears:
    "I am the resurrection. I am life."

All shall be judged,
  the greatest and the least,
    and all be loved,
till every hurt is healed, all wrong set right.
In bread and wine
we taste the great homecoming feast,
    and in the midst of death we are in life.

© 1993 (No. 153) and 1983 (No. 154) Hope Publishing Company for the USA, Canada, Australia and New Zealand and Stainer & Bell Limited for all other territories. All rights reserved.

No. 153 - October 1989. For the memorial service for John Rodland, colleague, friend, and distinguished member of the Presbyterian Hymnal Committee, and with love to Joanne Rodland.
    Metre: 4.4.4.4.8.8.   John 20:19-22
No. 154 - April 1976, revised 1994. First written as a gesture of friendship for two friends whose wedding took place a week after the sudden death of the bridegroom's father.
    Metre: 10.4.10.4.8.10.
John 11:25; 14:1 and 14:17; 1 Corinthians 2:9; Ephesians 3:18-19; Revelation 21:3.

Our Human Story

155

When joy is drowned
in heartbreak and dejection
that give no guarantee
of resurrection
we struggle to retain
the echo of Christ's name
though hope runs dry, and faith gives no protection.

If we must scour
the depths of desolation
and make of grey despair
a blood relation,
God, in our bleakest hell,
let but your silence tell
how love, in love, was once by love forsaken.

We cannot speed
the moment of our waking
by rage, or acts of will
to stem the aching,
but only recognise
a stillness of surprise
when clouds have passed, and dawn at last is breaking.

In any grief
of parting or rejection
there is no guarantee
of resurrection,
yet in our darkest hour
love's unexpected power
can raise us up to life and joyful action.

© 1983 Hope Publishing Company for the USA, Canada, Australia and New Zealand and Stainer & Bell Limited for all other territories. All rights reserved.

October 1976. Grieving is not a process with ordered, manageable stages, as I learned from listening to one person's experience of the second year of bereavement.
Metre: 4.7.6.5.6.6.11.   Matthew 27:46 (Stanza 2)

Mortality and Hope

156

God, let me welcome timely death,
and, filled with hope, be bold to say
that life should flourish, age, and end,
and generations pass away.

As weavers of a living web
the generations follow on
and history is on the loom
till all is ended and begun.

    Our pioneers of knowledge seek
      new frontiers for death and birth,
        and lure us with the ancient dream
          of immortality on earth.

        Yet who would live, at whose expense,
        if in a brave new world sublime,
        elites enjoyed extended powers
        while millions starved before their time?

        And who could tell tomorrow's child
        to go and reap where we have sown,
      if elders ruled for endless years
      and youth could never claim its own?

God, let me love you all my life,
and of my ending simply say,
"To you I come, my joy, my home,
while generations pass away."

© 1986 Hope Publishing Company for the USA, Canada, Australia and New Zealand and Stainer & Bell Limited for all other territories. All rights reserved.

January 1984, revised 1996. Written at Jane Marshall's request, for a commission that did not materialise. For memorial services, use stanzas 1, 2 and 5. On other occasions, the middle stanzas can be read aloud, the congregation singing the remainder.
Long Metre   Psalm 90

Our Human Story

157

We are the music angels sing:
short or long,
each life a song,
a treasured offering.

A child, brief skylark, soaring young,
fell from sight,
yet all that flight
by Gabriel is sung.

The melody, though short it seems,
deeper grows:
heav'ns music flows,
developing its themes.

Discordant grief and aching night,
love-transposed,
will be composed
in symphonies of light,

And every human pain and wrong
shall be healed,
for Christ revealed
a new and better song.

We are the music angels sing:
short or long,
each life a song,
a treasured offering.

© 1989 Hope Publishing Company for the USA, Canada, Australia and New Zealand and Stainer & Bell Limited for all other territories. All rights reserved.

May 1988. Commissioned by Roger and Evelyn Rietberg, to commemorate their son, Thomas Mark Rietberg, who died at the age of eight.
Metre: 8.3.4.6.

Mortality and Hope

158

Let hope and sorrow now unite
    to consecrate life's ending,
and praise good friends now gone from sight,
    through grief and loss are rending.
The story in a well-loved face,
the years and days our thoughts retrace,
    are treasures worth defending.

With faith, or doubt, or open mind,
    we whisper life's great question.
The ebb and flow of space and time
    surpass our small perception.
Yet knowledge grows with joyful gains
and finds out wonders far more strange
    than hopes of resurrection.

Be glad for life, in age or youth:
    its worth is past conceiving.
And stand by justice, love and truth,
    as patterns for believing.
Give thanks for all each person gives;
*as faith comes true, and Jesus lives,
    there'll be an end to grieving.

*To respect the integrity of diverse faiths and persuasions, a recommended variant is, "if faith comes true" (See note below).

© 1983 Hope Publishing Company for the USA, Canada, Australia and New Zealand and Stainer & Bell Limited for all other territories. All rights reserved.

June 1979, revised 1988. Written for the funeral service of my dear uncle, William Wren, which I conducted. Uncle Will stood by "justice, love and truth," without being a Christian, and the funeral service gathered people of diverse convictions. To do justice to the integrity of the mourners, the penultimate line originally read, "if faith comes true." Amended for publication in *Hymnal - A Worship Book* (USA-1992), it is a recommended variant when believers and non-believers gather together.   Metre: 8.7.8.7.8.8.7.

"All Things New"

159

This is a day of new beginnings,
time to remember, and move on,
time to believe what love is bringing,
laying to rest the pain that's gone.

For by the life and death of Jesus,
love's mighty Spirit, now as then,
can make for us a world of difference
as faith and hope are born again.

Then let us, with the Spirit's daring,
step from the past, and leave behind
our disappointment, guilt and grieving,
seeking new paths, and sure to find.

Christ is alive, and goes before us
to show and share what love can do.
This is a day of new beginnings;
our God is making all things new.

Alternative stanza 4, at communion:

*In faith we'll gather round the table
to show and share what love can do.
This is a day of new beginnings;
our God is making all things new.*

© 1983, 1987 Hope Publishing Company for the USA, Canada, Australia and New Zealand and Stainer & Bell Limited for all other territories. All rights reserved.

January 1978, revised 1987. Written for New Year's Day Sunday, Church of the Holy Family, Blackbird Leys, Oxford, England. Because the New Year is an arbitrary mark on the calendar, its ability to bring renewal is questionable, so the original began, "*Is* this a day of new beginnings?", followed by a second stanza asking, "How can the seasons of a planet, / mindlessly spinning round its sun, / with just a human name and number,/ say that some new thing has begun?" The revision, made at the request of the United Methodist Hymnal Revision Committee (USA), simplified the hymn, to make it more widely usable. *The communion stanza is an alternative, not an addition.*
Metre: 9.8.9.8.
2 Corinthians 5:17; Philippians 3:12-14; Revelation 21:5.

In The End, God

Eternal Life and New Creation

In our end is our beginning,
in our time, infinity,
in our doubt there is believing,
in our life, eternity,
in our death, a resurrection;
at the last, a victory
unrevealed until its season,
something God alone can see.

Natalie Sleeth (1930-1992)

© 1986 Hope Publishing Company,
Carol Stream, IL 60188, USA.
All rights reserved.

Beyond Time And Thought
160

Will God be Judge, and will there be a time,
    time-less, yet final, in a world new-born,
when all is weighed, accounted for, made good?
        Faith says, Amen,
           we know not how or when,
but pray and hope for justice seen and done.

Will God be judged, and satisfy the slain,
    destroyed by torture, genocide and greed?
Will God's perplexing ways be understood?
        Faith says, Amen,
           we know not how or when,
but say that love is real, and God is love.

Will Jew and Christian walk at last in love?
    Will clashing faiths be honoured and fulfilled
by pilgrims dance in galaxies of truth?
        Faith says, Amen,
           we know not how or when,
but being found, are seeking yet to find.

Christ is our sign, our window into God:
    this freeing life, unfinished by a cross,
awakens hope, and points a way ahead.
        Let faith's Amen
           be changing us for good,
to live as friends of God, and practise love.

© 1993 Hope Publishing Company for the USA, Canada, Australia and New Zealand and Stainer & Bell Limited for all other territories. All rights reserved.

November 1988 - January 1989. Since we must live with weighty questions, it is better to sing about them than ignore them.
Metre: 10.10.10.4 6.10.
Psalm 82

Exploring Our Final Destiny

161

When all is ended, time and troubles past,
shall all be mended, sin and death out-cast?
in hope we sing, and hope to sing at last:
  Alleluia!

As in the night, when lightning flickers free,
and gives a glimpse of distant hill and tree,
each flash of good discloses what will be:
  Alleluia!

Against all hope, our weary times have known
wars ended, peace declared, compassion shown,
great days of freedom, tyrants overthrown:
  Alleluia!

Then do not cheat the poor, who long for bread,
with dream-worlds in the sky or in the head,
but sing of slaves set free, and children fed:
  Alleluia!

With earthy faith we sing a song of heaven:
all life fulfilled, all loved, all wrong forgiven.
Christ is our sign of hope, for Christ is risen:
  Alleluia!

With all creation, pain and anger past,
evil exhausted, love supreme at last,
alive in God, we'll sing an unsurpassed
  Alleluia!

© 1989 Hope Publishing Company for the USA, Canada, Australia and New Zealand and Stainer & Bell Limited for all other territories. All rights reserved.

December 1988, inspired by William Rowan's tune YOGANANDA. From singing the melody, I felt an image of God bringing all things to a good end in spite of evil. Stanza 4, pivotal to the whole, came from conversations with Revd Betsy King (Temple Cowley United Reformed Church, Oxford). Metre: 10.10.10. with Alleluias

Beyond Time And Thought
162

With humble justice clad and crowned,
the Christ of God will come again
and sing in every land on earth
the song begun at Bethlehem,
and justice shall defend the poor
as barn and warehouse give their grain,
and all the hungry, richly filled,
shall feel that Christ has come again.

The Word of truth will free the oppressed,
and, justly judging every need,
will end the power of flaunted wealth,
and cruel, quiet, systemic greed.
The violence of selfish lust
to have and hold at any cost
will know at last that God is just,
and face the final Pentecost:

As thunderclouds of love rain down
life-giving, universal showers,
the meek will rule, and thus redeem
earth's high authorities and powers,
as workers dance with heads of state,
and all unite, embrace and bring
the richest fruits of hand and brain
in homage to the humblest king.

Say not that justice never dawns,
that peace on earth will never come.
The promise shines from Bethlehem,
for all, forever, like the sun.
Along the highway of the weak,
the poorest and the most distressed,
Christ comes again, and yet again,
till earth, and all on earth, are blessed.

© 1993 Hope Publishing Company for the USA, Canada, Australia and New Zealand and Stainer & Bell Limited for all other territories. All rights reserved.

February 1986, revised 1989, a paraphrase and interpretation of Psalm 72, believing that through Christ, in the age of the Holy Spirit, the hope first vested in Israel's kings becomes ultimate, yet not unearthly. Stanza 1 is based on Psalm 72:1-3, stanza 2 on Psalm 72:12-14 and 7-9. Stanza 3 echoes Psalm 72:6-11 and Matthew 5:5-6 (in line 3), while stanza 4 refers to Psalm 72:17-19. Long Metre Double (LMD/DLM)

Exploring Our Final Destiny
163

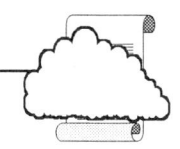

Christ will come again,
God's justice to complete,
to reap the fields of time
and sift the weeds from wheat:
then let us passionately care
for peace and justice here on earth,
and evil's rage restrain with love,
till Christ shall come again.

Christ will come again
and life shall be complete.
The waters from the throne
shall wash the nations' feet:
then let us passionately care
for health and wholeness here on earth,
and ease our neighbour's pain with love,
till Christ shall come again.

Christ will come again,
and joy shall be complete
as flames of lightning love
bedeck the judgment seat:
then let us passionately share
the whole great gospel here on earth,
until all things attain their end,
when Christ shall come again.

© 1989 Hope Publishing Company for the USA, Canada, Australia and New Zealand and Stainer & Bell Limited for all other territories. All rights reserved.

July 1987. Written at Glacier View Ranch during the Seventh Day Adventist Musicians Convention. I wanted to honour my hosts with a hymn on the Second Advent which, whether understood literally or symbolically, would connect ultimate hope with current action for peace, justice, healing and evangelism.
Metre: 5.6.6.6.8.8.8.6.
Matthew 13:24-30; 2 Corinthians 5:10; Revelation 22:1-2.

"History Shall Dry Its Tears"
164

Arise,
shine out,
your light has come,
unfolding City of our dreams.
On distant hills a glory gleams: the new creation has begun.

Above earth's valleys, thick with night,
high on your walls the dawn appears,
and history shall dry its tears,
as nations stream towards your light.

From walls surpassing time and space,
unnumbered gates, like open hands,
shall gather gifts from all the lands,
and welcome all the human race.

The sounds
of violence
shall cease
as dwellings
of salvation rise
to sparkle in eternal skies
from avenues of praise and peace.

The dancing air shall glow with light
and sun and moon give up their place
when Love shines out of every face:
our Good, our Glory, our Delight.

© 1989 Hope Publishing Company for the USA, Canada, Australia and New Zealand and Stainer & Bell Limited for all other territories. All rights reserved.

April 1987, commissioned by the United Methodist Church Hymnal Revision Committee (USA), as a selective paraphrase of Isaiah 60:1-19 (vv 1-3, 11a, 14c, 18-19 NEB). First published in *New Songs of Praise 4*, Oxford University Press, 1988.
Long Metre
Isaiah 60:1-19; Revelation 21:1-4, 22-27 and 22:1-5.

Our Lives Be Praise

Praising God: Creator, Mystery, Trinity

I'll praise my Maker while I've breath,
and when my voice is lost in death
praise shall employ my nobler powers.
My days of praise shall ne'er be past
while life and thought and being last
or immortality endures.

Isaac Watts (1674-1748)

Praising God

ALLELUIA

165

Praise God, the Giver and the Gift.
Hearts, minds and voices now uplift:
Alleluia! Alleluia!
Praise, praise the Breath of glad surprise,
freeing, uplifting, opening eyes,
Three-in-Oneness, Love Communing,
Alleluia! Alleluia!
Alleluia!

166

Eternal Wisdom, timely Friend,
each cell, each self, reveals your art,
and we, the children of your heart,
upon your faithfulness depend.

Within your boundless care and thought,
set free by your creative grace,
we marvel that you give us space
to grow, and move in ways untaught.

We do not know if we alone
can know ourselves, the world, and you,
or if, in other spaces too,
awakened minds have flexed and grown.

Your purpose, weaving dark and light,
as deep and restless as the sea,
is overcast with mystery,
and ranges far beyond our sight.

We only know, from all we find
in Christ, that you will not forget
the earth or us, but keep us yet
in love, in being, and in mind.

Nos. 165 and 166 © 1989 Hope Publishing Company for the USA, Canada, Australia and New Zealand and Stainer & Bell Limited for all other territories. All rights reserved.

No. 165 - The doxologies in this section use traditional tunes, for ease of singing (See Nos. 172 and 180). "Praise God, the Giver and the Gift" was written at a 1987 workshop on *The Languages of Worship* (Schuyler Institute for Worship and the Arts / Boston University School of Theology).
    Long Metre with Alleluias
No. 166 - April 1989. To my brother Keith, written on his birthday, praising God and accepting our humble place in the universe, reacting against the arrogant belief that the human race is God's only achievement or concern.
    Long Metre   Isaiah 45:7; John 1:13; 1 John 3:1-2.

Lover of Creation

167

Let all creation dance
in energies sublime,
as order turns with chance,
unfolding space and time,
for nature's art
in glory grows,
and newly shows
God's mind and heart.

God's breath each force unfurls,
igniting from a spark
expanding starry swirls,
with whirlpools dense and dark.
Though moon and sun
seem mindless things,
each orbit sings:
"Your will be done."

Our own amazing earth,
with sunlight, cloud and storms
and life's abundant growth
in lovely shapes and forms,
is made for praise,
a fragile whole,
and from its soul
heav'n's music plays.

Lift heart and soul and voice:
in Christ all praises meet
and nature shall rejoice
as all is made complete.
In hope be strong,
all life befriend
and kindly tend
creation's song.

© 1991 Hope Publishing Company for the USA, Canada, Australia and New Zealand and Stainer & Bell Limited for all other territories. All rights reserved.

July 1989, to commemorate the 200th anniversary of the death of John Darwall (1731-1789), Anglican cleric and composer. I am told that Darwall composed tunes for all 150 metrical Psalms. One of them, named "DARWALL'S 148TH" because it was for Psalm 148, has been sung ever since. I decided to reunite the Psalm with the tune, by re-visioning the Psalmist's portrayal of all creation praising God. Together with No. 119, this hymn was part of my contribution to a Presbyterian Association of Musicians' Conference in New Wilmington, Pennsylvania.
Metre: 6.6.6.6.4.4.4.4.   Psalm 148

> **Covenanted Praise!** I believe, though cannot prove, that the act of giving heartfelt, genuine praise to another is therapeutic, able to "change our heart's condition" (103), directing us toward others while making us more fully ourselves. So "praise lifts our spirit high, out of gloom and grieving, into new believing" (171), and in relation to God, "praise is our destiny, duty and joy, melting our pride and pretending, ousting our stubborness, easing our pain, failure and folly transcending, never demeaning, always right, gateway to glory unending" (169). I praise God as trinity, because that is how the mystery of the ultimate has been made known to Christian faith, in the unfolding story of the One, historic Liberator who is also Origin of all things, then known humanly in Jesus, then received empoweringly as Spirit, such that it has not made sense to collapse that threefoldness into singleness, nor undo it into separateness. Trinity shows the divine as relational, the origin and sustenance of community, and as partner more than monarch. Because God covenants with us, we also covenant with God, so "sing to God" at all times, thankfully or angrily, in gladness and in bleakness (150). We do not abandon God, but "walk beside you, come what may" even when all we can do is "sing an honest, aching song" (119).

Praising God

168

ALLELUIA

Acclaim with jubilation
    and sing in harmony
with nature's old, evolving,
    unfolding symphony;
the blazing of a comet,
the greening of a planet,
    are songs without a voice
    that bid us all rejoice.

The shrieking of the storm-wind,
    the surging of the seas,
the awestruck alleluias
    that whisper through the trees,
the rushing, booming surf-beat,
the thumping, pulsing heart-beat,
    resound through blood and bone
    to praise the Holy One.

Be still, to muse and marvel
    how every creature sings.
The chattering of dolphins,
    the chirp of cricket-wings,
the coughing of a lion,
the thrilling trill of birdsong,
    our highest skills invite
    to share in their delight.

Then flex your hearts and voices,
    your fingers and your feet;
bring music cool or classic,
    or drum a driving beat.
With orchestra and organ
expand the celebration
    till earth and ocean ring
    and all the people sing.

Acclaim with jubilation
    the Singer and the Song.
Come out of isolation:
    to sing is to belong.
To God, whose mighty singing
sets all creation ringing,
    lift heart and soul and voice,
    be thankful and rejoice!

© 1993 Hope Publishing Company for the USA, Canada, Australia and New Zealand and Stainer & Bell Limited for all other territories. All rights reserved.

October 1990. Commissioned by Warner Memorial Presbyterian Church, Kensington, Maryland, for the dedication of their new organ. I found an old Swedish tune, BEREDEN VÄG FÖR HERRAN, and let it suggest the mood. The theme was suggested by my composer friend, John Horman, who is on the staff of Warner Memorial.
Metre: 7.6.7.6.7.7.6.6.

Lover of Creation

169

Praise to the Maker who paints with a thought,
   spreading and shaping and seeing
oceans of galaxies, islands of life,
   measureless wonders of being,
     whose purpose, ever good and right,
     ranges through realms beyond our sight,
   endlessly flowing and freeing.

Praise to the Servant who chooses a clown,
   wisdom in folly concealing -
laughable, beautiful Body of Christ,
   bungler, and bearer of healing.
     With awkward limbs and comic face
     we mime the mysteries of grace,
   God's pain and glory revealing.

Praise to the Spirit who mends with a song,
   quilting and liltingly weaving
peoples and histories, beauty and pain,
   wickedness, glory and grieving,
     whose healing, love-revealing choice
     gives to the Church's answering voice
   ballads of joy in believing.

Praise is our destiny, duty and joy,
   melting our pride and pretending,
ousting our stubbornness, easing our pain,
   failure and folly transcending,
     never demeaning, always right,
     freeing, fulfilling, love's delight,
   gateway to glory unending.

© 1993 Hope Publishing Company for the USA, Canada, Australia and New Zealand and Stainer & Bell Limited for all other territories. All rights reserved.

April-May 1990. I worked on this, on and off, for a couple of years, till it seemed ready for use.
Metre: 10.8.10.8.8.8.8.

Praising God

170
ALLELUIA

As a mother comforts her child,
the Holy One comforts her people
with all-embracing love.

As an eagle watches the nest,
spreading her sheltering wings,
and carries her fledglings aloft,
teaching them to fly,
> So God befriends the Church
> with patient, teaching love.

As a bear, deprived of her young,
rises with grief-stricken rage
and catches the thieves unaware,
crushing flesh and bone,
> So God defends the oppressed
> with angry, grieving love.

As a mother governs her child,
the Holy One governs the nations
with all-perceiving love.

As a woman looks for a coin,
bending and sweeping the room,
and finding it, calls to her friends,
"Come and share my joy,"
> So God retrieves the lost
> with seeking, joyful love.

As a midwife watches a birth,
guiding with capable hands,
and washes and carries the child
safe to mother's arms,
> So God awakes new life
> with skilful, birthing love.

As a mother watches her child,
the Holy One watches creation
with all-sustaining love.

© 1989 Hope Publishing Company for the USA, Canada, Australia and New Zealand and Stainer & Bell Limited for all other territories. All rights reserved.

March 1989, written for Denver South Seventh Day Adventist Church, as an anthem text for Mother's Day. If it gives new insight into the richness of scripture, it will prove helpful, provided it is not used to reinforce stereotypes of motherhood.
Metre: 8.7.8.5.6.6. Refr.
Deuteronomy 32:11; Psalm 22:9; Isaiah 66:13; Hosea 13:8; Luke 15:8-10.

Lover of Creation

171

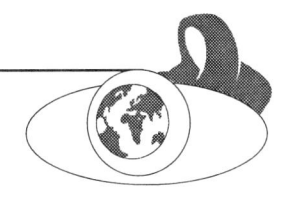

Praise lifts our spirit high,
out of gloom and grieving,
   into new believing,
   gazing at the mystery
   far beyond our seeing,
well and womb of being.
    Alleluia!

Praise brings our spirit home
to the Word of glory
   in our human story,
   love's eternal mystery,
   now in Jesus spoken,
beautiful, and broken.
    Alleluia!

Praise leads our spirit on
to a dance surprising,
   meeting Christ arising.
   Touch the hem of mystery,
   sighing, seeking, groping,
holding, healing, hoping.
    Alleluia!

Praise fills our spirit's flight,
climbing, swooping, soaring,
   growing and exploring
   on the breath of mystery,
   till we're resurrected
in a world perfected.
    Alleluia!

172

Praise God, from whom all blessings flow.
Praise God, all creatures high and low.
Praise God, in Jesus fully known:
Creator, Word and Spirit One.

© 1995 (No. 171) and 1989 (No. 172) Hope Publishing Company for the USA, Canada, Australia and New Zealand and Stainer & Bell Limited for all other territories. All rights reserved.

No. 171 - August 1995. To celebrate and honour the 50th birthday of a friend, Heather Hobbs.
Metre: 6.6.6.7.6.6. with Alleluia
No. 172 - 1989. A revision of the traditional doxology.
Long Metre

Praising God

173
ALLELUIA

Bring many names,
    beautiful and good,
celebrate, in parable and story,
    holiness in glory,
    living, loving God.
Hail and Hosanna!
bring many names!

Strong mother God,
    working night and day,
planning all the wonders of creation,
    setting each equation,
    genius at play:
Hail and Hosanna,
strong mother God!

Warm father God,
    hugging every child,
feeling all the strains of human living,
    caring and forgiving
    till we're reconciled:
Hail and Hosanna,
warm father God!

Old, aching God,
    grey with endless care,
calmly piercing evil's new disguises,
    glad of good surprises,
    wiser than despair:
Hail and Hosanna,
old, aching God!

Young, growing God,
    eager, on the move,
saying no to falsehood and unkindness,
    crying out for justice,
    giving all you have:
Hail and Hosanna,
young, growing God!

Great, living God,
    never fully known,
joyful darkness far beyond our seeing,
    closer yet than breathing,
    everlasting home:
Hail and Hosanna,
great, living God!

© 1989 Hope Publishing Company for the USA, Canada, Australia and New Zealand and Stainer & Bell Limited for all other territories. All rights reserved.

February 1986, revised 1987, 1988 and 1994. Because femaleness and maleness are created jointly in the image and likeness of God (Genesis 1:27), both genders can reveal the divine, and since we live in a developmental life cycle, both youth and age can give glimpses of God. Reversing gender stereotypes in stanzas 2 and 3 makes visible the many women whose genius can "set equations," and gives a picture of fatherhood in tune with the Abba to whom Jesus prayed (Matthew 6:26, 7:11). The Bible speaks of God as the white haired "ancient one" (Daniel 7:9). At Christmas, Christians celebrate God revealed in the infant-ness of a new born. God's passion for justice is well expressed in youthful intolerance of "falsehood and unkindness" (see, e.g., Isaiah 2:13-17; Amos 5:21-24).
Metre: 4.5.10.6.5.5.4.
Genesis 1:27; Isaiah 2:13-17; Daniel 7:9; Amos 5:21-24; Matthew 6:26 and 7:11.

Mysterious and Wonderful

174

Name Unnamed, hidden and shown, knowing and known: Gloria!

Beautiful Movement, ceaselessly forming,
    growing, emerging with awesome delight,
Maker of Rainbows, glowing with colour, arching in wonder,
    energy flowing in darkness and light:
Name Unnamed, hidden and shown, knowing and known: Gloria!

Spinner of Chaos, pulling and twisting,
    freeing the fibres of pattern and form,
Weaver of stories, famed or unspoken, tangled or broken,
    shaping a tapestry vivid and warm:
Name Unnamed, hidden and shown, knowing and known: Gloria!

Nudging Discomforter, prodding and shaking,
    waking our lives to creative unease,
Straight-Talking Lover, checking and humbling jargon and grumbling,
    speaking the truth that refreshes and frees:
Name Unnamed, hidden and shown, knowing and known: Gloria!

Midwife of Changes, skilfully guiding,
    drawing us out through the shock of the new,
Mother of Wisdom, deeply perceiving, never deceiving,
    freeing and leading in all that we do:
Name Unnamed, hidden and shown, knowing and known: Gloria!

Dare-devil Gambler, risking and loving,
    giving us freedom to shatter your dreams,
Life-giving Loser, wounded and weeping, dancing and leaping,
    sharing the caring that heals and redeems:
Name Unnamed, hidden and shown, knowing and known: Gloria!

© 1989 Hope Publishing Company for the USA, Canada, Australia and New Zealand and Stainer & Bell Limited for all other territories. All rights reserved.

July 1986. On the second day of the Summer Workshops in Music at San Francisco Theological Seminary, the fifty members of my workshop wrote one-sentence prayers using varied metaphors for God. I wrote this text using their work, and shared the writing process with them over the following days. The refrain begins and ends with the mystery of God ("Name Un-Named"), and continually returns to it from stanzas parading a pageant of metaphors for the divine.
Metre: Irregular

Praising God

175

Tree of Fire, in sapphire flame outspreading,
   centre of holy ground, of pain and healing,
Rock of Dreams, red in the desert rising,
   measure and mark of time, each age recording: Alleluia!
     Holy is the Name Unnamed,
       good unbounded, uncontained,
         God in Jesus touched and seen:
           worship, wonder, praise we bring.

Hill of Feasts, with milk and honey flowing,
   giver of ample good, all creatures feeding,
Cave of Sighs, latent with whispered longing,
   stillness of growth unseen, and womb of waiting: Alleluia!
     Holy is the Name Unnamed,
       good unbounded, uncontained,
         God in Jesus touched and seen:
           worship, wonder, praise we bring.

Cloud of Dark, all speech and thought dissolving,
   terror of tugging void and stark unknowing,
Wheel of Light, rainbow of shimmered swirling,
   whirlpool of dizzied change, and dread disturbing: Alleluia!
     Holy is the Name Unnamed,
       good unbounded, uncontained,
         God in Jesus touched and seen:
           worship, wonder, praise we bring.

Sea of Tears, despair and evil drowning,
   ocean of restless care, all hate eroding,
Well of Gifts, measureless depth of being,
   gladness of life revived, and hope's refreshing: Alleluia!
     Holy is the Name Unnamed,
       good unbounded, uncontained,
         God in Jesus touched and seen:
           worship, wonder, praise we bring.

© 1993 Hope Publishing Company for the USA, Canada, Australia and New Zealand and Stainer & Bell Limited for all other territories. All rights reserved.

August 1989. These powerful images had gripped me for some time, so the hymn had to be written.
Metre: 10.11.10.11.4. Refr.
Exodus 3:1-8 and 20:21; Ezekiel 1:4-21; Joel 3:18.

Mysterious and Wonderful
176

Dear Mother God,
you held me at my birth.
You sang my name, were glad to see my face.
You are my sky, my shining sun,
and in your love there's always room
to be, and grow, yet find a home,
a settled place.

Dear Brother God,
in Christ your love rings true.
The mighty, high and haughty lose their sway.
Your service, free from servitude,
draws out a love that, strong to give,
can show and tell, inspire and live
a better way.

Dear Sister God,
you give the listening love
(when people meet, and trust, as sharing grows)
that murmurs yes, and yes again,
as sighs and hurts too deep for words
are hailed, embraced, accepted, heard,
and courage flows.

Dear Father God,
with strong and gentle hands
you plant, and prune, and tend the living earth.
Your will be done, your freedom come,
till none exploit, or win, or lose,
but cherish life, and spread the news
of second birth.

© 1980 Hope Publishing Company for the USA, Canada, Australia and New Zealand and Stainer & Bell Limited for all other territories. All rights reserved.

March 1980. Originally "Dear Sister God," written for a Wives' Club Anniversary at Hockley and Hawkwell United Reformed Church, Essex, England, where I was Minister from 1965-70. The metaphors (Mother, Brother, Sister and Father) are poetry, not creed: they are not a "quaternity" replacing the Trinity, but four relational windows into the trinitarian Oneness of the divine.
Metre: 10.10.8.8.8.4.
Isaiah 66:13; Hosea 11:1-4; Luke 24:24-27; John 15:1 and 20:15; Romans 8:26.

Praising God

177

ALLELUIA

Praise the God who changes places,
    leaves the lofty seat,
welcomes us with warm embraces,
    stoops to wash our feet.
> *Friends, be strong!*
> *Hold your heads high!*
> *Freedom is our song! Alleluia!*

Praise the Rabbi, speaking, doing
    all that God intends,
dying, rising, faith renewing,
    calling us his friends.
> *Friends, be strong!*
> *Hold your heads high!*
> *Freedom is our song! Alleluia!*

Praise the Breath of Love, whose freedom
    spreads our waking wings,
lifting every blight and burden
    till our spirit sings:
> *Friends, be strong!*
> *Hold your heads high!*
> *Freedom is our song! Alleluia!*

Praise, until we join the singing
    far beyond our sight,
with the Ending - and - Beginning,
    dancing in the light.
> *Friends, be strong!*
> *Hold your heads high!*
> *Freedom is our song! Alleluia!*

© 1986 Hope Publishing Company for the USA, Canada, Australia and New Zealand and Stainer & Bell Limited for all other territories. All rights reserved.

February 1985, revised 1995. Trinitarian praise using non-traditional imagery.
Metre: 8.5.8.5. Refr.
Isaiah 40:31: Philippians 2:5-11; John 1:38; 3:2; 3:26 and 15:12-17; 2 Corinthians 3:17; Revelation 1:8.

Glorious Trinity

178

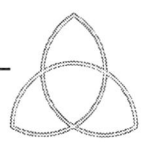

I met three children in the street.
    They did not give me trick or treat
but whispered, laughed, and called my name.
    I nearly walked away,
    but something made me stay
and join them in their game.

"Now let's pretend that we are God,"
    they said, and ran to where I stood.
They danced around me in a ring
    and sang, "You must agree
    to give us questions three,
so ask us anything."

They waited, sitting on the ground,
    and did not move or make a sound.
I thought and puzzled long that day,
    and then, to my surprise,
    I looked into their eyes,
and knew what I would say:

"Now listen to my questions three,"
    I said, "and you must answer me:
What is your name? and *Are you real?*
    and *Can you see and know
    how humans think and grow,
and fathom how we feel?*"

The first child stood up tall,
and suddenly I felt quite small
as solemnly she said:
    "We never give our name away,
    but listen hard to what I say:
    God is not a she, God is not a he,
    God is not an it or a maybe.
    God is a moving, loving,
    knowing, growing mystery."

The second child moved so fast
I hardly saw her spinning past
as all around she sang:
    "I'll dance my dance of destiny
    till you are all as real as me:
    I made you. I know you.
    I love you."

The third child took my hand
and whispered, "Yes, we understand.
I know what children think and do,
for I have been a child like you.
I know how it feels to walk and run,
to sing and shout, and play in the sun,
    or cry in the night,
    or fall to the ground,
    or tremble with fright,
    or be lost and found.
I know how it feels to look at the sky
and keep on asking why and why."

I met three children on my way,
    and never knew, in all our play,
their age or name or why they came,
    yet all the world is new,
    and everything I do
will never be the same.

    God is not a she,
    God is not a he,
    God is not an it or a maybe.
God is a moving,
    loving,
      knowing,
        growing
          mystery.

© 1996 Hope Publishing Company for the USA, Canada, Australia and New Zealand and Stainer & Bell Limited for all other territories. All rights reserved.

Book for a Cantata on the Trinity, composed by John Horman (music not yet published).

Praising God

179

ALLELUIA

God is One, unique and holy,
    endless dance of love and light,
only source of mind and body,
    star-cloud, atom, day and night:
        everything that is or could be
        tells God's anguish and delight.

God is Oneness-by-Communion:
    never distant or alone,
at the heart of all belonging:
    loyal friendship, loving home,
        common mind and shared agreement,
        common loaf and sung Shalom.

Through the pain that loving Wisdom
    could foresee, but not forestall,
God is One, though torn and anguished
    in the Christ's forsaken call,
        One through death and resurrection,
        One in Spirit, One for all.

180

Praise the Lover of Creation,
Praise the Spirit, Friend of Friends,
Praise the true Beloved, our Saviour,
    Praise the God who makes and mends,
    strong, surrendered, many-splendoured,
    Three whose Oneness never ends.

© 1983, 1995 (No. 179) and 1989 (No. 180) Hope Publishing Company for the USA, Canada, Australia and New Zealand and Stainer & Bell Limited for all other territories. All rights reserved.

No. 179 - September 1980, revised 1993. One source was Jürgen Moltmann, *The Trinity and the Kingdom of God.*
    Metre: 8.7.8.7.8.7.   Deuteronomy 5:6-7 and 6:4-5 (NRSV- see marginal note); Mark 15:33-39; John 10:30 and 14:6-11; 1 Corinthians 2:1-13; Ephesians 4:3; Colossians 3:14.
No. 180 - Based on St. Augustine (see also No. 182).
    Metre: 8.7.8.7.8.7.

Glorious Trinity

181

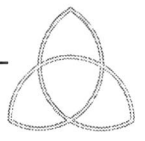

When minds and bodies meet as one
   and find their true affinity,
we join the dance in God begun
   and move within the Trinity,
so praise the good that's seen and done
   in loving, giving unity,
revealing God, forever One,
   whose nature is Community.

When leaders meet with angry sound,
   yet bridle their hostility
to bargain for a common ground
   and end with unanimity,
be glad for all the hope that's won
   in every gleam of unity,
revealing God, forever One,
   whose nature is Community.

When teamwork serves a common aim
   and players move in sympathy,
the flowing rhythm of the game
   is beauty in simplicity,
so praise the good that's seen and done
   in swiftly moving unity,
revealing God, forever One,
   whose nature is Community.

When people feel the lashing claws
   of greed and inhumanity,
yet struggle in a rightful cause
   with love and solidarity,
be glad for all the hope that's won
   in freedom-loving unity,
revealing God, forever One,
   whose nature is Community.

In Christ we come to break and bless
   the bread of new society,
created for togetherness
   from infinite variety,
so praise the good that's seen and done
   in Spirit-given unity,
revealing God, forever One,
   whose nature is Community.

© 1980 Hope Publishing Company for the USA, Canada, Australia and New Zealand and Stainer & Bell Limited for all other territories. All rights reserved.

1980, revised 1994. The doctrine of the Trinity is not a mathematical formula but a serious attempt to make sense of Christian experience. This carol celebrates the Trinity and connects the doctrine with contemporary experience.
Long Metre Double

Alleluia!
182

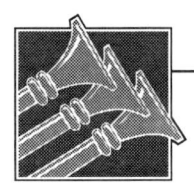

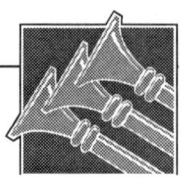

How wonderful the Three-in-One,
whose energies of dancing light
are undivided, pure and good,
communing love in shared delight!

Before the flow of dawn and dark,
Creation's Lover dreamed of earth,
and with a caring deep and wise,
all things conceived and brought to birth.

The Lover's own Belov'd, in time,
between a cradle and a cross,
at home in flesh, gave love and life
to heal our brokenness and loss

Their Equal Friend all life sustains
with greening power and loving care,
and calls us, born again by grace,
in Love's communing life to share.

How wonderful the Living God:
Divine Beloved, Empow'ring Friend,
Eternal Lover, Three-in-One,
our hope's beginning, way and end!

© 1989 Hope Publishing Company for the USA, Canada, Australia and New Zealand and Stainer & Bell Limited for all other territories. All rights reserved.

February 1988. St. Augustine suggested that Christian experience of God as Trinity can be pictured in terms of one who loves (the Origin, the Creator), one who is loved (Jesus Christ, the Word of God in human flesh) and the love-bond between them (the Holy Spirit, poured out on all who believe). The hymn develops Augustine's metaphor by recognizing that the Holy Spirit is a full expression of divine "personhood," so not secondary or lesser (as is arguably implied by the phrase, "bond of love"). Augustine's metaphor enables us to speak of God as Trinity in terms fully personal, not limited to male or female gender, and true to the fundamental biblical revelation that God is Love. The hymn arises from a chapter in my book, *What Language Shall I Borrow?* (New York: Crossroad Books, 1989).
Long Metre

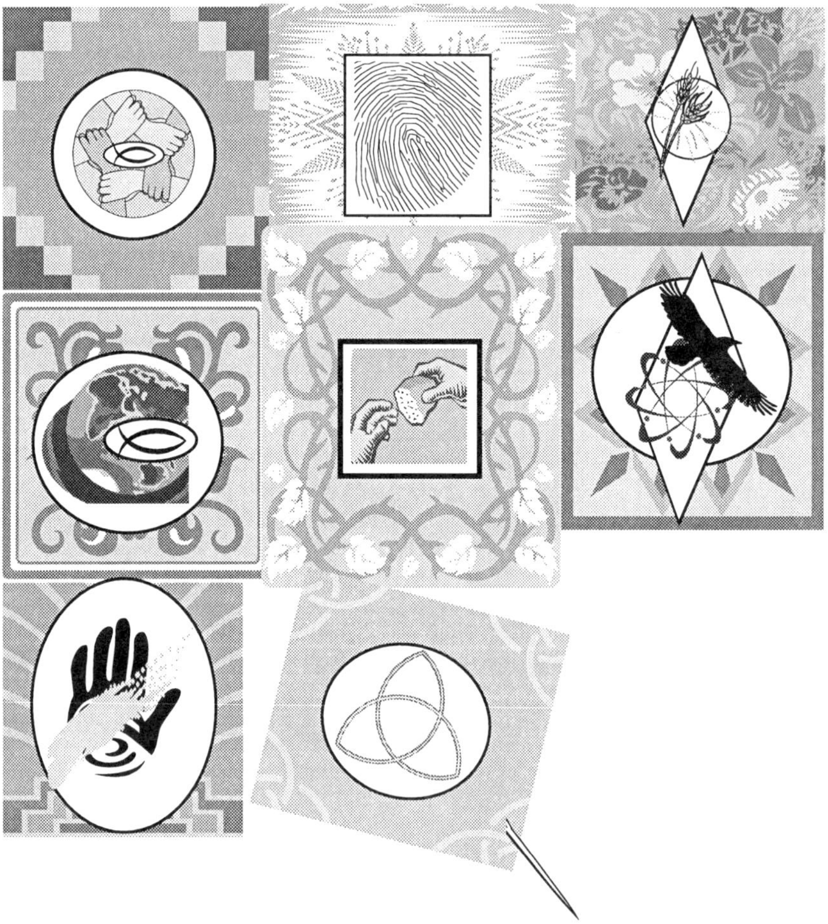

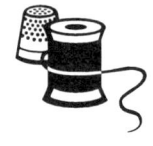

Appendix

Contents

- A hymnic setting of the Eucharistic Prayer, placed here because it is a unit, with adaptations of traditional hymns as well as original material.

- Items omitted from the anthology because they are only partially mine (188), thematically repetitious (185, 191), outdated, or otherwise out of place.

- Various Poems and Song Lyrics.

Lift Heart and Voice
The Great Thanksgiving in Song

- This may be sung, or partly sung and partly read (which takes less time)
- Plain type is sung or read by worship leader(s); bold is sung or read by all.
- For the prayer to be worshipful, THE MUSIC MUST BE FAMILIAR; make sure the tunes are well known before using them.
- For their meaning to be understood in the flow of the prayer, the texts are printed as poetry. DO NOT INTERLINE THEM WITH MUSIC, except optionally for worship leaders. For congregations, only the texts are needed.

" Lift up Your Hearts"
183   May God Be With You!
Brian Wren - Tune: BUNESSAN (5.5.5.4.D.)

May God be with you!
And with you also!
Lift hearts and voices
gladly to God.
**Everywhere, always,
this is the right thing,
praising our Maker,
holy and good.**

God's Works in Creation
For the Beauty of the Earth (Foliot S. Pierpoint, adapted) Tune: DIX

For the beauty of the earth,
for the glory of the skies,
for the love which from our birth
over and around us lies,
**Source of all, to thee we raise
this our sacrifice of praise.**

For the joy of ear and eye,
touch and tasting, sound and sight,
times and seasons flowing by,
love's desire and mind's delight,
**Source of all, to thee we raise
this our sacrifice of praise.**

For the joy of human love,
brother, sister, parent, child,
friends on earth and friends above,
foes forgiven, reconciled,
**Source of all, to thee we raise
this our sacrifice of praise.**

Original versions of adapted hymns are public domain. Adaptations, Brian Wren texts, and "Lift Heart and Voice" as a whole are © 1995 Hope Publishing Company for the USA, Canada, Australia and New Zealand, and Stainer & Bell Limited for all other territories. All rights reserved.

" Holy, Holy, Holy"

Reginald Heber, adapted. Tune: NICAEA

Holy, Holy, Holy, Merciful and Mighty,
all thy works shall praise thy name in earth and sky and sea.
Only thou art holy; there is none beside thee,
God in three persons, blessed Trinity!

Holy, holy, holy, saving and restoring,
Blessed is the One who comes, thy glory to proclaim.
with the saints we praise thee, thankfully adoring.
Hail and hosanna, hallowed be thy name!

God in Christ

(i) "We Would See Jesus" (J. Edgar Park) and (ii) "All praise to thee" (F. Bland Tucker).
Tunes: (i) INTERCESSOR; (ii) ENGLEBERG or SINE NOMINE.

We would see Jesus, Mary's son most holy,
light of the village life from day to day;
shining revealed through every task most lowly,
the Christ of God, the life, the truth, the way.

Thou came'st to us in lowliness of thought;
by thee the outcast and the poor were sought,
and by thy death was God's salvation wrought:
    Alleluia!

We would see Jesus, in his work of healing,
at eventide, before the sun was set;
divine and human, in his deep revealing
of God made flesh, in loving service met.

Let this mind be in us, which was in thee,
who wast a servant, that we might be free,
humbling thyself to death on Calvary:
    Alleluia!

Original versions of adapted hymns are public domain. Adaptations, Brian Wren texts, and "Lift Heart and Voice" as a whole are © 1995 Hope Publishing Company for the USA, Canada, Australia and New Zealand, and Stainer & Bell Limited for all other territories. All rights reserved.

"In Remembrance of Me"

(i) "On the Night Before He Died" (Brian Wren - No. 37 in main anthology)
(ii) "O Thou, Who This Mysterious Bread" (Charles Wesley)
Tunes: (i) STOOKEY or ABERYSTWYTH; (ii) LAND OF REST.

On the night before he died,
to the government betrayed,
at his people's freedom meal,
Jesus broke the bread, and said:
"Take and eat my broken self.
Share in all I say and do.
Though I go, I shall return:
God is making all things new."

When the meal was nearly done,
and his blood would soon be shed,
Jesus lifted up the cup,
"All must drink of this," he said,
"When the powers of earth prevail,
and my blood is shed for you,
taste the sign within the wine:
God is making all things new."

O thou, who this mysterious bread
didst in Emmaeus break,
return, herewith our souls to feed,
and to thy followers speak.

Enkindle now the heavenly zeal,
and make thy mercy known,
and give our pardoned souls to feel
that God and love are one.

One in the Spirit

(i) "Great is the Mystery" (Brian Wren) Metre: 5.5.6.5.6.5.6.5. Refr.
(ii) "All praise to thee" (F. Bland Tucker).
Tunes: (i) JUDAS MACCABEUS; (ii) ENGLEBERG or SINE NOMINE.

184 Great is the Mystery

Great is the myst'ry; faith shall say: Amen! -
Christ who died is risen; Christ will come again!
Lift the cup of blessing, share the broken bread,
Taste and see Christ Jesus, risen from the dead.
One in the Spirit, gladly sing "Amen,
Christ who died is risen; Christ will come again!"

Let every tongue confess with one accord
in heaven and earth, that Jesus Christ is Lord;
and God the Father be by all adored:
Alleluia! Alleluia!

Most of the tunes are widely published. CUSHMAN, STOOKEY, and LAND OF REST are in the *United Methodist Hymnal*, USA 1989, Nos. 256, 627 and 613.

Original versions of adapted hymns are public domain. Adaptations, Brian Wren texts, and "Lift Heart and Voice" as a whole are © 1995 Hope Publishing Company for the USA, Canada, Australia and New Zealand, and Stainer & Bell Limited for all other territories. All rights reserved.

Hymns Not Included

185 As Man and Woman We Were Made

Love
As man and woman we were made
   that love be found and life begun
so praise the Lord who made us two
   and praise the Lord when two are one:
praise for the love that comes to life
through child or parent, husband, wife.

Joy
Now Jesus lived and gave his love
   to make our life and loving new
so celebrate with him today
   and drink the joy he offers you
that makes the simple moment shine
and changes water into wine.

Hope
And Jesus died to live again
   so praise the love that, come what may,
can bring the dawn and clear the skies,
   and waits to wipe all tears away
and let us hope for what shall be
believing where we cannot see.

Peace
Then spread the table, clear the hall
   and celebrate till day is done;
let peace go deep between us all
   and joy be shared by everyone:
laugh and make merry with your friends
and praise the love that never ends!

© 1983 Hope Publishing Company for the USA, Canada, Australia and New Zealand and Stainer & Bell Limited for all other territories. All rights reserved.

1973. "When Love is Found" and "God the All-Holy" better express its themes. Metre: 8.8.8.8.8.8.
Tune: SUSSEX CAROL

186 Dear Christ, The Father's Loving Son

Dear Christ, the Father's loving Son,
whose work upon the cross was done
   to give and receive,
make all our scattered churches one
that the world may believe.

To make us one your prayers were said.
To make us one you broke the bread
   for all to receive.
It's pieces scatter us instead:
how can others believe?

Free us, forgive us, make us new!
What our designs could never do
   your love can achieve.
Our prayers, our work, we bring to you
that the world may believe.

We will not question or refuse
the way you work, the means you choose
   the pattern you weave,
but reconcile our warring views
that the world may believe.

© 1972, 1996 Hope Publishing Company for the USA, Canada, Australia and New Zealand and Stainer & Bell Limited for all other territories. All rights reserved.

March 1962, revised 1968, 1995. My second usable hymn, published quite widely in the 1960s. Though I'm happy with the revision, its theme of unity in Christ is amply covered in the main text.
Metre: 8.8.5.8.6. Tune HAMPTON POYLE, Peter Cutts, *Faith Looking Forward*, 1983: Hope Publishing Company (USA) and Oxford University Press (UK).

187 For the Bread

For the bread that we have eaten,
for the wine that we have tasted,
for the life that you have given,
   Father, Son and Holy Spirit,
   we will praise you.

For the life of Christ within us,
turning all our fears to freedom,
Helping us to live for others,
   Father, Son and Holy Spirit,
   we will praise you.

For the strength of Christ to lead us
in our living and our dying,
in the end, with all your people,
   Father, Son and Holy Spirit,
   we will praise you.

Copyright © 1965 SCM Press Ltd. Used by Permission. All Rights Reserved.
First published in *Contemporary Prayers for Public Worship*, Ed. Caryl Micklem, SCM Press (UK) and Eerdmans (USA), 1967 - one of several prayers I contributed to that collection.
Metre: 8.8.8.8.4. Tune: MAYFIELD, Peter Cutts, *Faith Looking Forward*, 1983: Hope Publishing Company (USA) and Oxford University Press (UK).

---

188 God, Your Glory We Have Seen

God, your glory we have seen in your Son,
Full of truth, full of heavenly grace;
In Christ make us live, his love shine on our face,
And the nations will see in us the triumph you have won.

In the fields of this world his good news he has sown,
And sends us out to reap till the harvest is done: *God, your glory...*

In his love like a fire that consumes he passed by;
The flame has touched our lips; let us shout: 'Here am I!': *God, your glory...*

He was broken for us, God-forsaken his cry,
And still the bread he breaks; to ourselves we must die: *God, your glory...*

He has trampled the grapes of new life on his cross;
Now drink the cup and live; he has filled it for us: *God, your glory...*

He has founded a kingdom that none shall destroy;
The corner-stone is laid; go to work, build with joy! *God, your glory...*

Verses © Hope Publishing Company for USA, Canada, Australia and New Zealand and Stainer & Bell Limited for all other territories. Refrain reprinted by permission.

Translation from the French by Didier Rimaud (1922-). I translated the verses and the refrain was translated by Sir Ronald Johnson (1913-). Metre: 12.12.with refrain. Tune: DIEU, NOUS AVONS VU, *Cantate Domino, Rejoice and Sing* (UK), *Rejoice in the Lord* (USA).

189 Half the World is Hungry, Lord

Half the world is hungry, Lord.
   Christian people, sleekly fed,
Christian comforts can afford —
   Worship, faith, and heavenly bread.
Others crave for earthly food;
   Starving, have no strength to pray.
Glib, we sing how God is good —
   We shall eat and drink today.

Wealthy, white, and selfish lands,
   Hurling space-probes at the sky,
Give, then take with eager hands,
   Buying cheap and selling high;
Proud of aid that's merely loaned
(crumbs from tables rich with food)
They will fight to keep their own:
   Half the world is hungry, Lord...

We your well-fed people, Lord,
   Blind and deaf have lived too long.
By the love that burst the tomb
   Men must fight a man-made wrong.
Wealth and comfort are our chains;
   Full, we fear to pay your price.
By your suffering set us free —
   Free to love and sacrifice.

© 1971 Hope Publishing Company for the USA, Canada, Australia and New Zealand and Stainer & Bell Limited for all other territories. All rights reserved.

More a protest than a hymn and couched in irredeemable sexist language, written for a Christian Aid pamphlet on *Hunger and Justice*, using the tune ABERYSTWYTH. The tune HALF THE WORLD IS HUNGRY by John Hastings is in *One World Songs* (Methodist Church Division of Social Responsibility-UK). Metre: 7.7.7.7.D.

---

190 Holy Spirit, Hear Us As We Pray

Holy Spirit, hear us as we pray.
Take the faltering and stumbling words we say
   and turn them into songs.
So you will help us give to God
   the praise we want to give.

Holy Spirit, speak to us as we pray.
Bring merciful and forgiving words today
   from God the Father.
So you will help us find in God
   the peace we need to find.

Holy Spirit, come to us today.
Tell of the dying and rising of Christ the Lord
   and give us joy.
So you will help us live for God
   the life we ought to live.

Copyright © 1964 SCM Press Ltd. Used by Permission. All Rights Reserved.
First published in *Contemporary Prayers for Public Worship* (1967: Ed. Caryl Micklem, SCM Press (UK) and Eerdmans (USA) - one of several prayers I contributed to that collection.

Metre: Irregular. Tune: PETITION, Peter Cutts, *Faith Looking Forward*, 1983: Hope Publishing Company (USA) and Oxford University Press (UK).

191 When I Have Failed

When I have failed
  I want a new start,
    a clean heart,
      and Holy Breath
    to change my ways
  as I appraise
how I have failed.

Each time I fall,
  I start a new game
    with rash claim
      of better faith,
    then start to play
  the same old way,
and so I fall.

A deeper love
  that kneels to serve me,
    might nerve me
      to see and shift
    my patterned wrong
  and sing my song
to Christ alone.

Come, Holy Breath,
  to seek and know me
    and show me
      how I can walk
    in better ways
  alive with praise
for Christ alone.

© 1993 Hope Publishing Company for the USA, Canada, Australia and New Zealand, and Stainer & Bell Limited for all other territories. All rights reserved.

November 1989 - January 1990. A hymn equivalent of the song-lyric, "Come Holy Breath," whose wording it closely follows. Metre: 4.5 3.4.4 4.4. Tune: AFTON, Lawrence Wareing, *New Beginnings*, 30

Poems and Lyrics

192 Cucumber Hearts

Across the lake, the evening sun
shines bright upon the water,
where power-boats scalpel their incisions.
Within the room, arriving guests
give hugs, and handshakes, smile and speak, move on,
as music murmurs its continuo.
A silver tray appears, on unobtrusive hands,
and moves from point to point,
adorned with tiny hearts, exquisite, delicate.
In passing, hands reach out,
and fingertips, like tweezers, lift them, one by one
to parting lips, that taste, and smile with sudden pleasure.
Cucumber at the base, they touch the tongue
as chords of coolness, with a fishy descant.

In heaven's halls, that tray of hearts
stands on a Chippendale
beneath a Michelangelo.

© 1996 Hope Publishing Company for the USA, Canada, Australia and New Zealand and Stainer & Bell Limited for all other territories. All rights reserved.

May 1994, a thank-you to my hosts, during a visit to Seattle.

193 Easter Light

River, with the flow of grace abounding,
Thunder, with the roar of love resounding,
Rainbow, with a gleam of hope surprising,
Sunlight, in the dawn of faith arising -
Christ of God, deep in the hell of pain,
bearing away our sinning,
birthing a new beginning,
Christ our Love, leaving the womb of night,
filling the world with Easter light.

Come, with the care that carries our shame,
bearing away our sinning,
birthing a new beginning.
Come, with the love that calls us by name,
filling the world with Easter light.

Speaker, for the poor and weak protesting,
Partner, bond of love in earth investing,
Healer, all our broken stories mending,
Singer, with a song of joy unending,
Christ of God, walking along our way,
putting the powers of death to flight.

Come, with the peace the world cannot give,
sharing our joy and weeping,
holding us in safe keeping.
Come, with the love that frees us to live,
filling the world with Easter light.

© 1996 Hope Publishing Company for the USA, Canada, Australia and New Zealand and Stainer & Bell Limited for all other territories. All rights reserved.

Lyrics for music by Andrew Stallman, commissioned by Revd Sallie E. Shippen, then Rector of Grace Episcopal Church, Astoria, Oregon, and sung at the church's Easter Vigil on April 14th, 1989.

---

194 I Promise (Farewell Song)

I promise, I promise from the heart,
to hear your story, and sing your song.
I promise, I promise from the heart,
to remember that we met, and keep your face in mind.

To be loved and understood is a treasure and a gift.
To respect and understand takes everything we have,
There's a bridge to be built from each to the other.
There are letters to write and friendships to discover.

So I ask, I ask from the heart,
Will you hear my story, and sing my song
as we promise, we promise from the heart,
to remember that we met, and keep your face in mind?

Fare well, goodbye, till every story's heard,
and every song is sung.

© 1996 Hope Publishing Company for the USA, Canada, Australia and New Zealand and Stainer & Bell Limited for all other territories. All rights reserved.

August 1989, for Starfire Youth Choir, Los Altos United Methodist Church, California.

195 Listening

Paleface people need to listen
to people of colour.
Don't say, "I hear you."
People of colour will tell us
when we've heard them.

Men need to listen to women.
Don't say, "Yes, I understand."
Women will tell us
what we've understood.

Adults need to listen to children,
walkers to riders in wheelchairs,
quick talkers to non-speakers.
They cannot always tell us
if we're listening:
all the more reason, then,
to listen, listen,
and more than listen.

Suburb, Main Line,
and First World people
need to listen, and more than listen,
to Inner City, Side-lined,
Third World people.

All of us need to listen,
and more than listen,

but quick talking, fast-walking,
main line, first world, paleface
Men
need the biggest ears,

because we need to listen
to everyone.

(PS. Dumbo had big ears
and learned to fly.)

© 1989 Hope Publishing Company for the USA, Canada, Australia and New Zealand and Stainer & Bell Limited for all other territories. All rights reserved.

Bryn Mawr, Pennsylvania, June 1988, revised 1994. First published in the introduction to *Bring Many Names* (1989: Hope Publishing Company, USA, distributed in the UK and Europe by Stainer & Bell Limited).

196 Only One Earth

Only one earth, we can't make another,
only one earth, our human home,
only one life to find each other
only one time, and the time is now,
only one sky, and only one ocean,
only one race, the whole human race,
only one past and only one future,
only one time, and the time is now.

There are fish and insects, animals and birds,
there's life in the forest and life in the sea,
there's wisdom and wonder in every kind of life,
and every kind of life has the right to be
in only one earth.....etc.

There's a thousand generations waiting to be born,
there's a future for earth that we'll never see,
there's wisdom and wonder in every age to come,
and every age to come has the right to be
in only one earth....etc.

Now our children perhaps will visit the stars,
and our grandchildren's children may live to see
the wisdom and wonder of other worlds of life,
but only if today we can all agree
that there's only one earth....etc.

August 1989, for Starfire, Los Altos United Methodist Church, California, and Dirk and Carol Damonte.

© 1996 Hope Publishing Company for the USA, Canada, Australia and New Zealand and Stainer & Bell Limited for all other territories. All rights reserved.

197 Old Dog: A Tribute to Alfie

Old Dog,
veteran of summers,
earth keeps you; we hold you
in memory.

Inside the door
your spirit wags
in silent welcome.
Faint-echoed in the walls
your phantom bark
gladdens our coming.

Behind the chair,
your shadow sleeps,
twitching dog dreams
of youthful glory.

Old Dog,
your name was Welcome;
your soul, a Smile;
your walk, Affection.

May 1992, for George and Nancy Shorney, with love.

© 1996 Hope Publishing Company for the USA, Canada, Australia and New Zealand and Stainer & Bell Limited for all other territories. All rights reserved.

---

198 Onward, Christian Rambos!

Onward, Christian Rambos,
spoiling for a fight,
wave the flag for Jesus,
knowing that we're right:
load the gospel rifle,
throw grenades of prayer,
blast the Spirit's napalm:
evil's over there -
Onward, Christian Rambos,
spoiling for a fight,
wave the flag for Jesus,
knowing that we're right.

Like a panzer army
we shall blitz the foe.
Rugged Cross, old glory,
lead us as we go!
Hail or heil your leader,
drilled to do or die,
under Holy Orders,
never asking "why?" -
Onward, Christian Rambos,
spoiling for a fight,
wave the flag for Jesus,
knowing that we're right.

Feel the thrill of bloodshed,
guns, and holy wars.
We don't really mean it,
its all metaphors.
Nuke the Devil's Empire,
for in God we trust.
Yes, we'll love our enemies,
when they bite the dust.
Onward, Christian Rambos,
spoiling for a fight,
wave the flag for Jesus,
knowing that we're right.

© 1996 Hope Publishing Company for the USA, Canada, Australia and New Zealand and Stainer & Bell Limited for all other territories. All rights reserved.

1987. A tongue-in-cheek spoof for the United Methodist Church hymnal revision committee, following national controversy as to whether "Onward, Christian soldiers" should be kept in the new hymnal.

199 The Owl That Sat In Wesley's Place

The owl that sat in Wesley's place
  must soon take wing, and all the birds
will wheel and hover, lost for words,
  and sadly view the empty space.
On stormy days he'd calmly sit,
  aware of every groaning branch,
and help our labours to advance
  with wisdom, courtesy and wit.
Go well, good Owl. With love we'll look
  wherever next you wing your way.
Beyond all honours we can pay
  a singing Church, an open book,
will be your emblem and reward:
  the song is mightier than the sword.

© 1996 Hope Publishing Company for the USA, Canada, Australia and New Zealand and Stainer & Bell Limited for all other territories. All rights reserved.

1989. For Dr. Carlton Young, these verses inadequately celebrate his great work of scholarship and enablement for the Hymnal Revision Committee of the United Methodist Church 1984-1989 and were written with pleasure at the Committee's request.

---

200 The Walls of Separation

The walls of separation
are high and thick and wide.
We cannot sneak around them
or tunnel underneath them,
for though they stand between us,
they're also built within us -

*And so we want, we want to find
a peaceful way, a careful way,
step by step, brick by brick,
stone by stone,
to take them down.*

The walls are strong and solid,
with hard and heavy stones -
the strangeness of the stranger
and memories of danger,
the terror of invasion,
the fear of losing freedom -

*And so we need, we really need
a listening way, a lasting way,
step by step, brick by brick,
stone by stone,
to take them down.*

(Continued on next page)

August 1989, a song lyric for Starfire (Youth Choir), Los Altos United Methodist Church, California.

Yet sometimes,
in a moment of surprise,
we hear the heart that's speaking,
and meet each other's eyes,
our fears dissolve,
and misconceptions fall,
and for a breathing space
there's no dividing wall.

So though our song is ending
and many walls remain,
we hope this loving greeting,
with every honest meeting,
each good negotiation,
each little celebration,

can give us all, for good and all,
a peaceful way, a lasting way,
step by step, brick by brick,
stone by stone,
to take them down.

© 1996 Hope Publishing Company for the USA, Canada, Australia and New Zealand and Stainer & Bell Limited for all other territories. All rights reserved.

201 We Cannot Be Beguiled By Pleasant Sounds

We cannot be beguiled by pleasant sounds.
The cadences of Cranmer and King James
caress the palate, smooth as ancient wine,
yet clothe the humble power of love divine
in Tudor pomp, and Absolutist claims,
while soaring plainsong from a thousand tongues
sent Inquisition victims to the flames.
We cannot be beguiled by pleasant sounds.

© 1996 Hope Publishing Company for the USA, Canada, Australia and New Zealand and Stainer & Bell Limited for all other territories. All rights reserved.

1991, in response to a magazine article on inclusive language.

202 Wedding Wishes

In a corner of life's puzzle, two pieces meet. Their angled edges, curves and corners, beautiful apart, now dovetail into unity. Together, they are stronger, more complete, and give a flash of meaning to the wider picture. And this is true, and false: for each remains unique, apart though now at one. Their joining is not seamless, losing either in the other. Together, they will trim some corners, shape new lines, and smooth hard edges. Yet bumps and indentations, knobs, and awkward angles will remain, to be forgiven, held, and loved, as week by week, their joining is redone. May they continue thus, till other pieces say, "A good fit. Its clear that they belong together."

© 1996 Hope Publishing Company for the USA, Canada, Australia and New Zealand and Stainer & Bell Limited for all other territories. All rights reserved.

December 1995, for Debi and Dwight Pensiero, on the occasion of their wedding.

Index of Metres

CM (Common Metre: 8.6.8.6.)
- A woman in a world — 55
- Come let us praise — 11
- Dear Christ, uplifted — 44
- I come with joy — 97
- If I could visit Bethlehem — 21
- The gifts of God — 142
- This is a story full of love — 10

CMD (Common Metre Double)
- Come, celebrate the call — 67
- Deep in the shadows — 86
- Give thanks for music-making — 69
- We meet as friends at table — 96
- When pain and terror — 41

CMT (8.6.8.6. Triple)
- The horrors of our history — 118

LM (Long Metre: 8.8.8.8.)
- A man of ancient time — 30
- Arise, shine out — 164
- Christ is alive! — 52
- Come, build the Church — 93
- Eternal Wisdom — 166
- Go now in peace — 148
- God, give us freedom — 119
- God, let me welcome — 156
- Great Lover, calling us — 134
- How great the mystery — 79
- How wonderful — 182
- Look back and see — 72
- Praise God from whom — 172
- The gospel came — 92

LM with Alleluias
- Praise God, the Giver — 165

LMD (Long Metre Double)
- By contact with the Crucified — 66
- Once, from a European — 91
- When minds and bodies — 181
- With humble justice — 162

SM (Short Metre: 6.6.8.6.)
- How deep our Maker's grief — 117
- In Christ, our humble head — 71
- Lead us in paths of truth — 132

SM with Refrain
- How good to thank — 80

SMD (Short Metre Double)
- How can we name? — 136

2.4.5.5.5. Refr.
- True friends — 143

3.3.3.3:3.4.3.3.
- Who is God? — 5

3.6.5.6.6.5.6.D. Refr.
- Jesus, as we tell — 59

3.6.5.6.6.D.
- Who is She? — 4

3.7.6.5.D.3.
- Here am I — 57

4.4.4.4.8.8.
- Grief of ending — 153

4.4.4.4.D.
- When love is found — 146

4.4.7.
- Look at this man — 33

4.5.3.4.4 4.4.
- *When I have failed* — 191

4.5.10.6.5.5.4.
- Bring many names — 173

4.5.5.5.5.4.5.
- Born into love — 138

4.7.6.5.6 6.11.
- When joy is drowned — 155

4.8.4.5.5.7.5.
- We want to love — 133

4.8.4.8.
- Love makes a bridge — 147

4.8.6.6.8.6.4.6.8.6.
- Who comes? — 12

4.8.8.4.8.8 8.
- Outgoing God — 87

4.8.8.7.
- I love this land — 124

5.5.5.4.D.
- God, the All-Holy — 145
- *May God be with you!* — 183
- Wonder of wonders — 137

5.5.5.5. Refr.
   Woman in the night   29
5.5.5.5.6.5.6.5.
   In water we grow   61
5.5.6.5.6.5.6.5. Refr.
   Great is the myst'ry   184
5.5.7.4.4.7.
   Oh, how joyfully!   17
5.5.8 8.5.5.
   Jesus is with God   56
5.5.8.8.D. Refr.
   God of many Names   7
5.6.7.5.6.6.5.8.
   God remembers   42
5.6.11.5.6.8.8.8.
   Prophets give us hope   128
5.6.6.4.
   Water in the snow   113
5.6.6.6.8.8.8.6.
   Christ will come again   163
5.6.8.6.8.8.6.
   Jesus comes today   13
5.7.5.6.4.
   Child, when Herod wakes   22
5.7.8.5.8.
   Faith moving onward   54
5.8.7.8. Refr.
   When anyone is in Christ   95
6 4.4.4.8.4.
   All saints?   70
6.4.6.8.8. Refr.
   A dancer's body   48
6.5.6.5.D.
   All-perceiving Lover   149
6.5.6.6.6.6.
   Painting many pictures   75
6.6.12.6.12. Refr.
   Where shall Wisdom?   65
6.6.6.6.5.D. Refr.
   Ever-journeying Friend   107
6.6.6.6.4.4.4.4.
   Let all creation dance   167
6.6.6.6.8.4.4.8.
   By purpose and by chance   81
6.6.6.7.6.6. with Alleluia
   Praise lifts our spirit high   171

6.6.6.D.
   Acclaim God's saving news   8
6.6.8.6.8.6.6.
   You were a babe of mine   20
6.6.8.D.6.6.6.
   Love alone unites us   64
6.7.4.4.5.6.6.9.
   How shall I sing to God?   150
6.7.6.7.
   Hail, undiminished love   15
6.7.6.7.6 6.7.
   Sing praises old and new   85
6.8.6.8.6.6.8.8. Refr.
   God, thank you for the Jews   90
7.5.5.4.6.
   I'll try, my love, to love you   140
7.6.7.6.
   Here hangs a man discarded   39
7.6.7.6.7.7.6 6.
   Acclaim with jubilation   168
7.6.7.6.D. Iambic
   Her baby, newly breathing   19
   Made one in Christ   78
   To Christ our hearts   102
   What was your vow?   25
7.6.7.6.D. Trochaic
   When on life a darkness   151
7.6.7.6.D. Refr.
   We plough and sow   115
7.7.7.7.
   Doom and danger Jesus knows   36
   Dying love has been my birth   43
   There's a spirit in the air   101
7.7.7.7. Refr.
   At the table of the world   98
7.7.6.4.5.6.5.6.5.4.
   When a baby   18
7.7.7.7.7.
   Holy Spirit, storm of love   40
7.7.7.7.D.
   Half the world is hungry   189
   On the night before he died   37
   Water, splashing hands   60
7.8.5.6.6.8. Refr.
   Dust and ashes   83
7.8.7.8.4.
   Jesus on the mountain peak   34

7.8.7.8.7.6.7.7.6.
    Daughter Mary   28
8.8.5.8.6.
    Dear Christ, the Father's   186
8.3.4.6.
    We are the music   157
8.3.8.8.5.5.7.7.
    Can a man be kind?   31
8.5.4.10.8.Refr.
    Thank you God, for times   135
8.5.8.5. Refr.
    Praise the God who changes   177
8.6.8.8.8.8.
    As Jeremiah took a jar   38
8.7.5.5.7.7.7.
    Sing together on our journey   108
8.7.6.6.8.5.
    Each seeking faith   6
8.7.8.5.6.6. Refr.
    As a mother comforts   170
8.7.8.6. Refr.
    Break the bread   125
8.7.8.7. with Alleluias
    Far and wide the gospel   103
8.7.8.7.7.7.8.8.
    Sing and tell   9
8.7.8.7.8.5.7.7.
    Speechless in a world   116
8.7.8.7.8.7.
    God is One, unique   179
    Life is great!   144
    Praise the Lover   180
8.7.8.7.8.8.7.
    Let hope and sorrow   158
8.7.8.7.8.8.8.7.
    Joy has blossomed   89
8.7.8.7.D. Iambic
    A prophet-woman   68
8.7.8.7.D. Trochaic
    Christ is risen! Shout   49
    Source of All   73
8.8.8.8.4.
    For the bread   187

8.8.8.8.8.8.
    A body broken   58
    A stranger, knocking   88
    As man and woman   185
    Great God, your love   84
    Not only acts   121
8.8.8.8.8.8.8.
    A child, a woman   126
8.8.8.8.9.9.8.8.8.
    The light of God   139
8.8.8.9.
    May the Sending One   110
8.8.8.D.
    In great Calcutta   104
8.9.8.5.
    We are not our own   62
9.10.10.9.
    Thank you, God, for water   111
9.8.9.8.
    This is a day of new   159
9.8.9.8.8 8.
    You are my body   100
9.8.9.8.8.7.
    A cloud of witnesses   74
9.9.9.9.
    Jesus is good news   50
10.10.10. with Alleluias
    When all is ended   161
10.10.10.10. Iambic
    Weep for the dead   120
10.10.10.10.10. Dactylic
    Good is the flesh   23
10.10.10.10.10. Refr.
    How perilous   26
10.10.10.10.10.
    I have no bucket   1
    What shall we love?   3
10.10.10.4.6.10.
    Will God be Judge?   160
10.10.11.10.
    Joyful is the dark   45
10.10.8.8.8.4.
    Dear Mother God   176
10.11.10.11.4.Refr.
    Tree of fire   175

10.4.10.4.8.10.	
When grief is raw	154
10.4.7.11.5.	
Holy Weaver	76
10.6.10.10.10.6.10.	
This we can do	129
10.8.10.8.8.8.	
Praise to the Maker	169
10.8.5.6.5. Refr.	
Love is the only hope	123
10.8.8.6.D. with Alleluias	
As in a clear dawn	47
11.10.10.11.	
Christ loves the Church	94
11.10.11.10. Iambic	
Come, cradle all	112
Go forth in faith	106
Spirit of Jesus	131
We offer Christ	105
When illness meets denial	152
11.10.11.10. Dactylic	
Welcome the wild one	24
11.11.11.11.	
Praise God for the harvest	114
12.12.14.10.	
Will you come and see?	14
12.12. Refr.	
God, your glory	188
12.8.12.8.8.8.	
Great soaring Spirit	130
13.13.14.13.	
God of Jeremiah	127
Irregular	
A woman in the crowd	27
Are you the friendly?	2
Christ crucified now	51
Come, Holy Breath	82
Here and now	32
Holy Spirit, hear us	190
I am going to Calvary	35
I met three children	178
Name Unnamed	174
Peace is my parting-gift	109
Say "No" to peace	122
Sing my song backwards	53
The waiting night	46
We are your people	63
We bring, you take	99
When children pray	141
When God is a child	16

Index of Box Notes on Theological Themes

These notes are indexed by their page number

Christians and Other Faiths .... **page** 7	Divine Pronouns .... **page** 5
Christians and Jews:	God's Holy Name 6
Covenant 10	The Weaver 3
Living Faith 12	Guilt or Lament 84
Was Paul Converted? 139	Jesus:
Church:	Christ 23
Who has the Gospel? 96	Choice and Chance 40
Worship Order 71	For Women and Men? 35
Darkness and Light 46	Human Stranger 17
Finality (Eschatology) 129	Justice:
God:	Easter Joy-Action for Justice 48
And Evil 42	Justice, Peace and Love 92
Can God grow? 133	"Sin" 74
Covenanted Praise 157	What Kind of Theology? 104

Index of Scripture References

- Hymns are listed in plain type, by hymn number. Box Note references are in italics, by page number, thus: *Psalm 51:7.....BN p.46*. The sign § = Stanza, thus: "45-§2 " means "Hymn 45, stanza 2."
- I mostly use the New Revised Standard Version (NRSV), plus the New English Bible (NEB), King James Version (KJV), and Revised English Bible (REB).

Genesis
1: 2	45-§2; 130
1: 27	84; 173
1: 31	23; 112
1: 26-28	4-§1
3: 19	83
3: 1-24	95
12: 1-9	10-§2
18: 22-23	*BN p. 133*
18: 27	83

Exodus
3: 1-8	175
3: 7-12	10 -§3
3: 13-15	3; 7; 86
3: 14, 20-33	*BN p. 133*
8: 20	11-§2
14-15	11-§2
15: 1-5	60
20: 18-21	45
20: 21	175
33: 7	93

Leviticus
16: 20-22 ("Scapegoat") 126

Numbers
20: 9-11	1-§4; 9-§5; 65

Deuteronomy
5: 6-7	3; 179
6: 4-5	3; 179
14: 2	90
24: 14-22	125
32: 11-13	130; 170

Joshua
24: 14-15	3

1 Kings
8: 10-13	45

Job
19: 8	151
28: 12	65
42: 6	83

Psalms
18: 8-12	45
22: 9	170
23: 4	148
34: 1	150
51: 7	*BN p. 46*
51: 10	126
72	162
82	160
85: 10	51-§4; 80-§4
88	119
90	156
92: 1-3	80-§1
98: 1-2	22
104: 29-30	7-§1
114: 4-6	51-§5
118: 19	51-§1
148	167

Proverbs
3: 19-20	10-§2
8: 22-31	10-§2

Isaiah
2: 13-17	173-§5
5: 20	22
9: 1-6	25
9: 6-7	120
11: 6	95
11: 6-11	120
12: 2	16-Refr.
35: 3-4	16-Refr.
40: 1-3	11-§3
40: 31	130; 177

43: 1-2	84
43: 19-21	87
43: 16-21	11-§3
45: 7	166
45: 1-7, 13-14	11-§4
49: 5-6	90
50: 4-5	65
51: 1	72
53: 1-3	25
53: 4	152
53: 11 (NEB)	51-§1
58: 5-9	83
60: 1-19	164
66: 13	170; 176

Jeremiah
6: 14	127
7: 1-11	80-§3
8: 18 - 9: 1	127
19: 1-15	38
19: 1-3, 10-12	127
29: 4-14	127
32: 6-15	127
36, esp. v. 23	127

Lamentations
3: 22-23	11-§1; 47

Ezekiel
1: 4-21	175
11: 19-20	126

Daniel
7: 9	173-§4

Hosea
8: 7	127
11: 1-4	4-§2; 176
13: 8	170

Joel			Mark			15: 8-10	79; 170
3: 18	175		1: 9-11	25		18: 25-43	36
			1: 1-14	24		19: 1-10	36
Amos			1: 12-13	26		22: 24-27	64
4: 12	13		1: 40-45	30		23: 34	35-§4
5: 24	9-§5		*1: 41*	*BN p. 40*		23: 49	58
5: 21-24	80-§2; 173-§5		2: 13-14	13-§3		23: 55 - 24: 10	29
7: 10-17	128		3: 1-6	31		24: 1-11	68
			3: 20-35	28		24: 8-11	55
Jonah			4: 1	4		24: 13-35	117
2: 5-9	83		5: 25-34	27		24: 24-27	176
3: 10	*BN p.133*		5: 24-34	29; 48		24: 30-40	88
			7: 24-29	*BN p. 40*			
Micah			9: 2-8	34		**John**	
4: 3	95; 122-§4		10: 17-22	131		1: 1-3	9-§3
6: 8	80-§2		10: 31	14-§4; 16-Refr.		1: 5	14-§5
			10: 46	36		1: 1-16	10-§4
Matthew			11: 1-11	36		1: 13	166
2: 1-2	14-§1		14. 3-9	68		1: 14	19-§3; 23
3: 1-17	24		14: 17-25	37; 38		1: 29	126
2: 7-18	22		14: 33-34	40-§2		1: 38	7-§2; 30; 177
3: 13-17	25		15: 32-33	53		3: 1-16	43
3: 16-18	30		15: 34	12-§3; 39; 116		3: 2, 26	7-§2; 30; 177
4: 1-11	26		15: 33-39	179		3: 3-5	121
5: 1-11	32		16: 2	78		3: 5-8	66
5: 6	128		16: 2-4	85		*4: 1-29*	*BN p. 40*
5: 6-9	109		16: 1-8	47		4: 7-30	29
5: 7-9	126					4: 11-15	1
5: 41	66		**Luke**			4: 13-14	83
5: 43-44	51-§4		1: 26-38	28		6: 15	48
5: 45	112		1: 46-55	14-§4; 28		6: 37	96
6: 24	50, 104-§4		1: 51-53	55		7: 37-38	1
6: 26	173-§3		2: 6-7	12-§1; 29		8: 12	14
6: 33	50		2: 8-20	47		9: 1-41	27
6: 39	128		2: 14	53		10: 7-9	59; 151
7: 11	173§3		2: 16-20	13 §1		10: 11 16	88
10: 16	121		3: 1-22	24		10: 30	179
11: 2-15	14-§3		3: 21-22	25		11: 47-53	22
13: 33	128		4: 1-30	26		11: 25	154
13: 24-30	163		4: 16-21	12-§2		11: 35	31; *BN p. 40*
15: 21-28	27		*5: 12*	*BN p. 40*		12: 32	35-§5; 44
17: 1-9	34		7: 11-15	31		13: 1-20	26
19: 24	104-§5		7: 36-50	29		13: 1-17	84
20: 20-28	26		8: 1-3	29		13: 3-5	64; 88
21: 1-10	36		9: 28-36	34		14: 1 & 17	154
25: 31-45	56; 57; 74		9: 51	36		14: 6	52; 151
25: 31-33	90		12: 50	52		14: 6-11	179
26: 48-50	2		13: 34	130		14:12	71
27: 32-56	118, 119		14: 15-24	59		14: 27	109; 151
27: 46	155-§2						
28: 20	59						

191

15: 1	176	2: 9	154	1: 13-20	10-§5-6
15: 15	49; 88	3: 11	151	2: 12	61; 66
15: 12-17	143; 177	6: 19-20	62	2: 9-15	10-§5-6
16: 20-22	43	10: 4	9-§5	2: 13-14	103
17: 20-21	64	11: 23-26	37; 38	2: 14-15	104-§3; 129
18: 33 - 19: 16	48	12: 4-11	63; 68; 75	3: 1-4	56
19: 2	121	12: 12-13	100	3: 3-4	42
19: 23	111-§4	13	123; 144-§4	3: 14	179
19: 25-27	28	13: 5 REB	64		
19: 25	29	13: 6 REB	146-§4	**1 Timothy**	
20: 11-18	68	13: 12	69	3: 16	79
20: 15	176	16: 2	78		
20: 22	64			**2 Timothy**	
20: 19-22	153	**2 Corinthians**		4: 2 KJV	127
20: 24-29	88	1: 2-7	104-§2		
21: 9-13	99	3: 17	84; 177	**Hebrews**	
		3:18	BN p. 35	1: 1-4	56
Acts		4: 7	94	11: 1 - 12: 2	106
2: 1-2	59	4: 7-12	104-§2	12: 1-2	62; 70; 74
2: 3	12-§1	5: 10	84; 163		
2: 1-13	47	5: 16-18	20-§5	**1 Peter**	
2: 17-18	52; 68; 95	5: 17	95; 159	2: 4-5	62
2: 38-39	51	5: 21	40-§3	2: 21-25	40-§3; 126
2: 43-45	131	12: 10	16-Refr	3: 21	61
17: 6	51-§5, Line 2				
20: 7	78	**Galatians**		**1 John**	
22: 16	61	2: 20	20-§5	3: 1-2	166
26: 12-23	149	3: 27-28	68	3: 2	69; 70
				4: 7-8.	80-§6
Romans		**Ephesians**		4: 7-12	64
1: 7	70	1: 20-23	56		
3: 21-26	84	2: 8	64	**Revelation**	
5: 8	82	2: 14-15	68; 91	1: 8	177
6: 3-4	52	3: 18-19	154	3: 8	56-§3; 87
6: 3-11	40-§4; 61	4: 3	179	3: 20	88
7: 14 - 8: 5	82	4: 1-4, 11-16	66	5: 9a	22
8: 26	176	5: 19	80-§5	7: 16-17	142
8: 38-39	123			11: 15	104-§3
12: 9-17	133	**Philippians**		21: 3	154
15: 7	44	2: 5-11	177	21: 5	159
		3: 12-14	159	21: 1-5	4-§4; 164
1 Corinthians				21: 22-27	164
1: 2	70	**Colossians**		22: 2, 13	49
1: 18-31	10; 41-§4-5	1:17	145-§3	22: 1-5	12; 163; 164
1: 26-31	58; 81; 104	1: 18	64; 100	22: 13	10-§7; 59; 71
2: 1-13	179	1: 24	52		
2: 6-8	10-§5				

Index of First Lines with Tunes

```
                            Key
First line                              Hymn number
(from the Appendix if in italics)       (Not page number)

    Are you the friendly God? ................................................. 2
    COMSIA, Mikkel Thompson, Praising a Mystery, 5
   /              \              \
Tune Name      Composer      Source (see details below)
```

Tune Sources are listed thus:
Available - published in several hymnals, including four recent standard works (listed separately if the tune is not in all four)
    United Methodist Hymnal (1989: United Methodist Publishing House, Nashville, Tennessee, USA) - UMH
    Presbyterian Hymnal (1990: Westminster John Knox Press, Louisville, Kentucky, USA - 1990) - PH
    Hymns Ancient and Modern, New Standard (1983: Hymns Ancient and Modern Ltd, UK) - A&MNS
    Rejoice and Sing (1991: Oxford University Press, Oxford, England, for the United Reformed Church) - R&S

Forthcoming - planned for publication in the next collection of Brian Wren hymn-texts-with-tunes (Hope Publishing Company, USA, distributed in the UK and Europe by Stainer & Bell Limited).

Unpublished - the tune is not in print.

If so specified, the tune is published in a Brian Wren hymn collection: either
Faith Looking Forward (1983: Hope Publishing Co., USA; Oxford University Press in UK), or one of the following, published by Hope Publishing Company, USA, distributed in the UK and Europe by Stainer & Bell Limited:
    Praising a Mystery (1986)   *Bring Many Names* (1989)
    New Beginnings (1993)   *Faith Renewed* (1995)

Published in or by the following (mentioned in the index):
    A New Hymnal For Colleges and Schools (New Haven: Yale UP 1992)
    The Al Fedak Hymnary (1990: Selah Publishing Co., Kingston, NY 12401, USA)
    Hymns for Today's Church (London: Hodder & Stoughton, 1982)
    Lutheran Book of Worship (Minneapolis: Augsburg Fortress, 1978)
    New Songs of Praise-2 (Oxford University Press and the BBC, 1986)
    Rejoice in the Lord (Grand Rapids, Michigan: Wm B. Eerdmans, 1985)
    Sacred Music Press, Box 802, Dayton, OH 45401-0802, USA.
    Selah Publishing Co., Kingston, NY 12401, USA.
    Supplement 96, Hope Publishing Co., Carol Stream, IL 60188, USA

A body broken on a cross 58
      POWER TO CHANGE, Valerie Ruddle, *Bring Many Names*, 1
A child, a woman and a man 126
      DURNBAUGH, William Rowan, *Praising a Mystery*, 1
A cloud of witnesses around us 74
      ESBEE MAX, Carlton R. Young: *Forthcoming*
A dancer's body leaps and falls 48
      DANCING DAY, Kathy Wonson Eddy, *Bring Many Names*, 2
A man of ancient time and place 30
      COSTLY LOVE, Austin Lovelace, *New Beginnings*, 2
A prophet-woman broke a jar 68
      MEGERRAN, Walter K. Stanton, *New Beginnings*, 4
A Stranger, knocking on a door 88
      CASAD, Lawrence Wareing, *New Beginnings*, 13
A woman in a world of men 55
      LARCHES, Veronica Bennetts, *Bring Many Names*, 8
      AZMON (PH, UMH) and SAINT MAGNUS (A&MNS, R&S)
A woman in the crowd 27
      GOD IS GOOD, Hal H. Hopson, *Praising a Mystery*, 27
Acclaim God's saving news 8
      LAUDES DOMINI, Joseph Barnby: *Available*
Acclaim with jubilation 168
      BEREDEN VÄG FÖR HERRAN, arr. Hal Hopson, *New Beginnings*, 1
Against the clock 77
      Unpublished tune ("Sunday Show") by Dirk & Carol Damonte.
All-perceiving Lover 149
      KING'S WESTON, R. Vaughan Williams, *Bring Many Names*, 3
All saints? 70
      HUNTER'S HILL, Brian Wren arr. R. Wagner, *Bring Many Names*, 4
Are you the friendly God? 2
      COMSIA, Mikkel Thompson, *Bring Many Names*, 5
Arise, shine out, your light has come 164
      BLACKWELL, Robert A. Harris, *Bring Many Names*, 6
      DUNEDIN (UMH, A&MNS), GONFALON ROYAL (not UMH)
As a mother comforts her child 170
      Choral setting, Hal. H. Hopson, *Unpublished*
As in a clear dawn 47
      CRAWFORD, Hal H. Hopson, *Supplement 96*
As Jeremiah took a jar 38
      Tune by Joan Collier Fogg: *Unpublished*
As man and woman we were made 185
      SUSSEX CAROL, *Available* (not PH)
At the table of the world 98
      CONCELEBRATION, Anthony Fedell, *Bring Many Names*, 7
Born into love 138
      NAMESAKE, Anthony Fedell, *New Beginnings*, 6
Break the bread of belonging 125
      TRAVELLERS, Hedley Roberts, *Praising a Mystery*, 2

Bring many names 173
    WESTCHASE, Carlton Young, *Bring Many Names*, 9
By contact with the Crucified 66
    ASKERSWELL, Peter Cutts, *Praising a Mystery*, 3
By purpose and by chance 81
    RHOSYMEDRE, Available, and *New Beginnings*, 10
Can a man be kind and caring? 31
    JEDI SONG, Brian Wren arr. Joan Collier Fogg, *Praising a Mystery*, 4
Child, when Herod wakes 22
    CHRISTMAS NOW, Peter Cutts, *Faith Looking Forward*, 43
Christ crucified now is alive 51
    THE EAST IS RED, arr. Erik Routley, *Faith Looking Forward*, 39
Christ is alive! 52
    TRURO: *Available*, and *Faith Renewed*, 1
Christ is risen! Shout hosanna! 49
    JACKSON NEW, William Rowan, *Praising a Mystery*, 5
    W ZLOBIE LEZY (INFANT HOLY): *Available* - R&S, UMH, PH
Christ loves the Church 94
    HIGH STREET, Jane Marshall, *Praising a Mystery*, 6
Christ will come again 163
    IDA, Joan Collier Fogg, *Bring Many Names*, 10
    GLACIER VIEW, Melvin West, *Bring Many Names*, 10
Come, build the Church 93
    ADVENT NEW, Peter Cutts, *Praising a Mystery*, 7
Come, celebrate the call of God 67
    ALIDA'S TUNE, Hal H. Hopson, *New Beginnings*, 17
Come, cradle all the future generations 112
    SAN CARLOS, Annette Bender, *Faith Renewed*, 2
Come, Holy Breath 82
    HOLY BREATH, Susan Heafield, *New Beginnings*, 31
Come let us praise what God has done, ... 11
    DUNDEE: *Available* (not UMH)
Cucumber Hearts 192
    Poem: no tune
Daughter Mary 28
    ROSEWOOD, Veronica Bennetts, *Bring Many Names*, 11
Dear Christ, uplifted from the earth 44
    ST BOTOLPH, Gordon Slater, *Faith Looking Forward*, 24
Dear Christ, the Father's loving Son 186
    HAMPTON POYLE, Peter Cutts, *Faith Looking Forward*, 23
Dear Mother God 176
    MARYSVILLE, Dan Damon, *Faith Renewed*, 3
Deep in the shadows of the past 86
    NORTHOVER, Peter Cutts, *Faith Renewed*, 4
Doom and danger Jesus knows 36
    TORVANGER ROAD, Mikkel Thompson, *New Beginnings*, 9
Dust and ashes 83
    DUST AND ASHES, Hal H. Hopson, *Bring Many Names*, 12

Dying love has been my birth 43
    KEINE SCHÖNHEIT HAT DIE WELT, arr. Peter Cutts, *Faith Renewed*, 5
Each seeking faith 6
    THREE RIVERS, Joan Collier Fogg, *Bring Many Names*, 13
Easter Light 193
    Andrew Stallman, *Unpublished* choral setting
Eternal Wisdom, timely Friend 166
    KEITH'S TUNE, Hal H. Hopson, *New Beginnings*, 3
    TALLIS' CANON, *Available*
Ever-journeying Friend 107
    PIONEERS, Kim D. Sherman, *New Beginnings*, 25
Faith moving onward 54
    MARTYRS' MEMORIAL, Peter Cutts, *Faith Renewed*, 6
Far and wide the gospel travels 103
    RODLAND-TIMMONS, Deborah Holden-Holloway: *Forthcoming*
For the bread that we have eaten 187
    MAYFIELD, Peter Cutts, *Faith Looking Forward*, 26
Give thanks for music-making art 69
    ELLACOMBE: *Available* (not R&S), and *New Beginnings*, 32
Go forth in faith 106
    LARGENT, William Rowan, *Bring Many Names*, 15
Go now in peace 148
    TALLIS' CANON, *New Beginnings*, 12, and *Available*
God, give us freedom to lament 119
    WILMINGTON NEW, Hal H.Hopson, *New Beginnings*, 26
God is One, unique and holy 179
    TRINITY Peter Cutts, *Faith Renewed*, 7
God, let me welcome timely death 156
    MELCOMBE, *Praising a Mystery*, 19
God of Jeremiah 127
    KELVINGROVE, arr.Valerie Ruddle, *New Beginnings*, 7
God of many Names 7
    MANY NAMES, William Rowan, *Praising a Mystery*, 8, and UMH
God remembers 42
    MOUNT ROYAL, Joan Collier Fogg, *New Beginnings*, 14
God, thank you for the Jews 90
    STAR OF DAVID, William P Rowan, *Praising a Mystery*, 28
God, the All-Holy 145
    BUNESSAN, *Bring Many Names*, 14, and *Available*
God, your glory we have seen 188
    DIEU, NOUS AVONS VU, R&S and *Rejoice in the Lord*
Good is the flesh 23
    MAGNOLIA, Veronica Bennetts, *Bring Many Names*, 16
    STORBAKKEN, Lee Cobb: *Forthcoming.*
Great God, your love has called us here 84
    ABINGDON, Erik Routley, *Faith Renewed*, 8
    RYBURN, Norman Cocker, *Faith Renewed*, 8
Great is the myst'ry 184
    (JUDAS) MACCABAEUS, *Available*

Great Lover, calling us to share 134
    HAGEL, William Rowan, *Bring Many Names*, 17
    GONFALON ROYAL: *Available* (not UMH)
Great soaring Spirit 130
    McKENDRIE, Hal H. Hopson, *Bring Many Names*, 18
    SOLANO, Anthony Fedell, *Bring Many Names*, 18
Grief of ending 153
    MOUNT AUBURN, Peter Cutts, *New Beginnings*, 27
Hail, undiminished love 15
    CUMBERWORTH, Peter Cutts, *Praising a Mystery*, 9
Half the world is hungry, Lord 189
    ABERYSTWYTH, *Available*
Her baby, newly breathing 19
    MERLE'S TUNE, Hal Hopson, *Bring Many Names*, 19
Here am I 57
    STANISLAUS, Dan Damon, *Faith Renewed*, 9
Here and now, if you love 32
    ALCONBURY NINE, Brian Wren, arr. Peter Cutts, *Praising a Mystery*, 10
    Untitled tune by Kathy Wonson Eddy: *Forthcoming*.
Here hangs a man discarded 39
    SHRUB END, Peter Cutts, *Faith Renewed*, 10
Holy Spirit, hear us as we pray 190
    PETITION, Peter Cutts, *Faith Looking Forward*, 22
Holy Spirit, storm of love 40
    STORM OF LOVE, Valerie Ruddle, *Praising a Mystery*, 11
    NICHT SO TRAURIG, J.S. Bach, *New Songs of Praise-2*
Holy Weaver, deftly intertwining 76
    OPOCENSKY, trad. arr. Joan Collier Fogg, *Bring Many Names*, 20
How can we name a love? 136
    RICHES, Dan Damon, *Faith Renewed*, 11
How deep our Maker's grief 117
    SOUTHWELL: *Available* (not UMH)
How good to thank our God 80
    SING PRAISES, Hal H. Hopson, *New Beginnings*, 15
How great the mystery of faith 79
    GATHERING, Carol Doran, *Bring Many Names*, 21
How perilous the messianic call 26
    Alice Parker: *Forthcoming*.
How shall I sing to God? 150
    WEAVER MILL by Joan Collier Fogg, *Praising a Mystery*, 12
How wonderful the Three-in-One 182
    THYATIRA, Anthony Fedell, *Bring Many Names*, 22
I am going to Calvary 35
    SEE SAW SACCARA DOWN, arr. Charles Strange, *Faith Looking Forward*, 18
I come with joy 97
    LAND OF REST (PH, UMH); ST BOTOLPH (A&MNS, R&S)
    BALLACHULISH, Carl Schalk, *Faith Renewed*, 12

I have no bucket and the well is deep 1
        LIGHTCLIFFE, Paul Bateman, *Rejoice and Sing*, 340
        WELLSPRING, Hal H. Hopson, *Praising a Mystery*, 13
I love this land 124
        FAIR HAVEN, John Collier Fogg, *Praising a Mystery*, 14
I met three children in the street 178
        Cantata, by John Horman, *Unpublished*
I Promise (Farewell Song) 194
        Dirk & Carol Damonte, *Unpublished*
If I could visit Bethlehem 21
        PATHWAYS, Dan Damon, *New Beginnings*, 19
In Christ, our humble head 71
        ST. THOMAS: *Forthcoming*, and *Available*
In great Calcutta Christ is known 104
        CALCUTTA, Jane Marshall, *Praising a Mystery*, 15
In water we grow 61
        LAUDATE DOMINUM: *Available* (not UMH)
        HANOVER: *Available*
I'll try, my love, to love you 140
        MAKHASANENE, Brian Wren arr. Erik Routley, *Faith Looking Forward*, 30
Jesus, as we tell your story 59
        Untitled tune, Thom Bohlert: *Forthcoming*
Jesus comes today 13
        PREPARATION, Peter Cutts, *Praising a Mystery*, 16
Jesus is good news to all the poor 50
        RAILTON ROAD, Peter Cutts, *Faith Looking Forward*, 42
Jesus is with God 56
        BOLINAS, Joan Collier Fogg, *Praising a Mystery*, 17
Jesus on the mountain peak 34
        SHILLINGFORD, Peter Cutts, *Faith Renewed*, 13, and UMH
        MOWSLEY, Cyril Taylor, *Faith Renewed*, 13, and PH, R&S
Joy has blossomed out of sadness 89
        IN BABILONE: *Forthcoming* and *Available* (PH, UMH)
Joyful is the dark 45
        CEDARS, Veronica Bennetts, *Bring Many Names*, 23
        GEARY (Dan Damon) & LINDNER (Carlton Young) *Supplement* 96
Lead us in paths of truth 132
        ST. MICHAEL: *Available*
Let all creation dance 167
        DARWALL'S 148th, *Available*, and *New Beginnings*, 33
Let hope and sorrow now unite 158
        NUN FREUT EUCH, *Faith Renewed*, 14
Life is great 144
        LITHEROP, Peter Cutts, *Faith Looking Forward*, 11, and
        Hymns for Today's Church
Listening 195
        Poem: no tune
Look at this man 33
        Tune by Dirk & Carol Damonte: *Unpublished*

Look back and see the apostles' road 72
    BOW BRICKHILL, S.H. Nicholson, *Praising a Mystery*, 18
Love alone unites us 64
    DUNAWAY, Joan Collier Fogg, *Bring Many Names*, 24
    WUNDERBARER KÖNIG (GRONINGEN): *Forthcoming*, and R&S
Love is the only hope 123
    PRESTON, Joan Collier Fogg, *Praising a Mystery*, 20
Love makes a bridge 147
    GOLDEN GATE, Peter Cutts, *Faith Looking Forward*, 35
Made one in Christ, we gather 78
    ES FLOG EIN KLEINS WALDVÖGELEIN: *Forthcoming*, and PH
May God be with you! 183
    BUNESSAN, *Available*
May the Sending One sing in you 110
    ROLLINGBAY, Mikkel Thompson, *Bring Many Names*, 35
    Alice Parker, *Trinitarian Blessings* (SATB, Hope Publishing Company)
Name Unnamed 174
    CASTLE MONTGOMERY, Brian Wren arr. Wilbur Russell, *Bring Many Names*, 25
Not only acts of evil will 121
    VATER UNSER (OLD 112TH), *Bring Many Names*, 26, PH, UMH
Oh, how joyfully! 17
    SICILIAN MARINERS, PH, UMH, and *New Beginnings*, 28
Old Dog 197
    Poem: no tune
On the night before he died 37
    ABERYSTWYTH: *Available*; and STOOKEY, Carlton Young, UMH
Once, from a European shore 91
    ASKERSWELL, Peter Cutts, *Faith Renewed*, 15
Only One Earth 196
    Dirk & Carol Damonte, *Unpublished*
Onward, Christian Rambos! 198
    ST GERTRUDE, A&MNS AND UMH
Outgoing God 87
    TRINITY CHURCH NASHVILLE, Hal Hopson: *Forthcoming*
Painting many pictures 75
    TACOMA, Dan Damon, *Supplement 96*
Peace is my parting gift to you 109
    Anthem setting by John Horman, Sacred Music Press, USA
Praise God for the harvest 114
    MINIVER, Cyril Taylor, *Faith Looking Forward*, 9 (and A&MNS)
Praise God, from whom all blessings flow 172
    OLD HUNDREDTH, *Available*
Praise God, the Giver and the Gift 165
    LASST UNS ERFREUEN: *Available*
Praise lifts our spirit high 171
    Untitled tune, Susan Heafield, *Forthcoming*
Praise the God who changes places 177
    BOE, William P. Rowan, *Praising a Mystery*, 21

Praise the Lover of Creation 180
    REGENT SQUARE, *Available*
Praise to the Maker 169
    LOBT GOTT DEN HERREN, Melchior Vulpius, *New Beginnings*, 5
Prophets give us hope 128
    KNYSNA, Peter Cutts, *Faith Renewed*, 16
Say "No" to peace 122
    INGOMAR, Joan Collier Fogg, *Praising a Mystery*, 29
Sing and tell our Saviour's story 9
    GENEVAN PSALM 42: *Forthcoming*, also in *Rejoice in the Lord*
Sing my song backwards 53
    HILARY, Ann Loomes, *Faith Renewed*, 17
Sing praises old and new 85
    FONDREN, John Carter, *New Beginnings*, 8
    SPANISH HYMN (MADRID), PH and UMH
Sing together on our journey 108
    ALLINDRACK, Peter Cutts: *Forthcoming*
Source of All, Sustaining Spirit 73
    ABBOTSLEIGH and HYFRYDOL: *Available*
Speechless in a world that suffers 116
    BRYN CALFARIA: *Forthcoming*, also in PH
Spirit of Jesus 131
    TEGAN, Dan Damon, *Faith Renewed*, 18
Thank you, God, for times of growing 135
    DUBA'S TUNE, Hal. H. Hopson: *Forthcoming*
    McCONNELL'S MILL, Joan Collier Fogg: *Forthcoming*
Thank you, God, for water, soil and air 111
    AMSTEIN, John Weaver, *Faith Renewed*, 19
The gifts of God 142
    PTOMEY, Hal H. Hopson, *New Beginnings*, 24
The gospel came with foreign tongue 92
    GOD AND KING, Hal H. Hopson, *Faith Renewed*, 20
The horrors of our history 118
    GOD IS THERE, William P. Rowan, *Faith Renewed*, 21
The light of God is shining bright 139
    DANDYLION, Joan Collier Fogg, *Bring Many Names*, 27
The owl that sat in Wesley's place 199
    Poem: no tune
The waiting night 46
    SUNRISE, Peter Cutts, *Faith Looking Forward*, 36
The walls of separation 200
    Dirk & Carol Damonte, *Unpublished*
There's a spirit in the air 101
    LAUDS, John W. Wilson, *Faith Renewed*, 22 (and PH, A&MNS, R&S)
This is a day of new beginnings 159
    BEGINNINGS, Carlton Young, *Faith Renewed*, 23
This is a story full of love 10
    TIMOTHY, William Rowan, *Praising a Mystery*, 22

This we can do 129
    BRIDGE STREET, Kay Mutert, *Faith Renewed*, 24
To Christ our hearts now given 102
    WIE LIEBLICH IST DER MAIEN: *Forthcoming*, and PH
Tree of Fire 175
    SPECTRA, Sue Mitchell-Wallace, *New Beginnings*, 18
True friends 143
    EASTON, Joan Collier Fogg, *Praising a Mystery*, 23
Water in the snow 113
    WATER IN THE SNOW, Erik Routley, *New Orbit* (Stainer & Bell Ltd)
    and *Faith Looking Forward*, 10
Water, splashing hands and face 60
    SALZBURG (Hintze): *Available* (not UMH)
We are not our own 62
    YARNTON, Brian Wren arr. Fred Graham, *Bring Many Names*, 28
We are the music angels sing 157
    RIETBERG, Al Fedak, *The Al Fedak Hymnary*
We are your people 63
    WHITFIELD, John W. Wilson, *Faith Renewed*, 25, A&MNS, PH
We bring, you take 99
    BRIGHTHELM, Veronica Bennetts, *Bring Many Names*, 29
    HOST, Betty Pulkingham, *Supplement* 96
We cannot be beguiled by pleasant sounds 201
    Poem: no tune
We meet as friends at table 96
    MEAL OF LOVE, Hal H. Hopson: *Forthcoming*
We offer Christ 105
    ORANGEBURG, Hal H. Hopson, *Bring Many Names*, 32
We plough and sow 115
    HARVEST HYMN, Hal Hopson, *Faith Renewed*, 26
    WIR PFLÜGEN (A&MNS, R&S)
We want to love 133
    LLANMARCH, Brian Wren arr. Peter Cutts, *Praising a Mystery*, 24
    Untitled tune, Kathy Wonson Eddy: *Forthcoming*
Wedding Wishes 202
    Poem: no tune
Weep for the dead 120
    REMEMBRANCE, Hal H. Hopson, *Bring Many Names*, 30
Welcome the wild one 24
    HERALD, Sue Mitchell Wallace, *Bring Many Names*, 31
    McCURDY'S AIR, Brian Wren, arr. Pamela Payne, *Bring Many Names*, 31
What shall we love and honour most of all? 3
    Untitled tune by Kay Mutert: *Forthcoming*
What was your vow and vision? 25
    COMPLAINER, trad. arr. Hal H. Hopson, *Faith Renewed*, 27
When a baby in your arms 18
    FIRST CHRISTMAS, Susan Heafield, *New Beginnings*, 20
When all is ended 161
    YOGANANDA, William Rowan, *Bring Many Names*, 33

When anyone is in Christ 95
    CHARLOTTESVILLE, Hal H. Hopson, *Supplement 96*
When children pray 141
    Ann Wilson, Choral setting, Selah Publishing Co., USA
When God is a child 16
    MOON BEAMS, Joan Collier Fogg, *Bring Many Names, 34*
When grief is raw 154
    SHAWN, Hal H. Hopson, *Faith Renewed, 28*
When I have failed 191
    AFTON, Lawrence Wareing, *New Beginnings, 30*
When illness meets denial and rejection 152
    OREN, John Fowler: *Unpublished*
When joy is drowned 155
    UFFINGTON, Brian Wren arr. Peter Cutts, *Faith Looking Forward, 33*
When love is found 146
    GIFT OF LOVE, Hal H. Hopson, *Faith Renewed, 29*
When minds and bodies meet as one 181
    TRINITY CAROL, Peter Cutts, *Faith Renewed, 30*
When on life a darkness falls 151
    DROOPING SOULS, *Praising a Mystery, 25*
When pain and terror strike by chance 41
    KINGSFOLD, R. Vaughan Williams, *New Beginnings, 11*
    English Hymnal version, reading ♩ | ♩ ♫ ♩ ♩ *for "force, ready to rule and" (etc.)*
Where shall Wisdom be found? 65
    LINDSAY, Susan Heafield: *Forthcoming*
Who comes? 12
    MUIR WOODS, Joan Collier Fogg, *Praising a Mystery, 30*
Who is God? 5
    WALDEN CIRCLE, Joan Collier Fogg, *New Beginnings, 16*
Who is She? 4
    CRESCENT HILL, Brian Wren arr. Pamela Payne, *Praising a Mystery, 26*
    MARJORIE, Jane Marshall, *A New Hymnal For Colleges and Schools*
Will God be Judge? 160
    FOSTER, Dan Damon, *New Beginnings, 21*
Will you come and see the light? 14
    KELVINGROVE (arr. Valerie Ruddle), *New Beginnings, 22*
With humble justice clad and crowned 162
    RUITER-FEENSTRA, William P. Rowan, *New Beginnings, 29*
Woman in the night 29
    HAIZ, Charles Webb, *Faith Renewed, 31 and UMH*
    WOMAN IN THE NIGHT, Al Fedak, *A New Hymnal for Colleges and Schools*
    NEW DISCIPLES, Peter Cutts, *Faith Looking Forward, 15*
Wonder of wonders 137
    BUNESSAN, arr. Hal H. Hopson, *Faith Renewed, 32, and Available*
You are my body 100
    O DASS ICH TAUSENDZUNGEN HÄTTE (PH)
    WARNER, John Horman: *Forthcoming*
You were a babe of mine (Joseph's Carol) 20
    JOSEPH'S CAROL, Erik Routley, *Faith Renewed, 33*